the works of Hurston, West, and
Fauset to demonstrate how the folk,
bourgeois, and proletarian aesthetics
figure into their writings. The volume
concludes by discussing the writers
in relation to contemporary African
American women authors.

## About the Author

**SHARON L. JONES** is Assistant
Professor of English at Earlham
College, where she teaches African
American literature, humanities,
modern literature, 19th-century
literature, and contemporary
literature. She is coeditor of *The
Prentice Hall Anthology of African
American Literature* (2000).

# REREADING THE HARLEM RENAISSANCE

**Recent Titles in**
**Contributions in Afro-American and African Studies**

Critical Essays on Alice Walker
*Ikenna Dieke, editor*

Education and Independence: Education in South Africa, 1658–1988
*Simphiwe A. Hlatshwayo*

African American Autobiography and the Quest for Freedom
*Roland L. Williams, Jr.*

The White Image in the Black Mind: A Study of African American Literature
*Jane Davis*

Black Leadership for Social Change
*Jacob U. Gordon*

Mythatypes: Signatures and Signs of African/Diaspora and Black Goddesses
*Alexis Brooks De Vita*

African Visions: Literary Images, Political Change, and Social Struggle in
Contemporary Africa
*Cheryl B. Mwaria, Silvia Federici, and Joseph McLaren, editors*

Voices of the Fugitives: Runaway Slave Stories and Their Fictions of Self-
Creation
*Sterling Lecater Bland, Jr.*

Meditations on African Literature
*Dubem Okafor*

Achebe the Orator: The Art of Persuasion in Chinua Achebe's Novels
*Chinwe Christiana Okechukwu*

Rethinking the Slave Narrative: Slave Marriage and the Narratives of Henry
Bibb and William and Ellen Craft
*Charles J. Heglar*

The Harlem Group of Negro Writers
*Melvin B. Tolson*
*Edward J. Mullen, editor*

# "REREADING THE HARLEM RENAISSANCE"

Race, Class, and Gender in the Fiction of Jessie Fauset, Zora Neale Hurston, and Dorothy West

Sharon L. Jones

Contributions in Afro-American and African Studies, Number 207

GREENWOOD PRESS
*Westport, Connecticut · London*

**Library of Congress Cataloging-in-Publication Data**

Jones, Sharon L. (Sharon Lynette)
  Rereading the Harlem renaissance : race, class, and gender in the fiction of Jessie
Fauset, Zora Neale Hurston, and Dorothy West / Sharon L. Jones.
      p. cm.—(Contributions in Afro-American and African studies, ISSN
  0069–9624 ; no. 207)
  Includes bibliographic references (p.  ) and index.
  ISBN 0–313–32326–7 (alk. paper)
      1. American fiction—African American authors—History and
criticism.   2. Women and literature—United States—History—20th
century.   3. American fiction—Women authors—History and criticism.
4. American fiction—20th century—History and criticism.   5. West, Dorothy,
1909—Criticism and interpretation.   6. Fauset, Jessie Redmon—Criticism and
interpretation.   7. Hurston, Zora Neale—Criticism and interpretation.   8. African
American women in literature.   9. African Americans in literature.   10. Social
classes in literature.   11. Sex role in literature.   12. Race in literature.
13. Harlem Renaissance.   I. Title.   II. Series.
PS153.N5 J68 2002
813′.5209896073—dc21          2002067840

British Library Cataloguing in Publication Data is available.

Library of Congress Catalog Card Number: 2002067840

ISBN: 0–313–32326–7
ISSN: 0069–9624

First published in 2002

Greenwood Press, 88 Post Road West, Westport, CT 06881
An imprint of Greenwood Publishing Group, Inc.
www.greenwood.com

Printed in the United States of America

∞

The paper used in this book complies with the
Permanent Paper Standard issued by the National
Information Standards Organization (Z39.48–1984).

10 9 8 7 6 5 4 3 2 1

*This book is dedicated to Joe, Emily, and Keith Jones.*

# Contents

# Acknowledgments

I wish to thank the following people: Joe, Keith, and Emily Jones, the Earlham College Department of English, Phyllis Boanes, Sean Noel, Kristen Eberhard, Anne Marie Menta, Hugh Ruppersburg, R. Baxter Miller, Rosemary Franklin, Barbara McCaskill, Judith Ortiz Cofer, Brenda Cox, the staff of Earlham College's Lilly Library, Cheryl Collier, Rose Phillips, and Donna White.

# Introduction

When former president of the United States Bill Clinton opened his new office in Harlem during the summer of 2001, newspaper, radio, and television stations all over the world reported the historic event. The entrance of Bill Clinton into this mostly black mecca triggered a string of reactions among the media, who noted the former U.S. president's presence in Harlem as further proof of a second "renaissance" in Harlem. National magazines, such as *Vanity Fair*, heralded the advent of the "Second (Harlem) renaissance" and the revitalization of the area as evidenced by the popularity of Harlem nightclubs, restaurants, and galleries ("Harlem Renaissance" 2001: 193). The *Vanity Fair* layout included a map of Harlem's most popular sites. The affluent individuals moving into Harlem to renovate old brownstones and "gentrify" the area, and the escalating price of real estate in this mostly lower-class area of New York, made the area seem to be undergoing a revitalization. Tour buses travel to Harlem, stopping at historic restaurants, churches, and nightclubs to let tourists from all over the world learn about the glorious past and the promising future of Harlem. Bill Clinton's new offices, located on 125th Street, testify to the vitality and energy associated with this area of Harlem, which promises to become a thriving part of the community. Like the first renaissance that began in 1900 and ended in 1940, this current renaissance calls into mind the politics of race and socioeconomic class through the commercialization and commodification of Harlem as a site of "blackness" and urban American culture. In the 1920s and 1930s, upper-middle-class whites who wanted to be on the "cutting edge" of developments in music, art, and literature flocked to Harlem nightspots to listen to jazz, view art exhibits, and meet with promising African American intellectuals who fashioned themselves to be trailblazers in promoting the image of the "New Negro."

What will be the long-term effects of the "second renaissance" in Harlem? Only time will tell. During the first Harlem Renaissance, African American intellectuals showed an enthusiasm and hopefulness for the long-lasting implications of the movement. James Weldon Johnson (1997) lauded the possibilities of the "greatest Negro City in the world" (301). Alain Locke (1997), who edited *The New Negro,* pronounced the advent of "a spiritual Coming of Age" in Harlem that would be typified by African Americans articulating their social, economic, artistic, and cultural aspirations (16). While some contemporary Harlemites viewed Clinton's presence in Harlem and the promise of economic renewal that might accompany it with skepticism, others hoped that his presence would bring prestige and dollars to the local economy. It remains to be seen what his influence on the economic climate of Harlem will be, let alone the long-term effects. Nevertheless, the "second" renaissance in Harlem evokes memories of the "first" renaissance, when Harlem held center stage as a place of potential economic growth and cultural advancement in that flowering of creativity known as the "New Negro Movement." Nearly 100 years prior to Clinton's arrival in Harlem and the media spotlight on the area, blacks from Africa, the Caribbean, and other regions of the United States migrated to Harlem in search of the American Dream of economic prosperity and equality, often to find that the dream was elusive. While many of those individuals were blue-collar laborers and tradespeople or white-collar workers, a number of artists, musicians, and writers moved to Harlem due to New York City's preeminence as a center of the musical, artistic, and literary world. For black men, the politics of race and class often militated against their quest for fame and success. The black women, on the other hand, sometimes faced the triple jeopardy of race, class, and gender oppression.

In the 1920s, three African American women from different areas of the United States converged upon Harlem full of hope and vigor. Zora Neale Hurston relocated from Washington, D.C., to New York City in 1925 to pursue a career as a writer; Jessie Fauset moved to New York City in 1919 to serve as literary editor of the *Crisis;* and Dorothy West moved to New York City with her cousin Helene Johnson, a poet, in 1926, and she later sublet Hurston's New York City apartment. While the arrival did not garner the attention of Clinton's in 2001, one could argue that the longstanding effects of their entrance onto the Harlem scene would have even more powerful ramifications from their diligence at challenging stereotypes of race, class, and gender in literary expression, which laid a foundation for contemporary African American women writers such as Toni Morrison, Gloria Naylor, and Alice Walker. Not only does their work reveal the complexities of tripartite race, class, and gender relations, but their lives and the challenges they faced as writers all call attention to the double jeopardy of being black and female in pre–Civil Rights Movement America as they forged ahead in their desire to rewrite the American literary landscape.

While Jessie Fauset is often described as a member of the black bourgeoisie, she suggests a proletarian aesthetic as she advocates black unity in "Impressions of the Second Pan-African Congress." Blacks from various parts of the African diaspora had attended the 1921 conference in hopes of linking their common concerns. Fauset (1995) wrote of the conference, "The rod of the common oppressor had made them feel their own community of blood, of necessity, of problem" (368).[1] Although Hurston has been labeled a writer of folk literature, she called for more diversity in representations of African Americans in literature. Hurston (1995) wrote, "The realistic story around a Negro insurance official, dentist, general practitioner, undertaker and the like would be most revealing. Thinly disguised fiction around the well-known Negro names is not the answer, either" (954).[2] By the same token, West, because of her privileged upbringing as the daughter of a successful businessman, is often characterized as the epitome of the bourgeois aesthete, but she recognized the folk roots of the most affluent blacks. She states, " There are some who think that these blacks [living in Martha's Vineyard] sprang full-grown from the earth into preordained success. No, their advantage was that their forebears came out of slavery with a fierce will to make up for lost time, and few descendants have let their momentum slacken" (West 1995: 242). Her comments suggests the blurred lines between the black folk and the bourgeoisie, for they have a common origin. In addition, West's remarks evince a proletarian stance, evoking the importance of acknowledging the barriers African Americans face in their acquisition of the American Dream.

Fauset, Hurston, and West fought against narrow-mindedness and bigotry in an attempt to transcend racial, class, and gender boundaries that critics and publishers, and sometimes their fellow artists, tried to utilize to constrain them. Instead of portraying monolithic, one-dimensional portraits of black life, Hurston, West, and Fauset sought to present a multidimensional and complex view of African American experience through their deft handling of narrative technique, symbolism, imagery, and themes. Furthermore, their works represent an underlying understanding and a reconfiguration of the three aesthetics—the folk, the bourgeois, and the proletarian—that reverberated throughout African American literature during the Harlem Renaissance and beyond.

African American writers of the Harlem Renaissance period tend to be identified as expressing one of the three aforementioned categories exclusively in their works. As a consequence, stereotypical notions among critics regarding which aesthetic constitutes authentic African American literature affected the production and reception of works by these writers. The misreading of these writers' texts militated against their critical reception during their lifetimes and afterward, creating few outlets for publication. More importantly, these assumptions about the "proper" aesthetic for African American writers sometimes tainted their critical reception at the time in which they wrote, which, as a consequence, led to the canonization of African American writers who seemed to embody the folk aesthetic and the devaluing of authors who evoked the bourgeois or the proletarian aesthetic. Of the three writers profiled in this study, Zora Neale Hurston (an early-twentieth-century folk heroine) generates the most attention in terms of critical studies, conferences, and societies devoted to her work, and her book *Their Eyes Were Watching God* is a ubiquitous text on college, high school, and middle school reading lists. In contrast, Jessie Fauset and Dorothy West elicit considerably less attention, and to date, there are relatively few critical studies of their works, and typically, these authors appear on reading lists for literature courses with far less frequency than Hurston, mainly from misconceptions about their social class, background, and ideologies. Why has the folk been privileged as the "authentic" African American voice and experience? The elevation of the folk stems from a variety of complex social, economic, and political reasons. One can argue that the Harlem Renaissance represents an artificial movement constructed by intellectuals and activists such as W.E.B. Du Bois, Alain Locke, and Jessie Fauset who viewed art as a means of promotiong social, economic, and political change. Despite their roles as arbiters of the Talented Tenth (the top 10 percent of African Americans in terms of education and socioeconomic opportunity), they viewed the folk as the wellspring of African American history, life, and culture. At a time in which they sought to argue that African Americans possessed a longstanding tradition of artistic and cultural contributions to American society, they valorized the folk as a means of validating the roots of black oral and vernacular expression such as folktales, sermons, and spirituals. In *The Souls of Black Folk* (1903), Du Bois emphasizes that the black folk contributed story, song, sweat, and spirit to the United States as their legacy (214). Alain Locke (1997) notes the preeminence of Harlem as the center of African American creativity. He located Harlem "with those nascent movements of folk-expression and self-determination which are playing a creative part in the world to-day" (xxvii). In this Harlem Renaissance manifesto, Locke contributed "The Negro Spirituals"; the volume also includes Arthur Huff Fauset's "American Negro Folk Literature" and folktales such as "B'rer Rabbit Fools Lizard" and "Compromise (A Folk Play)," written by Willis Richardson. Thus, Locke, like Du Bois, sought to legitimize the folk as a means of understanding African American culture. Zora Neale Hurston's *Mules and Men* (1935) featured folktales, sermons, and songs, illustrating the importance of this tradition to the African American literary canon. The emphasis on the folk-framed discussions of African American literary and artistic production; on the one hand, the emphasis on the folk-validated African American oral expression; on the other hand, writers whose work seemingly reflected bourgeois or proletarian strains remained marginalized and devalued or dismissed as inauthentic representatives of African American experience. Dorothy West's nearly fifty-year hiatus from publishing any novel stemmed from critics' assertions that her work represented a bourgeois aesthetic, while Jessie Fauset faced challenges in publishing her novel *The Chinaberry Tree* because readers at the Frederick A. Stokes publishing company held stereotypical notions that African American experience only encompassed the folk and not the bourgeois or the proletarian. Harlem Renaissance literature consists of all three aesthetics intertwined, and these strains cannot be arbitrarily separated. Rereading the Harlem Renaissance from this new critical viewpoint redefines these writers' texts and their legacies, for women writers such as Zora Neale Hurston, Jessie Fauset, and Dorothy West make problematic the notion that a writer can fit comfortably into one category. Each of these three authors has been mislabeled in the past (e.g., Hurston as folk, Fauset as bourgeois, and West as bourgeois or proletarian).

As a consequence, the politics of publication and reception both assisted and militated against these writers in their attempts at publication as well as critical reception. Deconstructing the tripartite division of folk, bourgeois, and proletarian aesthetics and reconstructing this division into a whole and complete triangular configuration of aesthetics where the aesthetics mutually support and interconnect leads to a greater understanding of African American literature of the Harlem Renaissance. Questioning and interrogating previous critical assumptions regarding what constitutes "authenticity" in African American cultural expression opens up the canon and expands the American literary landscape, creating exciting implications for future directions of African American literary critical study and inquiry. In order to understand the social-historical context of the folk, bourgeois, and proletarian aesthetics, it is necessary to understand the appropriation of these terms in relation to African American history and culture. E. Franklin Frazier (1957) notes, "The folk culture of the American Negro developed out of his experiences on American soil" (100). According to Frazier, Africans transplanted to the New World created their own religious, artistic, and cultural traditions, which were neither completely African nor completely European. As Nathan Huggins (1971) states, "Sophisticated Negroes began to find value in the peasant character of the mass of American Negroes. After all, it was from the common man and the peasant stock that these ingenuous and fresh folk materials were being produced" (73). Educators such as Arthur Huff Fauset (1997), Jessie Fauset's half-brother, sought to preserve African American folklore as the basis of cultural traditions. He contends that folk literature is marked by a focus on nature and a universality of themes (242). Fauset's essay (originally published in 1925) reveals the relevance of folk literature and culture to the aims of the Harlem Renaissance.

The folk aesthetic played a vital role in the formation of African American literature during the Harlem Renaissance. In *Reconstructing Womanhood: The Emergence of the Afro-American Woman Novelist* (1987), Hazel V. Carby suggests that the conception of the folk as manifested in African American literature privileges the southern and rural over the northern and industrial in terms of setting and characterization. She notes, "In search for a tradition of black women writers of fiction a pattern has been established from Alice Walker back through Zora Neale Hurston which represents the rural folk as bearers of Afro-American literary history and preservers of Afro-American culture" (175). Carby rightly assesses the folk as members of a lower socioeconomic class from both southern rural and northern industrial communities who encounter racial, sexual, and class prejudice. Her commentary also suggests the preeminence of the folk aesthetic in the historical conceptualization of the African American women's literary tradition. Folk literature features characters from lower socioeconomic backgrounds, typically laborers in northern industrial settings or farmers in rural, agrarian environments. Writers of the folk aesthetic experiment with dialect and other forms of nonstandard American literature to capture the language of their characters. Folk texts focus on themes such as family, community, oral storytelling, history, and religion. Africanisms (cultural traditions retained from Africa) play an important role as exemplified in religious ceremonies and music. Isolated from the rest of the society through class or geography, these texts tend to feature close-knit communities.

The bourgeois aesthetic serves as a counterpoint to the folk. Angela Davis (1981) attributes the growth and development of the bourgeois class in the United States to the Industrial Revolution of the nineteenth century, which created separate spheres for middle-class men and women as the country changed from a farm-based economy to a machine-based one. While bourgeois middle-class men worked as merchants, judges, factory owners, or doctors in the new urban and industrial worlds, their female counterparts focused on the domestic sphere as wives and mothers (Davis 1981: 31–32). Black women would comprise a relatively small percentage of the bourgeois class due to racial, sexual, and class inequities created by the institution of slavery. Consequently, African Americans still faced disenfranchisement in post-Emancipation America. Historically, a disproportionate number of black women belonged to the working classes as a result of race, class, and gender oppression. In the nineteenth and early twentieth century, many worked for bourgeois white women as maids or nannies.

Literature of the bourgeois aesthetic focuses on the middle class. In African American history, culture, and tradition, the bourgeoisie tends to be viewed as the flipside of the folk, when in reality the two stem from the same background. Kathy Russell, Midge Wilson, and Ronald Hall (1992) emphasize the existence of a bourgeois class among African Americans emerging from a color/class stratification on the plantations among the house and field servants: "Coveted indoor assignments, including artisan, driver, valet, seamstress, cook, and housekeeper, were nearly always reserved for mulattos, while the physically grueling field work was typically left to slaves who were dark skinned" (18). The bourgeois class grew out of the plantation society, consisting of mulatto slaves and ex-slaves who assimilated European beliefs, customs, and traditions in their daily lives. After the Civil War, this elite mulatto class obtained positions of leadership among blacks in Reconstruction-era America. These families segregated themselves socially from the black masses, choosing to worship at Episcopal, Presbyterian, Catholic, and Congregational churches as opposed to the Methodist and Baptist churches attended by working-class blacks (Frazier 1957: 99). As Lawrence Otis Graham (1999) notes, the bifurcation between working-class and middle-class blacks in relation to church membership served as a marker of class distinction: "The Episcopal faith was attractive because of its formality, and both faiths [Episcopal and Congregational] were appealing because they were known for having well-educated clergy and a small number of members" (13). Even after the Civil War, the color/class stratification continued as the mulatto elite consisted of an upper class socially, economically, and politically separate from the black folk or masses: "The elitism that had begun before the Civil War became further entrenched after it, and still remains evident today in the color gap of power and privilege that divides the Black community" (Russell et al. 1992: 24).

Literature focusing on the black bourgeoisie presents an inner view of the rituals, customs, and traditions of the most affluent African Americans. As Bernard Bell (1987) notes, "By focusing on the morals and manners of well-educated members of black high society, they [Harlem Renaissance writers] introduced the novel of manners and genteel realism [the bourgeois aesthetic] into the tradition of the Afro-American novel" (106). Hazel Carby (1987) cites Jessie Fauset in particular when she notes the prevalence of the bourgeois aesthetic in texts by Harlem Renaissance writers: "Fauset's intellectual contribution was the development of an ideology for an emerging black middle-class which would establish it as being acceptably urbane and civilized and which would distinguish it from rural influx" (167). Carby's assessment of Fauset's work suggests that a bourgeois aesthetic encompasses the ideas of social refinement, gentility, and the promotion of middle-class traditional and conservative values. Literature of the bourgeois aesthetic mirrors the concerns of the black middle and upper-middle class of college-educated professionals and entrepreneurs. Characters eschew dialect and speak in a standard American English. As representatives of the Duboisian Talented Tenth, the characters in these texts view themselves as leaders in the African American community. These texts focus on middle and upper-middle-class mores and values of characters who have achieved or aspire to achieving the American Dream.

A third aesthetic, the proletarian, functions as the protest element of the Harlem Renaissance literature movement. Their assertion suggests the crux of the proletarian aesthetic in relation to protest and revolution. Angela Davis (1991) astutely points out that in American history, the rise of the proletariat parallels the emergence of the Industrial Revolution and manufacturing in the United States. Davis notes that black women have always been part of the labor force or proletariat in American history, as slaves, domestics, and factory workers, because of the social, political, and economic climate of the country. Citing statistics from the 1890 census, Davis notes that at the turn of the century, the U.S. population consisted of more than 2.7 million black females eleven years old or older. A large percentage were employed: "More than one million worked for wages: 38.7 percent in agriculture; 30.8 percent in household domestic service; 15.6 percent in laundry work; and a negligible 2.8 percent in manufacturing" (87–88). With the overwhelming presence of black females in the workforce, it should be no surprise that African American women writers of the Harlem Renaissance would depict their plight in fiction as a way of connecting with black women of all socioeconomic levels and calling attention to the interstices of race, class, and gender oppression by employing a proletarian aesthetic. In fact, the periodicals *Challenge* and *New Challenge* (1934–1937), edited by Dorothy West, provided a decidedly proletarian voice and outlet for African American writers. Writing for *New Challenge* in 1937, Richard Wright (2000) notes the existence of the bourgeois and folk classes in the African American community, contending that the writer can bridge the gap between the two worlds: "With the gradual decline of the moral authority of the Negro church, and with the increasing irresolution which is paralyzing Negro middle class leadership, a new role is devolving upon the Negro writer. He is being called upon to do no less than create values by which his race is to struggle, live and die" (969). The views of Wright and others suggest that the proletarian aesthetic embodies the spirit of the working class and revolution. Proletarian literature functions as propaganda and a vehicle for social change. Overtly critical of racial, class, and gender hierarchies, these texts may feature characters from the folk and/or bourgeois classes as a means to meditate on power dynamics and relations in American society.

In order to understand fully and appreciate the contributions of Jessie Fauset, Zora Neale Hurston, and Dorothy West and their aesthetic voices, it is necessary to place them within the context of the African American female literary tradition in the United States. As Hazel Carby (1987: 23) notes, black women faced discrimination when attempting to exert their voices due to the concept of "true womanhood"—which excluded black women. The African American women who wrote slave narratives during the nineteenth century were writing in the midst of the domestic ideology of true womanhood and had to negotiate their status as black women and slaves (ex-slaves) in relation to this concept, which focused on the ideal woman as being religious, passive, chaste, and white (Carby 1997). Writing in the face of a domestic ideology which often excluded them, the black female authors of slave narratives had to develop alternative conceptions of true womanhood that valorized blackness, power, ingenuity, subversiveness, physical strength, and sexual autonomy.

While writing within the conventions of the sentimental tradition and true womanhood domestic ideology, some African American women writers managed to provide cogent and compelling commentary on issues of race, class, and gender. Harriet Jacobs in *Incidents in the Life of a Slave Girl* (1861) and Harriet Wilson in *Our Nig* (1859), a novel set in the North depicting the life of a biracial indentured servant that illustrates that slavery existed in the North as well, also subverted these very conventions through the presentation of self-reliant black women. Their commentary on the religious hypocrisy of "true white women," their emphasis on sexual autonomy as a positive force, and their focus on the importance of the black female voice as a means of creating a nation encompassing the ideal of a true democracy for all people mark a crucial stage in the development of African American literature. By engaging in a new discourse on womanhood and particularly black womanhood in America, Jacobs and Wilson paved the way for the black women writers of the Harlem Renaissance such as Jessie Fauset, Zora Neale Hurston, and Dorothy West.

However, it is important to note the existence, significance, and prevalence of black women writers, orators, and club women at the turn of the century whose multiplicity of voices serve as a bridge between the slave narratives of Jacobs and Wilson and the fiction of Fauset, Hurston, and West. Black women such as Anna Julia Cooper, Mary Church Terrell, Ida B. Wells, and Frances E. W. Harper wrote novels, articles, poetry, and speeches critiquing the racial, sexual, and class prejudice in the United States. As part of the black women's club movement, these highly educated African American women formed organizations which advocated black women's rights. Educator, orator, and writer Anna Julia Cooper (1892) argues in favor of higher education for black women, criticizes the unfair discrimination black female artists face, and demands that the black female's voice be heard in the social, political, and economic areas of American society. Similarly, Frances E. W. Harper connects to the plight of the African American female. Her landmark novel *Iola Leroy* (1892) features a light-skinned heroine who chooses to live as a black woman (although she can pass for white) in the South to work toward spiritual, educational, and emotional uplift for rural blacks in North Carolina.

Like Cooper and Harper, Mary Church Terrell spoke about the importance of education, empowerment, and activism for black women through her association with the black women's club movement in speeches and essays, proving herself an able educator and orator. Ida B. Wells, a journalist and publisher, used the antilynching crusade to call attention to the presence of African American women in the political, literary, and social arena of the nineteenth century (Davis 1991: 135–36). Cooper, Harper, and Terrell express the multiplicity of voices among black women at the turn of the century as they serve as a point of contact between antebellum and postbellum American female writers. While Jacobs and Wilson commented on the need for emancipation of slaves, Cooper, Harper, Terrell, and Wells speak to the plight of the "emancipated" slave and the need for the country to address the social, economic, and political inequities African Americans faced in the twentieth century. Fauset, Hurston, and West would later function as a response to the call for racial, sexual, and class parity in their depiction of the African American experience in their exploration of folk, bourgeois, and proletarian aesthetics.

The Harlem Renaissance reflects an important stage in the development of African American literature. The emergence of the Harlem Renaissance can be traced back to the publication of Du Bois's *The Souls of Black Folks: Essays and Sketches* in 1903. This landmark text chronicles the color line in nineteenth- and twentieth-century America while exploring the artistic and cultural contributions of African Americans. The themes of double consciousness among African Americans (feeling both their identities as blacks of African descent and their present reality as Americans), along with his tribute to the work, toil, and spirit of the black masses, would set a context for the evolution of the New Negro—articulate, proactive, and committed to the ideas of racial equality and justice. The Great Black Migration from the rural, agrarian South to the urban, industrialized North, the end of World War I in 1918 and the return of African American soldiers committed to making the United States live up to its credo of "freedom and justice for all" created a social, political, and economic climate for the movement. The publication of Alain Locke's anthology *The New Negro* in 1925 also signifies an important date in the formative stages of the Harlem Renaissance as the text articulates the goals of social, economic, and political equality for African Americans. A variety of social and economic factors led to the end of the Harlem Renaissance, the 1929 stock market crash and the onset of the Great Depression of the 1930s. The Great Depression reduced the number of publishing companies and magazines that served as outlets for literary works. Publishing companies had less capital for manufacturing books and fewer consumers with monetary resources to buy them, and so they contracted fewer books. Similarly, visual artists found themselves with fewer outlets for selling artworks.

Prior to the Harlem Renaissance, there had not been such a self-conscious and widespread collective movement among African Americans to revise stereotypical notions of African Americans through art, literature, and politics. Through journals such as *Fire!!*, the *Crisis, Opportunity,* the *Messenger, Challenge,* and *New Challenge,* African American writers, activists, and visual and performing artists sought to reconceptualize the "New Negro," who was strong, independent, self-actualized, and proud of his or her heritage as an American of African descent. The New Negro Movement also promoted the idea of Pan-Africanism, a philosophy that called for unity among blacks of African descent worldwide and an end to racial injustice and oppression. In the meantime, African American political activists and educators, along with more liberal whites, worked collaboratively for black civil rights and social changes. Working for voting rights, anti-lynching legislation, and educational and employment opportunities, these organizations believed that art should be used for propagandistic purposes. They hoped that through artistic, literary, and musical achievement, African Americans could show their humanity and their equality while advocating social and political change. The NAACP, through the *Crisis,* and the Urban League, through *Opportunity,* gave voice and space to promising young Harlem writers during the heyday of the Harlem Renaissance. While literary editor of the *Crisis* from 1919 to 1926 and the *Brownies Book* (a magazine for children) from 1920 to 1921, Jessie Fauset published the works of notable writers such as Langston Hughes and Nella Larsen. As Diane Johnson Feelings notes, "Jessie Fauset deserves more recognition than she is generally given for her influential work as an editor" (19). Zora Neale Hurston won literary awards from *Opportunity* magazine, which published several of her short stories, including "Drenched in Light" (1924), "Spunk" (1925), and "Muttsy" (1926). Dorothy West won an award for her story "The Typewriter" in 1926 (the same year that Hurston won a prize from *Opportunity* magazine for her short story "Muttsy" and her play *Color Struck*). The efforts of the NAACP and the Urban League were also fueled by the militancy and frustration African Americans felt after World War I; many black men served valiantly and heroically overseas only to return to the United States to be treated like second-class citizens.

The Harlem Renaissance also coincides with the modernist movement. The sense of fragmentation, alienation, and deterioration brought about by World War I created a malaise among writers, intellectuals, and artists during the 1920s and 1930s. The Western World, which many viewed as the origin of civilization, had been destroyed, and a new world would emerge. Harlem artists sought to conceptualize the new world despite their ambivalence about whether the future held more promise than the past. African American writers of the modernist period often thought globally as a result of their travels. Many of them lived overseas for various periods of time, like Claude McKay and Langston Hughes, or studied abroad like Fauset, or even traveled to Communist Europe—West and Hughes visited Russia in 1932. While Marcus Garvey and his followers exhorted African Americans to head back to the motherland in his Back to Africa Movement, African American intellectuals such as Du Bois and Fauset became involved in the Pan-African Movement, which sought unity and equality for blacks of African descent worldwide. Not surprisingly, Africa plays an important part in Harlem Renaissance literature as the ancestral home of black Americans. Countee Cullen's poem "Heritage" (Cullen 2000: 448) queries "What is Africa to me?" as he meditates on the meaning of Africa to African Americans. This movement, not surprisingly, relied heavily on the largesse of patrons of the arts, many of whom were white philanthropists. For example, Charlotte Osgood Mason provided money to both Langston Hughes and Zora Neale Hurston to support their writing and Hurston's folklore-collecting expeditions, but her imperious ways and her rigid concepts of what constituted "authentic" African American creativity erected a barrier that could not be breached between her and the writers she patronized: she held a notion that African American art should be "primitivistic." Another patron was Joel Spingarn, namesake of the Spingarn Medal, awarded to African Americans who demonstrated excellence. As David Levering Lewis (1989) points out, nearly half the winners during the period of 1924–1931 made their living as writers or artists (179–80). The philanthropist William E. Harmon also sponsored an award, with prizes for outstanding achievement in fine arts, music, and literature (Lewis 1989: 179).

The New Negro Movement ostensibly promoted an idea of egalitarianism and offered opportunities for individuals who had been marginalized, but a close study of the period suggests that sexual prejudice and oppression often permeated the doctrines and ideologies of the movement. As a consequence, black women writers had to strive harder to conquer the racial mountain in reconfiguring the literary landscape. As Gloria Hull (1987) notes, black women writers of the Harlem Renaissance faced marginalization from their gender and preconceived notions of appropriate behavior and vocations for women. Harlem Renaissance authors depended heavily on patronage or sponsorship, and individuals such as Alain Locke, who published the Harlem Renaissance manifesto *The New Negro* in 1925, discriminated against women writers. Hull writes, "The problem with Locke, however, is that he behaved misogynistically and actively favored men" (7). Locke went to great lengths to assist men in achieving publishing contracts and financial support but expressed no desire to assist women artists. As Hull notes, "This personality-patronage issue broadens into general revelations about the customary male circles of power and friendship, which during the period crossed racial lines" (9). In addition, acceptable modes of female behavior at the time prevented women from networking at bars or other establishments that men frequented to make contacts in the publishing world. They tended to lack the social freedom to travel alone or at the spur of the moment like men. Hull states, "They were much more likely to be tied to place via husbands, children, familial responsibilities, parental prohibitions, lack of fresh opportunities or the spirit of adventure, and so on" (12). Consequently, Hurston, West, and Fauset stand out in their abilities and opportunities to travel. Not surprisingly, West never married or had children. Fauset did not marry until 1929, when she was forty-seven years old (much older than the traditional bride at that time), and Hurston married and divorced twice, most likely from the pressures on her relationships from her desire to travel and to be independent. Not only did these three women writers challenge stereotypical notions of womanhood at the time, but they attempted to challenge stereotypical notions of what constituted authentic African American literature. Their rebellion often militated against them as they sought to explode the narrow confines of what constituted accepted African American artistic expression. Thus, the politics of publication during the Harlem Renaissance, which often privileged the folk or presented African Americans as the primitivistic and eroticized Other, profoundly affected the production and reception of African American writers such as Fauset, Hurston, and West.

Jessie Fauset, Zora Neale Hurston, and Dorothy West stand as a triumvirate in the canon of African American literature. Their work embodies the complexity and interstices of folk, bourgeois, and proletarian aesthetics. The literary legacies they bequeathed to the reading public differ in degree but not in kind. Through the appropriation of narrative strategies, including the bildungsroman and the kunstlerroman, the three women writers meditated on race, class, and gender in American society. Abrams (1993) stresses, "The subject of these novels is the development of the protagonist's mind and character, in the passage from childhood through varied experiences—and often through a spiritual crisis—into maturity and the recognition of his or her identity and role in the world" (132). For African American women writers, the bildungsroman may be an appealing narrative strategy in its focus on the individual's growth and perception of her place in the world. The bildungsroman narrative form enables the writer to approach a variety of subjects, including the roles race, class, and gender play in a person's conception of identity.

The kunstlerroman, the artist's coming of age, is a type of bildungsroman. According to Abrams (1993), "An important subtype of the Bildungsroman is the Kunstlerroman ('artist novel'), which represents the growth of a novelist or other artist into the stage of maturity that signalizes the recognition of the protagonist's artistic destiny and mastery of an artistic craft" (133). As literary artists, African American women writers may appropriate the kunstlerroman as a means of signifying the role race, class, and gender play in the source and development of their art. The kunstlerroman functions as a means of presenting the writer's own growth and development through the forum of literature. As a result, the kunstlerroman seems an effective vehicle for examining the black woman's struggle for voice and artistic expression. This rereading of the Harlem Renaissance examines the works of Jessie Fauset, Zora Neale Hurston, and Dorothy West by focusing on the connection between their use of narrative strategies such as the bildungsroman and the kunstlerroman to meditate on the African American experience. Analyzing the connection between narrative technique and more formal aspects of their work will reveal the complex arrangement of aesthetics in it—the folk, bourgeois, and proletarian—while shedding new light on the politics of race, class, and gender in their writing. Rereading their work in this way increases the understanding and appreciation of their literary artistry and innovations while illustrating that these aesthetics function together to create the totality of African American experience.

One of the most significant individuals in shaping the direction of the Harlem Renaissance was Jessie Fauset (1882–1961). Born in Camden County, New Jersey, Fauset grew up in Philadelphia, Pennsylvania. She attended Cornell University and graduated Phi Beta Kappa in 1905. She worked as a foreign language teacher of French and Latin in a Baltimore high school and later landed a position as a teacher at the prestigious M Street High School in Washington, D.C. She received an M.A. from the University of Pennsylvania in 1919 and also studied at the Sorbonne in Paris. She served as literary editor for the *Crisis* from 1919 to 1926. She wrote four novels that were published during her lifetime: *There Is Confusion* (1924), *Plum Bun* (1929), *The Chinaberry Tree* (1931), and *Comedy: American Style* (1933). This study will explore how Fauset employs the narrative strategies of bildungsroman and kunstlerroman in her four published novels, and several of her short stories from the *Crisis*, to meditate on folk, bourgeois, and proletarian aesthetics. Exploring the connection between narrative technique, theme, plot, symbolism, and characterization in Fauset's work provides a more sophisticated reading of her literary works.

Zora Neale Hurston (1891–1960) is often considered a writer who embodies the folk aesthetic, but there are strong bourgeois and proletarian strains in her work. Although it can be argued that she has folk origins because of her small-town southern background in Notasulga, Alabama, and Eatonville, Florida, she attended elite institutions of higher learning.[3] Her studies of literature and anthropology at Howard University and Barnard College provided her with a critical methodology for viewing individuals at all levels of society. *Jonah's Gourd Vine, Their Eyes Were Watching God, Moses, Man of the Mountain, Seraph on the Suwanee*, and several of her short stories exemplify her ability to appropriate narrative strategies such as the bildungsroman and the kunstlerroman to analyze the politics of race, class, and gender. Examining the connection between Hurston's narrative techniques and the themes, plots, symbols, and characterizations in her work provides a fresh look at the combination of aesthetics in her fiction—the folk, bourgeois, and proletarian.

Up to the time of her death, Dorothy West (1907–1998) was the oldest living writer of the Harlem Renaissance, and like Fauset, her work has been often overlooked or dismissed as "genteel" or "elite."[4] Born in Boston, she studied at both Boston University and the Columbia University School of Journalism. West won second prize in 1926 for her story "The Typewriter" in the *Opportunity* magazine short-story contest. Hurston earned a second-place prize for her story "Muttsy" that year as well. Through founding and editing *Challenge* and *New Challenge* from 1934 to 1937, West attempted to carry the fire and intensity generated by writers during the heyday of the Harlem Renaissance into the 1930s. Her books *The Living Is Easy* (1948), *The Wedding* (1995), and *The Richer, the Poorer* (1995) represent her provocative analysis of race, class, and gender. Of the three writers examined in the present study, considerably less attention has been paid to West's role in the Harlem Renaissance by studies of the period. This may be because her first novel was not published until after the Harlem Renaissance ended.

This examination of Fauset, Hurston, and West's works will also provide insights into the ways in which scholars of African American literature critique and assess the works of women writers of the Harlem Renaissance in terms of the folk aesthetic, the bourgeois aesthetic, and the proletarian aesthetic. A study of this scope and breadth calls for both historical and feminist critical approaches. A historical approach will provide the social, cultural, political, and economic context within which the women writers of the Harlem Renaissance negotiated their space as creative artists. The historical approach will also contextualize their fictional representations of the African American experience in their literature. The feminist approach will shed light on the connection between race and gender in their work as it relates to both the production of literature during the Harlem Renaissance and the depictions of the black female experience in their fiction. The two approaches, used in conjunction in this way, will illustrate how race and gender coincide with issues of class and political power in relation to the writers and their artistic creations and will offer enlightenment on the representations of the folk, bourgeois, and proletarian aesthetics in their literature. Examining formal elements of the texts (i.e., genre, point of view, irony) from historical and feminist perspectives allows us to remap and reconfigure the authors' literary contributions to the Harlem Renaissance.

Admittedly, employing historical and feminist approaches offers limitations for the scholar and critic. Viewing a work within a certain historical context may be problematic if one imposes or overemphasizes the relation of social, political, and economic events to the production of the text. Historical approaches sometimes obscure the formal elements of the text. Feminist approaches may be problematic as well by focusing on gender issues while obscuring other important elements or influences upon the work. Historical and feminist readings may obscure the role that other forces play in the text's composition, publication, and reception. Nevertheless, the historical and feminist perspectives offer the best tools for exploring folk, bourgeois, and proletarian aesthetics.

Fauset, Hurston, and West subvert the categories of the folk, the bourgeois, and the proletarian through their application of theme, plot, characterization, and symbolism from the bildungsroman and the kunstlerroman traditions. For example, in *There Is Confusion,* Jessie Fauset uses the narrative form of the kunstlerroman to chart the growth, development, and maturation of Joanna Marshall, an African American singer and dancer. In *Plum Bun,* Fauset appropriates the nursery rhyme, fairytale motifs, bildungsroman, and kunstlerroman in depicting the life of Angela Murray, a light-skinned black artist who passes for white. Fauset's *Chinaberry Tree* employs conventions of Greek tragedy, bildungsroman, and kunstlerroman to document the life of Laurentine Strange, a seamstress of mixed racial ancestry who succeeds in finding love and happiness despite the fact that her race and gender often militate against her. *Comedy: American Style,* Fauset's last novel, uses the bildungsroman form and narrative is organized according to elements of drama and the stage, in that the chapters contain headings such as "Setting," "Plot," "Acts," and "Final Curtain." The narrative technique highlights the tragic consequences of protagonist Olivia Cary's color consciousness as a light-skinned black woman, which destroys her family and sense of identity. In "The Sleeper Wakes" (the *Crisis* 1920), "Double Trouble" (the *Crisis* 1923), and "Mary Elizabeth" (the *Crisis* 1919), Fauset also meditates on the politics of race, class, and gender through folk, bourgeois, and proletarian narrative technique, theme, and imagery.

*Jonah's Gourd Vine, Their Eyes Were Watching God, Moses, Man of the Mountain,* and *Seraph on the Suwanee* represent Zora Neale Hurston's deft exploration of race, class, and gender. In *Jonah's Gourd Vine,* Hurston adopts the bildungsroman, kunstlerroman, and biblical allegory to chart the social, political, and economic rise of John Pearson, a black preacher. *Their Eyes Were Watching God* utilizes the bildungsroman and kunstlerroman in the depiction of Janie Crawford's quest for selfhood in the wake of three marriages to men of different social and economic classes. In *Moses, Man of the Mountain,* Hurston employs the bildungsroman and revises the biblical tale of Moses and the Exodus in her meditation on race, class, and gender. In *Seraph on the Suwanee,* Hurston uses the bildungsroman and biblical imagery in her exploration of the life of protagonist Arvay Henson, whose social and economic rise depicts the transformation from the Old South to the New South. Her short stories "Spunk" (*Opportunity* 1925), "Sweat" (*Fire!!* 1926), "The Gilded Six Bits" (*Story* 1933), and "The Bone of Contention" (1930–1935, unpublished during Hurston's lifetime) reflect the development of the formal components of her narrative technique as mediated through the triangle of folk, bourgeois, and proletarian aesthetics.

Dorothy West also employs a variety of narrative strategies, including bildungsroman, kunstlerroman, and first and third person narration, in *The Living Is Easy, The Wedding,* and *The Richer, the Poorer,* the last a comprehensive collection of her short fiction and autobiographical essays. In *The Living Is Easy,* West appropriates the bildungsroman in her exploration of Cleo Judson's coming of age in the South, her migration to the North in search of better economic opportunity, and her downward mobility as a result of her elitism and disrespect for other people. In *The Wedding,* West utilizes the bildungsroman as the underlying structure to the slave narrative form in her novel about the coming of age of the Coles family, who rise from the folk to the bourgeoisie socially and economically. West's *The Richer, the Poorer* features a variety of genres, including short story and nonfiction essay, as she adopts the bildungsroman and kunstlerroman as narrative strategies. Her appropriation of those techniques work in tandem with her exploration of race, class, and gender constructs in her explication of folk, "bourgeois," and proletarian elements in African American literature. Recent anthologies illustrate the prolific output of women writers of the Harlem Renaissance. Maureen Honey's *Shadowed Dreams: Women's Poetry of the Harlem Renaissance* (1989), Marcy Knopf's *Sleeper Wakes: Harlem Renaissance Stories by Women* (1993), Ann Allen Shockley's *Afro-American Women Writers 1746–1933: An Anthology and Critical Guide* (1987), David Levering Lewis's *Portable Harlem Renaissance Reader* (1994), and *Double-Take: A Revisionist Harlem Renaissance Anthology* (2001), coedited by Maureen Honey and Venetria K. Patton, reflect the growing interest in recovering texts by African American women writers. These texts feature works by Fauset, Hurston, and West, illustrating the ever-expanding number of anthologies devoted to presenting their literary legacy. Consequently, reviewing these three writers in context with one another offers a valuable rereading of racial, class, and gender politics in the Harlem Renaissance.

While exemplifying the bourgeoisie in her education and in her positions as literary editor of the *Crisis* and as a schoolteacher, Jessie Fauset's fiction and nonfiction call attention to the folk as the root of African American identity and heritage. Through her valorization of the folk, Fauset reveals a proletarian aesthetic of the brotherhood and sisterhood of humanity. While Zora Neale Hurston may have epitomized the folk through her self-representation as a product of the southern rural experience, she adopted methodologies learned at elite institutions of higher learning and negotiated bourgeois social circles to obtain patronage to fund her writing. Hurston's insistence on the dignity of all individuals regardless of race, class, and gender in her work suggests a proletarian aesthetic. In a career spanning more than half a century, Dorothy West illustrated that despite her bourgeois upbringing in Boston as the daughter of a wealthy black entrepreneur with the material wealth to own a home on Martha's Vineyard, she never forgot that her family's roots rest in the rural South and folk experience. Through her fiction and nonfiction, West critiqued racial, sexual, and class prejudice, which indicates the proletarian aesthetic underlying her work. Theoretical frameworks for African American women's writing must accommodate the notion that all three aesthetics work in conjunction with each other to present the richness and vitality of African American cultural expression. By rereading African American literature through a lens that acknowledges that a multiplicity of aesthetics exist in literary texts, we liberate the authors from arbitrary labels and we liberate ourselves as readers to appreciate the complexity of Harlem Renaissance writings while debunking simplistic and stereotypical notions of what constitutes authentic African American literature.

## NOTES

1. Fauset's essay illustrates her role as a participant in this conference held in Great Britain to address the social, political, and economic problems blacks faced worldwide in the early twentieth century

2. In her article, Hurston laments the lack of fiction on middle-class blacks due to white publishers' desires for stereotypical depictions of black life as one-dimensional or primitive.

3. Wall (1995) points out that Hurston was born in Notasulga, Alabama, and not Eatonville, Florida. Wall suggests that for blacks Eatonville symbolized the spirit of the "New Negro" as an all-black community in which blacks held social, political, and economic autonomy from whites.

4. The history of African American literary production is incomplete; previously unknown novels and stories continue to surface. Foster (1994) stresses that many African American novels lie embedded in newspapers and church periodicals as a result of the popularity of serialization.

## REFERENCES

Abrams, M. H. 1993. *A Glossary of Literary Terms.* Fort Worth, Tex.: Harcourt Brace.

Bell, Bernard. 1987. *The Afro-American Novel and Its Tradition.* Amherst: University of Massachusetts Press.

Carby, Hazel. 1987. *Reconstructing Womanhood: The Emergence of the Afro-American Woman Novelist.* New York: Oxford University Press.

Cooper, Anna Julia. 1892. *A Voice from the South.* New York: Oxford University Press.

Cullen, Countee. 2000. "Heritage," Pp. 448–51 in *The Prentice Hall Anthology of African American Literature,* eds. Rochelle Smith and Sharon L. Jones. Upper Saddle River, N.J.: Prentice Hall.

Davis, Angela Y. 1981. *Women, Race, and Class.* New York: Random House.

Fauset, Arthur Huff. 1997. "American Negro Folk Literature." Pp. 238–44 in *The New Negro: Voices of the Harlem Renaissance,* ed. Alain Locke. New York: Simon and Schuster.

Fauset, Jessie. 1995. "Impressions of the Second Pan-African Congress." Pp. 367–82 in *The Chinaberry Tree and Selected Writings,* ed. Richard Yarborough. Boston: Northeastern University Press. (Originally published in the *Crisis,* Nov. 1921, 12–18).

Foster, France Smith, ed. 1994. *Minnie's Sacrifice, Sowing and Reaping, Trial and Triumph: Three Rediscovered Novels by Frances E. W. Harper.* Boston: Beacon Publishers.

Frazier, E. Franklin. 1957. *Black Bourgeoisie: The Rise of a New Middle Class in the United States.* New York: Macmillan.

Graham, Lawrence Otis. 1999. *Our Kind of People: Inside America's Black Upper Class.* New York: Harper Collins.

"Harlem Renaissance." 2001. *Vanity Fair,* September, 192–93.

Huggins, Nathan. 1971. *Harlem Renaissance.* New York: Oxford University Press.

Hull, Gloria. 1987. *Color, Sex, and Poetry: Three Writers of the Harlem Renaissance.* Bloomington: Indiana University Press.

Hurston, Zora Neale. 1995. "What White Publishers Won't Print." Pp. 950–55 in *Folklore, Memoirs, and Other Writings,* ed. Cheryl Wall. New York: Library of America. (Originally published in Negro Digest, April 1950, 85–89).

Lewis, David Levering. 1989. *When Harlem Was in Vogue.* New York: Oxford University Press.

Locke, Alain, ed. 1997. *The New Negro: Voices of the Harlem Renaissance.* New York: Simon and Schuster. (Originally published in 1925).

Russell, Kathy; Midge Wilson; and Ronald Hall. 1992. *The Color Complex: The Politics of Skin Color among African Americans.* New York: Harcourt Brace Jovanovich.

Wall, Cheryl. 1995. *Women of the Harlem Renaissance.* Bloomington: Indiana University Press.

Weldon, James. 1997. "Harlem: The Culture Capital." Pp. 301–11 in *The New Negro: Voices of the Harlem Renaissance,* ed. Alain Locke. New York: Simon and Schuster. (Originally published in 1925).

West, Dorothy. 1995. "The Legend of Oak Bluffs." Pp. 235–42 in *The Richer, the Poorer.* New York: Doubleday.

Wright, Richard. 2000. "Blueprint for Negro Writing." Pp. 965–73 in *The Prentice Hall Anthology of African American Literature,* eds. Rochelle Smith and Sharon L. Jones. Upper Saddle River, N.J.: Prentice Hall.

# 1

# Deconstructing the Black Bourgeoisie: Subversions and Diversions in the Fiction of Jessie Fauset

When more than one hundred of the leading black and white writers, publishers, and editors of the 1920s met at New York's Civic Club on 21 March 1924, to celebrate the publication of Jessie Fauset's *There Is Confusion*, it served as the dress rehearsal for the Harlem Renaissance. The publication of Fauset's first novel was particularly significant because only a handful of blacks over the previous two decades, including W. E. B. Du Bois, James Weldon Johnson, Claude McKay, and Jean Toomer, had published notable works (Lewis 1989). The dress rehearsal, which brought together leading figures in the fields of arts and letters, spawned a special black literature issue of *The Survey Graphic*. The success of the special issue prompted Alain Locke to publish *The New Negro* in 1925, a manifesto of the artistic goals of the Harlem Renaissance. More importantly, the events occurring at the Civic Club dinner illustrate Fauset's contribution in laying the foundations for the Harlem Renaissance. The event also reveals the racial, sexual, and class politics of the movement: "What started out to be an informal gathering honoring Fauset turned into the well-orchestrated 'debut of the younger school of Negro writers.' The description is Charles S. Johnson's; the *Opportunity* editor was the event's guiding hand. If, as he would write afterward, there had been 'no formal, prearranged program,' the evening's unwritten agenda was crystal clear. So was the fact that the proceeding had little to do with Jessie Fauset" (Wall 1995: 69).

Ironically, the event showcasing *There Is Confusion* turned into a program that highlighted the promising futures of other, male, writers, nearly obscuring Fauset's own achievements.

Although Fauset served as the guest of honor, she played a minor role in the Civic Club dinner. Alain Locke served as master of ceremonies, and a number of black writers, including Langston Hughes, Gwendolyn Bennett, Eric Walrond, Walter White, and James Weldon Johnson, were introduced to luminaries in the publishing field. When Horace Liveright, whose company published *There Is Confusion*, addressed the audience, he spotlighted the publication of Jean Toomer's *Cane* (Wall 1995). Afterward, W. E. B. Du Bois, James Weldon Johnson, Carl Van Doren of *Century Magazine*, Walter White, Montgomery Gregory, and the art collector Albert Barnes addressed the audience about the importance of African American literature before Jessie Fauset had the opportunity to speak (Wall 1995). Consequently, in the same way Fauset's achievements were not foregrounded in a dinner held for the publication of her novel, chronicles of the Harlem Renaissance have often not highlighted her achievements despite her influential role in the literary movement as editor, writer, mentor, and confidante.

When *There Is Confusion* appeared in 1924, it received mostly favorable reviews. George Schuyler (the *Messenger*), Fred DeArmond (*Opportunity*), and reviewers from the *New York Times* "Book Review" section and the *Times Literary Supplement* praised its merits in presenting the African American experience (Sylvander 1981).[1]

The tendency to label Fauset's fiction as genteel still exists in more contemporary assessments of *There Is Confusion*. Nathan Huggins (1971) stresses the book's focus on the black bourgeoisie in its representation of African American culture and life. Similarly, Bernard Bell (1987) contends that Fauset's emphasis on middle-class African Americans reveals an author and narrator removed from the concerns and plight of the masses (107). These assessments of *There Is Confusion* emphasize the bourgeois aesthetic present in her works. However, a close reading of *There Is Confusion* and Fauset's second novel *Plum Bun* reveals a valorization of the folk as the basis for African American artistic, psychological, and cultural well-being and reveal as well a strong proletarian element in the protests against racial and sexual discrimination in American society.

Additionally, an understanding of Jessie Fauset's background reveals a real confluence of folk, bourgeois, and proletarian aesthetics, which further supports a rereading of her works to acknowledge the variety of its strains and impulses. While Jessie Fauset has often been described as a genteel woman from a bourgeois background, a close inspection of her life reveals this is not the case. Born in Camden County, New Jersey, on 27 April 1882, Fauset was the daughter of Annie Seamon Fauset and Redmon Fauset (Sylvander 1981). Her father held an exalted position in the community from his position as a minister for the African Methodist Episcopal (A.M.E.) Church. Redmon Fauset's position gave him prestige but little financial remuneration other than money collected from the church congregation (Sylvander 1981). A talented man, his unwillingness to hold back on his opinions may have contributed to his not reaching a higher status in the church. In her fiction, Fauset often portrays individuals with bourgeois aspirations who lack the financial resources to satisfy their intended lifestyle, which reflects the reality of her upbringing.

Fauset came from a large family of biological siblings and half-siblings. The family appeared to have all the trappings of the black middle class due to the prestige of her father's occupation and the genteel manner in which they led their daily lives, yet they possessed none of the capital or the financial resources associated with the black bourgeoisie. A strong-minded man, Redmon Fauset upset the upper-class establishment in Philadelphia in his strident display of his beliefs and attitudes: "Evidently outspoken, intelligent, intellectual, self-educated, controversial, and a strong influence on Jessie Fauset by her own evaluation, the real Reverend Redmon Fauset is not the kind of man who comes to mind when one reads of an old established Philadelphia family, or of a comfortable middle class life" (Sylvander 1981: 26). Unlike Dorothy West, who attended a private preparatory school in Boston, Fauset attended a racially integrated public school. The experience of being the sole black student in her high school classes caused some anxiety for her, which she replicates in her novels through the portrayal of segregation between blacks and whites in the North. Nevertheless, while attending the Philadelphia High School for Girls, she flourished academically, if not socially. Like other black women of the early twentieth century, Fauset pursued a higher education as a means of becoming a teacher, one of the few occupations available for a college-educated black women of the time (Sylvander 1981).

Fauset attended Cornell University on scholarship, which must have greatly relieved the financial tensions in the household. While there, Fauset studied Greek, German, French, English, political science, bibliography, archeology, ethics, and logic as well as history and psychology. Her firm foundation in these studies must have proven an important part of her development as an artist, since Fauset incorporates a variety of disciplines in her astute criticisms of social, political, historical, and economic aspects of American society. At Cornell University, she attended classes primarily with the white bourgeoisie, and was exposed to the customs, traditions, and rituals associated with the upper strata of society. In addition, her period of time at Cornell facilitated her meeting and correspondence with W. E. B. Du Bois. A white dean and head of sociology at Cornell named Walter Willcox corresponded with Du Bois on behalf of Fauset to inquire about obtaining a teaching position for her in 1903 (Sylvander 1981).

Later that year, Fauset herself wrote to Du Bois about a teaching job for the following year, preferably in the South, as a means of getting to know another stratum of the black population (Sylvander 1981). She relocated to Tennessee in the summer of 1904, where she taught grammar and American literature at Fisk University. Her desire to go to the South suggests a sense of adventure and a willingness to travel into uncharted territory, especially an environment more formally segregated than the one that she left. Despite the challenges of being a part of a small number of black students, Fauset graduated Phi Beta Kappa from Cornell University in 1905 (Sylvander 1981).

Between 1905 and 1918, Fauset taught at Douglass High School in Baltimore and the prestigious M Street High School (renamed Dunbar High School in

1916) in Washington, D.C., a school attended by the children of the black bourgeoisie (Sylvander 1981). The institution was considered to be "the jewel of black
public secondary schools" (Wall 1995: 42). The faculty of M Street High School
held degrees from the best institutions in the country, and here Fauset would
have found other individuals with excellent academic credentials. Nevertheless,
Fauset did not teach out of pure love for the vocation. Because of her modest
economic background and her father's meager income, she had to teach to survive economically, and she helped pay for the education of her sister Helen (Sylvander 1981). This, again, illustrates her modest economic means and challenges
the misconception that she was a full-fledged member of black bourgeoisie. As
Wall (1995) writes, "Fauset had no money of her own; neither did she have a
wealthy benefactor" (36). By the same token, between 1912 and 1919 (the year
she assumed literary editorship of the *Crisis*), Fauset steadily contributed short
fiction, poetry, and book reviews to the publication, a publication that had a wide
readership among black middle- and upper-class Americans. Furthermore, even
though she lived in Washington, D.C., for most of that period, she quietly
worked behind the scenes advising NAACP officials on policies and assisting
with their efforts to end racial discrimination (Sylvander 1981). In 1919 Fauset
had earned an M.A. degree in French from the University of Pennsylvania.

    Fauset's inclusion of folk, bourgeois, and proletarian aesthetics in her fiction
stems from her own socioeconomic background and an attempt to revamp and
redefine the predominant images of African Americans in American fiction prior
to the Harlem Renaissance. More importantly, it reveals the social, political, and
economic politics of literary production of the 1920s and earlier. Nineteenth-
century American literature often featured sentimentalized and stereotypical
portraits of African Americans as exemplified in Joel Chandler Harris's Uncle
Remus tales, Thomas Dixon's *Clansman: A Historical Romance* (1905), or
George Washington Cable's short stories, set in nineteenth-century Louisiana
(Brawley 2000). Writing both within and against the sentimental tradition of
the nineteenth century, African American writers such as Charles Chesnutt and
Paul Laurence Dunbar sought to challenge and transform earlier stereotypical
portraits of African American life. While Chesnutt and Dunbar made strides in
challenging sentimentalized portraits of African Americans in the nineteenth
century, their twentieth-century counterparts confronted similar problems in
refuting the one-dimensional and distorted images of African Americans in popular fiction. When World War I ended, white artists, thinkers, and writers began
to reevaluate themselves, the Western traditions, and their relation to world history. Feeling alienated, confused, and imprisoned, they portrayed Afro-American culture as vital, primitive, exotic, exciting, and uninhibited by the constraints
of Western civilization. Consequently, writers such as Jessie Fauset challenged
stereotypical notions of African American culture. While she adopted traditional
narrative forms such as the bildungsroman, the kunstlerroman, and fairytale
motifs, she subverted these genres and motifs through the sophisticated deconstruction of race, class, and gender.

Viewing Fauset's work within the social, political, and economic background of literary production and reception makes the publication of *There Is Confusion* all the more remarkable for its attempt to revise the perceptions of blacks in African American literature: "*There Is Confusion* was [T. S.] Stribling's *Birthright* [which had appeared in 1922] rewritten to the approved literary canons of the Talented Tenth, a saga of the sophisticated in which French and occasionally German tripped from the protagonists' tongues as readily as precise English; a novel about people with good bloodlines whose presence in the Algonquin Hotel dining room—but for a telltale swarthiness—would have been tout à fait comme il faut" (Lewis 1989: 124).[2] *Birthright* elicited controversy among African American intellectuals troubled by the novel's implication that to be African American and educated means to live a tragic existence because one does not fit comfortably in either the bourgeois world or the folk milieu. Fauset believed that *Birthright* presented a distorted portrayal of African American life and experience. The publication of *Birthright* prompted Fauset, Nella Larsen, and Walter White to write about African Americans from a black perspective (Wall 1995). As a creative writer and literary critic, Jessie Fauset worked within the worlds of both literary production and reception. Fauset sought to revise and reconstitute what she perceived as misperceptions and inaccuracies about African Americans of various socioeconomic levels, genders, geographical regions, and ideologies. Unlike *Birthright*, *There Is Confusion* does not portray the educated African American man or woman as a tragic and displaced individual but rather as an individual with the power to transform himself or herself and the community at large. The novel features African Americans who succeed in negotiating the folk, bourgeois, and proletarian aesthetics.

*There Is Confusion* appropriates the kunstlerroman, a variation of the bildungsroman (coming-of-age story), as the narrative form to comment on folk, bourgeois, and proletarian aesthetics in Fauset's exploration of the African American experience. She continues the use of the kunstlerroman, with minor variations, in her three later novels *Plum Bun, The Chinaberry Tree*, and *Comedy: American Style* as well as short stories such as "The Sleeper Wakes" (which appeared in the *Crisis* in 1920). Unlike the bildungsroman, the kunstlerroman focuses on the development of the artist (Holman and Harmon 1992). The bildungsroman and the kunstlerroman have long been adopted by American and British women writers to explore important social, political, and economic issues relating to women. Nineteenth-century British and American women writers—including Elizabeth Barrett Browning in *Aurora Leigh* (1856), Elizabeth Stuart Phelps in *The Story of Avis* (1877) and Kate Chopin in *The Awakening* (1899)—called attention to the difficulties women face in fulfilling the socially proscribed role of wife and mother when they also desire to express themselves artistically (DuPlessis 1985).

For African American women writers, the kunstlerroman serves as a useful vehicle for racializing the problems of sexual and class oppression and fictionalizing their own experiences as black women writers who often face the tripartite oppression of race, class, and gender. Nineteenth-century African American women writers such as Harriet Jacobs in *Incidents in the Life of a Slave Girl* (1861) and Frances E. W. Harper in *Iola Leroy* (1892) adopt the form of the bildungsroman to examine the interstices of race, class, and gender in American society through their focus on the growth, development, and maturation of African American women in the 1800s. These works also serve as kunstlerromans in the African American female literary canon insofar as the authors meditate on the problems of the African American female artist. Jacobs writes her autobiography to call for social change in an effort to support herself and her children financially, and Harper's novel calls attention to Iola's gift as a skilled orator and teacher—artistic abilities she employs in transforming society's racial, sexual, and social prejudices.

Jessie Fauset and other twentieth-century women writers appropriated the bildungsroman and kunstlerroman to address race, gender, and class in relation to the "New Woman" of the early twentieth century, who struggled to negotiate her way through changing perceptions of women's roles as wife, mother, and career woman. During the 1920s and 1930s, the bildungsroman and kunstlerroman by women writers flourished as illustrated by Zelda Fitzgerald's *Save Me the Waltz* (1932), Zora Neale Hurston's *Their Eyes Were Watching God* (1937), Nella Larsen's *Passing* (1929), and Virginia Woolf's *To the Lighthouse* (1927). As an unmarried college-educated African American woman with a flourishing career as a literary editor for the *Crisis,* Fauset could be considered the embodiment of this New Woman as she did not marry until 1929 at the age of forty-seven (Sylvander 1981).

Using the kunstlerroman as a narrative form, Fauset meditates on race, class, and gender at the turn of the century. Fauset centers *There Is Confusion* on Joanna Marshall's coming of age as an artist and human being, using her protagonist's family background, attitudes, and interpersonal relationships as a means of commenting on folk, bourgeois, and proletarian ideologies and aesthetics. The Marshalls represent the rising black middle class at the beginning of the twentieth century, yet Joel Marshall, the patriarch, is an ex-slave from Richmond, Virginia. By presenting a bourgeois middle-class black family with an ancestry of slavery in the South, Fauset illustrates that folk and the bourgeois are not mutually exclusive. The presence of the southern black experience in the Marshall family history reveals the folk as the basis of African American history, family, and culture. Fauset presents Joel Marshall as a cook for a wealthy white family who successfully starts his own restaurant business in Virginia and later moves to New York. Like several characters in Fauset novels—for example, Maggie Ellersley in *There Is Confusion,* Angela Murray in *Plum Bun,* and Olivia Cary in *Comedy: American Style*—Joel Marshall thinks marriage functions as an avenue into bourgeois society if one chooses the proper mate: "His wife had been a school teacher, and her precision of language and exactitude in small matters made Joel think again of the education and subsequent greatness which were to have been his" (*There Is Confusion:* 11). Fauset presents education, Standard American English, and social etiquette as markers of the black bourgeois class.

As the inheritor of Joel's bourgeois ambitions signified through a feminine version of his name, his daughter Joanna's desire to wed the "proper mate" and be a successful artist anticipates the portrayals of other black female artists in her fiction such as Angela Murray in *Plum Bun* and Marise Davies in *Comedy: American Style*. Joanna's desire to be an artist represents the complexities of the life for women from the bourgeois classes of the twentieth century. As Du-Plessis (1985) stresses, the appropriation of the kunstlerroman by women writers springs from the bourgeois ideology of the period: "Using the female artist as a literary motif dramatizes and heightens the already-present contradiction in bourgeois ideology between the ideals of striving, improvement, and visible public works, and the feminine version of that formula: passivity, 'accomplishments,' and invisible private acts" (84). Joanna attempts to negotiate her desire to be a female performing artist and attain fame, fortune, and social status with the pressure to conform to the socially prescribed roles of wife and mother, which may explain why at the end of Fauset's novel Joanna gives up her career to be a wife and mother to further the goals of the African American race. Her progeny become her work of art as she molds them to challenge prevailing racist, sexist, and class-based ideologies.

*There Is Confusion* illustrates how Joanna's artistic ambitions remain with her through adolescence and temper the ways she treats others. The bourgeois goals and elitism manifest themselves in her choice of friends and potential husband. As a child, she meets Peter Bye, who comes from an Old Philadelphia black family. Impressed by his knowledge of anatomy and his aspirations to be a doctor, Joanna approves of him. Like the Marshalls, the Bye family has folk roots and slave ancestry in its family history. Through the depiction of the Bye family tree, Fauset reveals the history of miscegenation in American society, anticipating the depiction of black and white sexual relations in her novel *The Chinaberry Tree* and her short story "Double Trouble" (which appeared in the *Crisis* in 1923). Fauset employs the genealogical history of the Bye family and the history of racial/class amalgamation as a means of meditating on race and class in the United States. By illustrating that blacks and whites often have the same biological roots, she explodes the idea of racial prejudice and promotes the two races' common humanity. Fauset suggests the absurdity of racial and class prejudice, for disliking members of another race becomes akin to self-hatred and denial of one's identity. Her presentation of the genealogy also contributes to the slave narrative tradition, the basis of African American literature. In landmark texts such as *Narrative of Life of Frederick Douglass* (1845) and Harriet Jacobs's *Incidents in the Life of a Slave Girl* (1861) as well as fictionalized slave narratives such as Frances E. W. Harper's *Iola Leroy* (1892), the authors call attention to the history of miscegenation between slaves and owners, stressing the irony of racism and class prejudice.

In *There Is Confusion* the Bye family history begins in the eighteenth century with a liaison between a slave named Judy and her master, Aaron Bye, a Quaker. After Aaron emancipates her, she bears her master's child and marries Ceazer Morton, a coachman. Her son Joshua (reared as a free black) marries Belle Potter and bears their son Isaiah, who represents the transition from folk to bourgeois for the family. Fauset's presentation of a family with a variety of social and racial backgrounds in its history makes a bold statement to her readership, which consisted of middle-class blacks and whites sympathetic to the New Negro Movement, for Fauset actually refutes the idea of the Talented Tenth propagated by Du Bois of the NAACP and other black leaders who felt that the top 10 percent of the African American population in terms of education and social position should be leaders. Fauset suggests that the Talented Tenth has its roots in the other 90 percent of the African American population. The Bye family's mixed racial and class history clearly undermines the complacency of the black and white bourgeoisie in their elite status.

Fauset's depiction of Isaiah's aspirations suggests the possibility of a rising black middle class under the proper social, economic, and educational conditions. Belle has bourgeois aspirations for her son, hoping that he can attain higher socioeconomic standing than she and her husband and fulfill his potential. Isaiah represents the possibilities of class ascension for the black Bye family through his bourgeois speech, manners, and access to educational opportunities. As a model of self-reliance and self-sufficiency, Isaiah works toward racial uplift by opening a school for blacks in Philadelphia, writing for A.M.E. Church newsletters, and acquiring real estate. A hard worker and a man with a vision, he marries when he is thirty-one and has a son, whom he names Meriwether. He invests his son with the desire to be great, and because becoming a doctor was such a remote dream for him, he instills that goal in his son. Ironically, Meriwether Bye represents a fall rather than a rise in the family fortunes, for he does not have the aptitude for math and science that would enable him to become a doctor. As a consequence, Meriwether abandons the bourgeois aspirations, marries a seamstress, and squanders the family's savings and real-estate holdings. Peter Bye, his son, relies on his family name to gain access into the upper echelons of African American society despite the family's reduced income. The interludes depicting the Marshall and Bye family history early in the novel also serve to provide a context for understanding the characters' motivations and desires for wealth, class, and fame.

Although Fauset has been criticized for not depicting blacks from lower socioeconomic levels, *There Is Confusion* features several folk characters with positive attributes. Maggie Ellersley represents the folk, for she and her mother live in a tenement in a low-rent district known for sexual immorality and crime. Her mother frequently rents out one of the three rooms in their apartment to men who work for the train station. Despite her environment, Maggie (like the protagonist of Stephen Crane's *Maggie: A Girl of the Streets*) blooms: "Out of it all Maggie bloomed—a strange word but somehow true. She was like a yellow calla lily in the deep cream of her skin, the slim straightness of her body" (*There Is Confusion:* 57).[3] Like other protagonists in Fauset novels such as Angela Murray in *Plum Bun*, Maggie sees marriage as a key to fulfilling her bourgeois aspirations of money and social standing. Maggie's family does not possess a history of gentility like Peter's, but the two share an affinity in their desire to associate with the Marshalls as a means of entering the world of the black bourgeoisie. The desire for a bourgeois respectability fuels the behavior of characters in *There Is Confusion*.

Joanna Marshall actively seeks to disrupt the burgeoning romantic relationship between her brother Philip and Maggie, but Maggie pursues Philip and later Henderson Neal, a gambler, in her quest for economic security. When Joanna writes a letter to Maggie claiming that she would not be a suitable mate for Philip due to her background and folk origins, Maggie marries Neal as a means of escaping what she perceives as a bleak future working in her family's boardinghouse. A gambler who stays at her family's boardinghouse from time to time, Neal has the material possessions of a respectable man—fashionable clothes and a car. Nevertheless, he lacks the social polish and prestige of the Marshalls. Still, for Maggie, he does represent a vehicle for leaving her environment. Despite her attraction to Philip Marshall, at times she feels more at ease with Neal, who shares her folk background.

The desire for financial security leads her to marry Neal, who promises he will take care of her. Like Nanny in Hurston's *Their Eyes Were Watching God*, Maggie believes financial security takes precedence over romantic love when considering a potential mate because of the limited options for black women at the turn of the century. Fauset's Maggie Ellersley bears affinity with Crane's Maggie. Crane's Maggie is of Irish American descent and Fauset's Maggie has an African American background, but both women are representatives of the folk marginalized due to gender and ethnic heritage and both women have bourgeois ambitions of marrying mates who will provide them with material comforts. Similarly, both women are artisans—Crane's Maggie is an expert seamstress, while Fauset's Maggie works as a hairdresser.

While not facing the same level of discrimination as African Americans at the turn of the century, Irish immigrants and their descendants were often denied equal access to the social, political, and economic power because of anti-Irish and anti-Catholic prejudices. In Crane's naturalistic novel, Maggie's ethnicity, lower socioeconomic level, and gender militate against her in moving up the socioeconomic ladder. After succumbing to sexual overtures by her brother's friend, Crane's Maggie has her romantic illusions shattered. Marginalized by her ethnicity, economic status, and reputation as a promiscuous woman, she becomes a streetwalker and eventually kills herself. Crane's deterministic and naturalistic novel suggests that she has no other way to break free from the racial, sexual, and class oppression. In contrast, Fauset's Maggie succeeds in educating herself, securing a husband, and later establishing her own business interests despite racial, sexual, and economic discrimination. Unlike Crane, Fauset suggests that free will and self-determination can counter or at least mitigate external factors that seek to oppress the individual. Contrary to previous critical assessments that posit that Fauset privileges the bourgeois class over the folk in her characterizations of African Americans, Fauset depicts blacks from lower socioeconomic levels in a more positive light in comparison to their more affluent counterparts—as revealed in her depiction of Maggie and Joanna. Admittedly, it could be argued that Fauset romanticizes the working class in her portrayals of them as symbols of endurance, fortitude, and female power, yet it must be noted that she also reveals negative aspects of her folk characters as well. Fauset portrays Maggie early in the novel as scheming, calculating, and materialistic in her desire to marry Henderson Neal and initially in her relationship with Philip Marshall. Also, Phebe Grant passes briefly for white and denies her racial heritage in order to obtain wealth and social status. Nevertheless, Fauset suggests in the endings of both *There Is Confusion* and *Comedy: American Style* that the folk hold the key to the emancipation and self-empowerment of African Americans as she portrays Maggie and Phebe both as enterprising businesswomen, suggesting that the African American community will not thrive unless all levels, including the folk, display initiative, drive, and resourcefulness.

Fauset presents the contrast in attitudes toward the folk among members of the bourgeois class through her depictions of Peter Bye and Philip Marshall in opposition to Joanna. Despite his desire to be a surgeon and fulfill his ancestor's dreams, Peter embodies the folk and proletarian aesthetics. In order to earn extra money while in medical school, he plays jazz and blues music, which connects him with his folk roots. Also, he considers all careers and vocations as necessary for the welfare of the country and mankind. Like Peter, Joanna's brother Philip valorizes the community over the individual. When Joanna initially discovers that her brother Philip plans to spend his summer teaching the folk in South Carolina, she reacts in horror and fears he has abandoned the family's bourgeois aspirations. Philip embodies the proletarian aesthetic in the novel in calling for change in society and taking an active role in effecting its transformation. After graduating Phi Beta Kappa from Harvard, Philip comes back home with very decisive ideas on the direction of the African American community. He proposes an organization and a magazine called the *Spur*. The goals include the end of lynching, voting rights, equal education, and participation in the government. Fauset's description of Philip's organization and publication the *Spur* bear a close affinity to the NAACP and the *Crisis*.

Fauset's story line suggests that she may have been attempting to infuse her novel with serious political commentary because of her own affiliation with the NAACP and the *Crisis*.[4] Philip's experiences also have other affinities with Fauset's life, suggesting that she may have modeled the character's proletarian leanings on her own career as a teacher in the South as well as her involvement in social and political organizations such as the NAACP and the Urban League. In 1904 Fauset, with the aid of Du Bois, secured a teaching position in Tennessee at Fisk University. A year earlier, she had written him a letter requesting aid in securing the position so that she could interact with blacks of other socioeco-nomic levels (Wall 1995). In 1921, Fauset participated in and reported on the Second Pan-African Congress, a convention dedicated to the social, political, and economic empowerment of blacks worldwide. In her speech before the assem-bly, she noted the role black women played in social uplift for the African Amer-ican community (Wall 1995).

In 1922 Fauset continued her activism through participating and reporting on the activities of the National Association of Colored Women in Richmond, Vir-ginia, a social, political, and economic organization that advanced the black race through the promotion of education, health, and black business. At the conven-tion, Fauset commented on the Pan-African Congress and their goals of im-proving the lives of all blacks (Wall 1995). Fauset's own social, political, and eco-nomic activities suggests proletarian leanings, which she may have fictionalized in her novels through the characterization of Philip Marshall. While Fauset came from a respectable and genteel family as the daughter of an A.M.E. preacher, the poverty she experienced as one of thirteen children in a large family may have led to her willingness and readiness to help the masses once her economic lot improved.

Like Philip, other characters in the novel must learn to negotiate the folk, the proletarian, and the bourgeois strains within them. Although a minor charac-ter, Vera Manning's role in the novel introduces the "passing" theme in Fauset's fiction, a focus for the resolution of folk, bourgeois, and proletarian aesthetics. Like Angela Murray in *Plum Bun*, Vera, a high school classmate of Joanna's, feels that passing as white will enable her to travel in the higher and wealthier white social circles. Although Vera once fell in love with a black man, her mother discouraged the relationship because the man was too dark. Fauset's character-ization of Mrs. Manning anticipates Olivia Cary of *Comedy: American Style*, who is also color conscious and forbids her daughter to marry a dark-skinned black man. Vera views passing as a way to enjoy what she sees as the rights and privileges she cannot enjoy as a black woman: "Vera Manning, although a minor character, is in many respects one of Fauset's most compelling portrayals in *There Is Confusion*. She is a light-skinned African American who temporarily passes for white. Vera's parents are upper-class blacks. Her mother is Negrophobic in reference to her children marrying anyone darker than they, and she aborts Vera's marriage to a dark-skinned man" (Lewis 1992: 379). Fauset's depiction of Vera's plight underscores the criticism of color and class prejudice among bour-geois blacks in the novel, of which Joanna Marshall is a compelling example.

Vera's passing leads to estrangement from her race and from her identity, as Joanna learns one day when she runs into her in New York. Vera represents a shift from bourgeois aspirations to a concern with the folk and consequently be-comes more concerned about the African American community as a whole than about her own aspirations. Vera also bears affinity to Fauset's characterizations of Angela Murray in *Plum Bun* and Amy in "The Sleeper Wakes," who also pass for white in pursuit of wealth, power, and status only to learn that the price of estrangement from one's identity is too high. Similarly, in Nella Larsen's *Passing* (1929), Clare Kendry and Irene Redfield learn the tragic consequences of light-skinned blacks passing for white in the pursuit of wealth and status when Clare Kendry falls out a window to an untimely death shortly after her husband discovers that she is African American. Vera's decision to leave the North and work for racial uplift in the South with the folk mirrors Philip's (and Fauset's) decision to head south to teach school. The depiction of Philip and Vera reflects a valorization of the folk and the proletarian or protest tradition in African American literature and culture, serving as a model for negotiating the folk, bourgeois and proletarian strains.

Like Peter and Vera, Joanna eventually learns to negotiate the folk, the bourgeois, and the proletarian voices within her that she has repressed out of her elitism. In *There Is Confusion*, Fauset suggests that African American artistic expression stems from the folk as exemplified in Joanna's appropriation of a children's street song for the Dance of Nations revue. Through her decision to use the song "Sissy in the Barn," Joanna reconnects to her own folk origins that she had abandoned earlier in her bourgeois aspirations. Joanna performs as America in the Dance of Nations and dons a mask to deflect attention from her true color. When asked to lift off the mask, she makes a powerful statement on the definition of an American:

There was a moment's silence, a moment's tenseness.
    Then Joanna smiled and spoke. "I hardly need to tell you that there is no one in the audience more American than I am. My great-grandfather fought in the Revolution, my uncle fought in the Civil War and my brother is 'over there' now." (*There Is Confusion*: 232)

The liberal Greenwich Village audience applauds her statement. The moment reflects both the folk and the proletarian strain in Fauset's work. As Nina Miller (1996) notes, "This performance is finally everything at once: the pinnacle of stage success couched in perfect personal and cultural integrity, and rightfully asserting the long-overdue equation of Negro and American identity" (211). Fauset's depiction of Joanna's Dance of Nations role and her speech reveals the folk as the root of African American art. More importantly, the children's street song promotes the idea that American art comes from "the masses and not the elite," underscoring the proletarian aesthetic in the novel.

*There Is Confusion* emphasizes the Americanness of African Americans as a means of embodying the proletarian aesthetic through the depiction of the Dance of Nations and black participation in World War I. While Joanna represents America in the Dance of Nations, Philip Marshall and Peter Bye represent America overseas in a fight against oppression in Europe. Ironically, as African American soldiers they face discrimination at home and in the military: "In Europe black troops experienced the same sort of inequity and prejudice at the hands of the military that they had encountered in the United States" (Wintz 1988: 12). Fauset presents an unflinching and realistic depiction of racism in the army during World War I among white American soldiers against their black colleagues as well as separate rest centers for black and white soldiers, such as the one in Chambery, France. For African American civil rights leaders of the early twentieth century, World War I posed a dilemma: Should they advocate joining the armed forces and fighting for freedom abroad when black soldiers were denied civil rights at home? In the end, leaders such as W. E. B. Du Bois supported the war effort as a means of African Americans proving their loyalty and right to be treated as equal citizens (Wintz 11). Fauset, as a devotee of Du Bois, suggests the same position in *There Is Confusion*.

The war interlude in *There Is Confusion* further emphasizes the proletarian or protest element of the novel, and it also serves as the setting for the reunion of Philip and Maggie in Europe, where she serves as an army nurse to atone for her past self-centered behavior. Once she and Philip are reunited, the two reconcile and vow to stay together despite the war injuries he has sustained, which have made him a near invalid. A change has occurred in Maggie: she now values Philip for the individual he is and not the class he represents. Maggie suggests that he can assist her in the hair salon business or that perhaps he can one day begin his magazine again, and she could work as his assistant. Through the marriage of Maggie and Philip, Fauset presents the possible union of folk, bourgeois, and proletarian classes and ideologies.

*There Is Confusion* illustrates the importance of community over individualism and class unity rather than stratification through the main characters' appropriations of folk, bourgeois, and proletarian aesthetics. When Peter returns from the war, passes his medical school exams, and reconciles with her, Joanna begins to review her past actions and behavior toward Maggie and those she considered socially beneath her. Her guilt from the way she treated Maggie prompts her to tell her brother Philip on his deathbed about the letter she sent Maggie. Joanna's admission of guilt and Philip's forgiveness reveal an important stage in Joanna's development as a human being and as an individual who sees beyond the superficiality of class differences, and it leads to her desire to wed Peter, give up her role as entertainer, and work for the advancement of blacks as a wife.

Fauset's depiction of Joanna's earlier desire to be a performing artist and her later decision to give up that career may reveal the conflicting and ambivalent feelings women of the early twentieth century experienced about the traditional role for women as wives and mothers and emerging vocational opportunities as female artists, educators, and businesswomen. The characterization of Joanna may reveal Fauset's own conflicting views on being a career woman and the pressures over the traditional views of women as wives and mothers. Joanna's decision to marry, have children, and work part time as a performing arts teacher when it does not interfere with her role as housewife represents an alternative means of negotiating the desire to be an artist while fulfilling the socially prescribed roles of mother and wife.

Fauset's portrayal of Maggie's evolution also illustrates the successful negotiation of folk, bourgeois, and proletarian aesthetics. Philip's death has a profound effect upon Maggie, who has grown into a self-reliant woman and no longer feels that she must have a man to offer her financial support. Fauset's depiction of Maggie as an enterprising businesswoman reflects the changing role of women in America at the turn of the century as they became integral parts of the workforce. Although Joanna gives up her career as a singer and dancer when she weds Peter, for the good of any future children, Fauset's portrait of Maggie as an enterprising entrepreneur who runs several salons reflects the modernity of her text. She grows from a young woman of folk origins with aspirations of entering the bourgeois class through marriage into a self-sufficient businesswoman.

Despite the label of "genteel realism" which has been ascribed to her fiction, Jessie Fauset's *There Is Confusion* presents a cross section of African American society. Admittedly, her novel features middle-class college-educated African Americans such as Peter Bye and Philip Marshall; however, representation from the folk appears in the form of Maggie Ellersley and Henderson Neal. Fauset portrays the South and the folk as the source of black art, black heritage, and spiritual growth and development. A strong protest or proletarian aesthetic runs through the novel in its criticism of discrimination against black soldiers during World War I, lynching, and the racial discrimination in the United States and abroad and the formation of civil-rights organizations. Fauset's life serves as the embodiment of the proletarian in her involvement with the NAACP, the National Black Women's Conference, and the Pan-African Congress. *There Is Confusion* reflects the first stage in Fauset's marriage of the folk, bourgeois and proletarian aesthetics. More importantly, the novel explores themes such as class prejudice, the color complex, the role of the female artist, and marriage, all of which Fauset later expands upon in *Plum Bun, The Chinaberry Tree, Comedy: American Style*, and short stories such as "Amy Elizabeth" (the *Crisis* 1919) "The Sleeper Wakes" (the *Crisis* 1920), and "Double Trouble" (the *Crisis* 1923).

*Plum Bun*, Fauset's second novel, which was published in 1929, reveals Fauset's concern with the plight of the black female artist during the 1920s and 1930s. Like her first novel, *Plum Bun* functions as a kunstlerroman; it depicts the coming of age of Angela Murray, a young, light-skinned, African American female who passes for white to succeed as an artist and secure a wealthy white husband. By adopting this narrative form, Fauset meditates on the role race, class, and gender play in the lives of black women artists. Considering Fauset's own role as a female writer and her relationship with other African American literary and visual artists of the period, it is not surprising that her novel treats the theme of the African American woman's struggle to create against the obstacles of race, class, and gender discrimination. In fact, biographical evidence suggests that Fauset championed women artists and made an effort to form a community with them. As a teacher at the M Street High School in Washington, D.C., where Fauset taught from 1906 to 1920, she established friendships with Angelina Weld Grimke and Georgia Douglas Johnson, two leading women poets, fiction writers, and playwrights of the Harlem Renaissance (Wall 1995).

As literary editor of the *Crisis* from 1919 and the *Brownie's Book* (a magazine for children), Fauset published the works of women writers, including Georgia Douglas Johnson, Effie Lee Newsome, and Nella Larsen as well as visual artists like Laura Wheeler Waring, Louise Latimer, and Hilda Wilkinson (Wall 1995). Fauset also championed the works of women in her reviews for the *Crisis*. Fauset's relationships with other black women writers and visual artists calls attention to the authenticity of her portrayal of their lives, struggles, and concerns.

In order to understand the significance of *Plum Bun* and Jessie Fauset's emergence as an important Harlem Renaissance writer and her articulation of black feminist themes, one must review her earlier short fiction, which served as a prototype of this novel. Regrettably, Fauset's short stories receive scant critical attention. This may be the result of a privileging of the novel or poetry in critical studies of the Harlem Renaissance. Fauset's short fiction merits mention, especially since they appeared in the *Crisis,* a magazine devoted to challenging racial stereotypes and using art as propaganda. "The Sleeper Wakes" and "Mary Elizabeth" serve as prototypes for *Plum Bun,* in its theme and characterization (Sylvander 1981). The kunstlerroman, the bildungsroman, and the fairytale provide the forms to explore folk, bourgeois, and proletarian aesthetics in "The Sleeper Wakes" as in *Plum Bun.* "The Sleeper Wakes" showcases Fauset's attempts to address provocative social, economic, and political issues through the form of a short story. Fauset makes Amy's heritage ambiguous, calling attention to the absurdity of race and color prejudice and shows the blurred lines between black and white identity. Furthermore, Amy's conscious decision to identify the mistreated black valet as her brother and her desire at the story's end to work for black uplift evokes a pro-black message in the story.

"The Sleeper Wakes" appropriates the fairytale story of the sleeping beauty who awakes when kissed by a handsome prince who fulfills all her hopes, dreams, and desires. Fauset alters the story line by creating an antagonist whose romantic interest (Stuart James Wynne) oppresses and constrains the heroine with his racist and sexist politics. Furthermore, when Amy tells him she is black, he divorces her; later, he pursues her in hopes that she will become his mistress. The protagonist, Amy, in turn, rejects his offer, and decides that ultimately a wealthy man is not the key to happiness and security. She awakens to the realization that she can be an agent for her own change and transformation and earn her own livelihood. Fauset's fiction ultimately condemns the fairytale ideology of love and marriage and debunks the idea that heterosexual marriage and bourgeois status lead to happiness and fulfillment. Like other women who have been indoctrinated with fairytales, Amy has a preoccupation with clothing, appearance, and marriage as a means to achieve social status. At the story's onset, Amy longingly looks at a sample dress, paying special attention to the interplay of the colors of the dress with her own complexion. When she tries on the dress and receives positive reactions from men, she becomes further convinced that she can use her beauty as a commodity to attract and entice the opposite sex. Through the right combinations of colors, she can create an illusion to mask her identity as the foster daughter in the home of an African American family with a modest income. Thoughts of color and appearance prompted her visit to the store in the first place after watching a romantic boy-meets-girl movie. In fact, she becomes so captivated with the movie and the visit to the store that she forgets to purchase the braid her foster mother wanted her to buy that day.

Fauset challenges the idea of race as biologically determined in her deconstruction of the color line in "The Sleeper Wakes." After the opening scene in which Amy tries on the dress, the narrator flashes back to Amy's childhood, where her blurring of racial lines began. When a social worker whisks Amy off to meet her foster family, the young girl queries, "Am I going to be colored now?" (2). The social worker replies affirmatively, and later the reader learns that Amy's foster mother, Mrs. Boldin, does not know her true racial identity. Because her racial identity is uncertain, she is placed with a black family rather than a white one, due to the color consciousness of the time period. While Amy may be a thoughtful child, she thrives on daydreaming and denying her mundane reality. Not prone to intellectual pursuits, she gains her stimulation from romance novels and fairytales. Amy likes the "rags to riches" or folk to bourgeois plots of these stories, and following that type of storyline becomes her ambition in life, as in the errand to purchase the braid, when the movie enchants her with its plot. She waxes effusive about the movie with Mrs. Boldin: "And oh, Mrs. Boldin, it was the most wonderful picture—a girl—such a pretty one—and she was poor, awfully. And somehow she met the most wonderful people and they were so kind to her. And she married a man who was just tremendously rich and he gave her everything" ("The Sleeper Wakes": 3). Amy's reaction to the movie illustrates her impressionability and her lack of realism, which Mrs. Boldin disapproves of greatly.

Fauset presents Amy's physical migration from New Jersey to New York in search of the American dream as a metaphor for the movement from folk to bourgeois. While in New York City, Amy passes for white and carves out a new identity for herself, initially living on savings she made from working as a seamstress. Living in a white YWCA, Amy obtains a job as a waitress and clerk in a candy shop and bakery. Her entrée into the artistic world occurs at the hands of Zora Harrison, a beautiful, sophisticated woman of humble origins who catapulted herself from the folk to bourgeois class. Zora seeks to fabricate a fiction out of Amy's life, creating character, a plot, and a resolution that culminates in Amy marrying a man of means. Her exhortation that Amy must marry a rich man infiltrates Amy's mind, a mind already entranced by movies and fairytales with similar plots. She creates a false identity for Amy, claiming that she originates from the Kildares, a prominent Philadelphia family, and contrives a story that Amy came to New York to study art, when this is not the case. "The Sleeper Wakes," which appeared in 1920, predates *Plum Bun* in publication by nine years, yet Amy bears affinity to Angela Murray, who heads to New York and passes for white in hopes of being a successful artist and marrying a wealthy white man. Like Amy, Angela befriends sophisticated whites who enable her to see a more affluent and cosmopolitan world.

Zora functions as a mentor for Amy, even allowing her to live with her as a model, a designer, and supervisor of household staff. Through Zora, Amy meets Stuart James Wynne, a prototype for Roger Fielding in *Plum Bun*. Like Roger, Stuart comes from a wealthy family and becomes the subject of the heroine's romantic and financial desires. He represents her modern Prince Charming, and he too succumbs to fairytale-like story lines as Zora weaves a tale of Amy as a woman of high birth but misfortune who needs a man to save her and restore her to her rightful place in society. Zora exhorts Amy to accept Stuart's proposal, for he will bring the young woman wealth, material possessions, and social status. He presents security and a new, established identity for the young woman of ambiguous origin and background. Nevertheless, the dream becomes a nightmare of racial, gender, and class oppression as she begins to see the consequences of selling herself as a commodity to such a rich and powerful man.

Fauset's characterization of Stuart functions as a criticism of color and class prejudice among the bourgeoisie. A product of a wealthy white racist family, he places Amy in his home near Richmond, Virginia. His xenophobia becomes apparent immediately from the racist terminology he uses in referring to blacks, Italians, and Hispanics. Nevertheless, she feels flattered that such a prominent man would take her as a wife and continues to delude herself that she has paid the right price for social affluence. Now that she finds herself a member of the bourgeoisie, her only contact with the folk derives from her experience with the staff at her home, who are all African American. Fauset portrays the servants in a sympathetic and humane light, which belies previous critical assumptions that her work neglects the folk experience. She also uses the black servants in the story to meditate on the fluidity of class among African Americans. Most of the servants in the text represent the folk, but they use their funds to catapult their relatives into the bourgeoisie. The cook is the mother of two Howard University students, and the valet Stephen holds ambitions of obtaining higher education. When Stephen and Stuart fight one day, Amy sides with Stephen, to the point of telling her husband that Stephen is her brother. In a sense, he becomes her brother through her recognition or realization of her possible racial heritage. Her admission gradually awakens her to a realization that he does not want a black wife, even if he is the only one who knows. He files for divorce and sets her up in a house he owns in New York, and he provides her with a staff of servants who are unaware of the true reason the couple have ended their relationship. Nevertheless, the separation proves fruitful as Amy seeks a way to occupy her time and express herself by working as a seamstress, contributing her money to the Red Cross during World War I.

When Stuart comes to visit her months later, she briefly hopes for a reconciliation, only to find that he wants her to live with him but not as his wife. Fauset uses the encounter between the two to comment on the politics of race class, and gender. Amy learns that Stuart cannot deal with being married to a black woman because of his status as an upper-class white man. He wants her to become his sexual chattel, reminiscent of white male slaveholders who exploited and abused black female slaves. The encounter also calls attention to the ambivalence of the white male bourgeoisie to the black female body. Stuart James Wynne finds himself simultaneously repulsed by and attracted to her. Put off by the ideology he espouses, she decides to relocate to the black community and to move to New Rochelle to be closer to other African Americans. Fauset insightfully analyzes this paradox of eroticizing the Other: "It seemed to her that his attitude toward her—hate and yet desire, was the attitude in microcosm of the whole white world toward her own, toward that world to which those few possible strains of black blood so tenuously and yet so tenaciously linked her" ("The Sleeper Wakes": 22). The relationship between Amy and Stuart becomes a metaphor for black–white, male–female, rich–poor relationships. By extension, it becomes a metaphor for the black artists' relationship to the white consumers, particularly during the period of the Harlem Renaissance, when black artists sometimes owed their livelihood to white patrons with stereotypical views of African Americans. This section of the story also reflects the proletarian criticism embedded within the story, as Amy sees a parallel between Stuart's exploitation of her and white European colonization and exploitation of nonwhites throughout the world. His treatment of her reminds Amy of European exploitation of Africans, and of nonwhites in Tasmania, the island off the coast of Australia. Through this incident, Fauset espouses the ideas of Pan-Africanism, the desire among blacks of African descent worldwide to form sympathetic ties with each other in the face of white European exploitation and coordinate their active efforts to condemn the evils of colonialism. In fact, in 1921 Jessie Fauset attended the Second Pan-African Congress in London. Here, Fauset would be further inspired and awakened to the common oppression and injustice blacks face worldwide. As Wilbert Jenkins (1986) notes, "Fauset was fascinated by the display of brotherhood between Black Americans and Africans at the Congress. She discovered that Blacks in America and Africa not only shared a commonality of blood, but also were plagued by some of the same social and political problems. American Blacks and most African Blacks suffered similarly from the lack of political power; and many African Blacks shared with American blacks the limitations which segregationist policies imposed upon them" (16).

"The Sleeper Wakes" appeared in the *Crisis* a year before Fauset's trip, yet the story suggests that Fauset was already formulating Pan Africanist ideas and incorporating the ideology into her fiction. Furthermore, the reference to the island of Tasmania suggests an affinity for dark skinned individuals of non-African descent as well, revealing a desire to empathize with any group exploited or dominated by European powers. Fauset's representation of Amy's epiphany on white–nonwhite power dynamics also reveals the political activism in her short fiction.

Amy's recognition that her situation with Stuart reflects a broader and more deeply entrenched race, class, and gender power dynamic mirrored in the larger world prompts the beginning of her true awakening to her history and her self-hood. She also decides to write to the Boldin family in a desire to return home to her heritage and to a group of individuals who accepted her even though they were unsure of her true racial identity. She recognizes that her stay with the Boldin family will be temporary due to her desire for adventure and sets about musing on the possibilities of setting up her own business for white women interested in the superficiality of fashion and then later to work with African Americans. In a bold deconstruction of racial identity, Fauset leaves Amy's heritage ambiguous, for the protagonist decides that she will make no effort to find her true racial origins. By the story's end Amy awakens, like Sleeping Beauty, but not to a prince who will save her. Amy realizes that she possesses the key to her own success, and through hard work and determination, she can make a life for herself. "The Sleeper Wakes" illustrates how Fauset revises or appropriates traditional forms of the kunstlerroman, the bildungsroman, and the fairytale to convey a message of female empowerment and self actualization. Additionally, the story represents Fauset's deft interweaving of folk, bourgeois, and proletarian aesthetics as a means of representing the African American experience of the early twentieth century while promoting an ethos of Pan-Africanism.

Another story that may serve as a prototype for *Plum Bun* is "Mary Elizabeth." The story belies the notion that Jessie Fauset focuses only on the bourgeois or black middle class and ignores the common folk. The servant Mary Elizabeth is a prototype for the character Hetty in *Plum Bun*, the black servant of Angela and Virginia Murray after their parents die. Angela, an aspiring artist with bourgeois fantasies centered on marrying a wealthy white man, ironically uses folk themes in her art. She draws a picture of her servant Hetty, much to Hetty's surprise, to reveal the beauty of the black working class, and she also renders a portrait of the working class in her creation *Fourteenth Street Types*. The story "Mary Elizabeth" portrays a young black middle-class couple, the Piersons, who earn enough money to afford domestic help. The narrator, Sally Pierson, learns the meaning of love, understanding, and marriage through her servant Mary Elizabeth, the daughter of slaves. The story suggests that the folk past must be understood in order to understand the bourgeois present for the rising black middle class at the turn of the twentieth century. The story, in turn, becomes a proletarian statement on the politics of race, class, and gender.

Jessie Fauset's use of history as a prominent theme in this story reflects her black cultural nationalist politics. Black cultural nationalist writers promoted the study and teaching of black history. Fauset's own past and interests placed her in a pivotal position to use history to challenge the politics of race, class, and gender. Jenkins (1986) notes, "Fauset's adamant belief that Blacks could only develop a racial consciousness and pride through the acknowledgment of their past, was persistently reflected in articles she wrote on major black historical figures in the pages of *The Crisis Magazine*" (15). Fauset's nonfiction essays in the *Crisis* advocate the study of black history, reinforcing the emphasis on recognizing the contributions of blacks in the past by proponents of the Harlem Renaissance movement. Furthermore, Fauset's short stories in the *Crisis* also mirror this position. The servant Mary Elizabeth functions as a symbol of the past for her affluent employers. Mary Elizabeth's history lesson on the legacy of slavery not only teaches the narrator an important lesson, but the *Crisis* readers as well. The story illustrates the heroism of the common folk, the wellspring of African American creativity and the repository of the past.

At the onset of the story, the narrator finds herself in despair because her servant is late and she must fix breakfast herself. Her shortcomings as a homemaker become apparent when she overcooks the coffee, and her husband becomes severely irritated. The narrator longs for the appearance of her cook to take care of the demands of the household. Fauset paints a complex portrait of a domestic servant and her power to affect and even transform the lives of those who may seem above her socially and economically. For the narrator, nearly every aspect of Mary Elizabeth's being evokes the Other or the past for her, including her language. The narrator notes Mary Elizabeth's nonstandard use of American English, which has a folktale quality to it. Her language evokes a past that the narrator finds distant, yet ironically it reveals their common heritage as ancestors of slaves. When Mary Elizabeth recounts for Sally Pierson the story of her family, Sally learns in microcosm the heritage of the African American. Mary Elizabeth comments that her parents never formally married. White slave owners prohibited slaves from formal wedding ceremonies. Mary Elizabeth recounts how her father was sold to another owner shortly after she was born, and her mother did not see him until years later after they both had remarried. Even though Mary Elizabeth's father returned twenty-six years later to find his wife and his child, the two did not reunite as a couple. For Sally Pierson, the story evokes the horrible consequences of slavery; nevertheless, Mary Elizabeth speaks with candid matter-of-factness about this tragic part of her past, and by extension, this time in African American history when families were divided by the system of slavery. The story touches the narrator, Mrs. Pierson, who begins to appreciate her marriage, and she sends Mary Elizabeth back home to be with her own ailing husband.

Mrs. Piersen imparts Mary Elizabeth's story to her husband, who informs her that if he had been Cassius (Mary Elizabeth's father), he never would have tolerated her marrying someone else because she is his true love. Fauset writes, "So, thus, and not otherwise, Mary Elizabeth healed the breach" ("Mary Elizabeth": 47). This story reveals Fauset's willingness to deal with the past in a realistic manner, particularly the legacy of slavery and its repercussions, which echoed well into the twentieth century. The story reminds the reader of the common legacy among all African Americans, for even if Mrs. Pierson's parents and grandparents were not slaves, most likely her earlier ancestors shared the same fate as Mary Elizabeth's family members. The story, published in the *Crisis* in December 1919, also reminds the readers that slavery functions as a part of the more recent past. Readers of the *Crisis* were often the descendents of slaves, whose experiences mirror those of Mary Elizabeth. In "Mary Elizabeth," the folk woman saves the bourgeois couple by reminding them of the legacy of slavery and their good fortune in not having to suffer separation at the hands or whims of others. In turn, Fauset strikes a proletarian note in her criticism of race, class, and sexual politics in "Mary Elizabeth." Far from being a writer out of touch with the folk, Fauset's story suggests an empathy with the black working classes and advocates the idea that the folk can teach the black bourgeoisie or the Duboisian Talented Tenth lessons about life. Many of the readers would have been members of the black middle class, and this narrative suggests to them the importance of not having a condescending attitude toward the black masses or folk; rather, the story suggests the importance of respecting their wisdom, dignity, and candor. Jessie Fauset's "Mary Elizabeth" functions as an attempt to bridge the gap between the black working and middle classes during the Harlem Renaissance. Similarly, in *Plum Bun,* Fauset tries to bridge the gap through her characterization of Hetty, the black housekeeper. By making Hetty the subject of an artistic work by the protagonist Angela Murray, Fauset suggests that the folk remain suitable and compelling subjects because they represent the foundations of African American culture, life, and experience.

Like *There Is Confusion, Plum Bun* presents folk, bourgeois, and proletarian aesthetics. The folk represents the source of African American artistic expression as manifested in Angela Murray's portrait of a black housekeeper and rendering of the masses on New York's 14th Street and her classmate Miss Powell's *Street in Harlem,* which valorizes the folk. While Angela's artwork stems from the folk experience, her desire for wealth, fame, and social status exemplify the bourgeois aesthetic as she passes for white to gain entry into the upper-crust social circles and marry a rich white husband. Although *Plum Bun* has been characterized as a bourgeois novel of manners, the novel exemplifies the proletarian strain through the valorization of the folk as the center of black art as well as Angela's admission of her black heritage to protest discrimination against Miss Powell by the Americans on the admissions board of a French art school.

When *Plum Bun* first appeared in 1929, reviews in the *New Republic,* the *New York Times,* and the *Saturday Review* focused on the sentimentality and melodrama in Fauset's text (Sylvander 1981). Nevertheless, Deborah McDowell's (1990) comments counter previous readings. She notes, "*Plum Bun* baits the reader with a range of familiar expectations about women and blacks, found both in and out of literature, but then refuses to fulfill them, particularly those that conform to the culturally coded exegeses of race and gender" (xxix). Fauset's *Plum Bun* presents a nonmonolithic portrait of African American life and experience, ranging from the folk to the proletarian and bourgeois in her presentation of the black female artist's struggle to create art in a world marked by race, class, and gender prejudices.

In *Plum Bun,* Fauset presents the bourgeois aesthetic through the depiction of Angela Murray's socioeconomic ambitions. Growing up as the daughter of a carpenter (Junius) and an ex-seamstress and domestic (Mattie) in Philadelphia, Angela and her sister Virginia have a comfortable if not luxurious existence. As young girls, Virginia and Angela have markedly different interests, skin shades, and dispositions. Angela and her mother share light complexions and enjoy excursions through the city of Philadelphia, window-shopping and going to fancy tea rooms as they pass for white: "Her mother is a 'mixed blood' whom whites refer to as a 'white nigger,' and her father is very dark-skinned. Angela discovers at a very early age that looking white has many advantages" (Lewis 1992: 380). These experiences have a profound effect upon Angela's identity as she begins to associate freedom, happiness, wealth, power, and prestige with being white.

Like Olivia Cary in *Comedy: American Style,* and Amy in "The Sleeper Wakes," Angela considers whiteness as central to financial success and fulfillment. In contrast, her dark-skinned sister Virginia cannot pass for white. She enjoys singing, playing the piano, and domestic chores. Art does not function for her as a vehicle by which she can gain access to bourgeois social circles. Virginia desires to become an excellent music teacher and develop a new method in piano instruction. Angela sees art as a means to an end—fame, money, and freedom. She views her family's life in Philadelphia as stifling and moribund. Becoming an artist is a way of breaking free from what she views as a rather pedestrian existence. Fauset presents both the advantages and disadvantages of black women pursuing roles as artists in a world marked by racism, sexism, and class prejudice. Fully aware of the racism and sexism that black female artists face, Mattie and Junius want their daughters to be able to support themselves financially. Like many black female artists of the 1920s and 1930s, Virginia and Angela attend college to train as teachers. Fauset presents the reality many black female visual, musical, and literary artists faced when their race, class, and gender militated against them. Fauset's own experiences call attention to the lack of vocational opportunities for black women and the reliance on teaching as a means of support for budding black women artists.

Fauset's own experiences as a teacher reveal the limited options for educated and uneducated black women of the period. For those with college degrees, social work, teaching, and nursing provided professional careers. Even the most educated often worked in positions that did not require a great deal of formal education, including domestic worker, custodian, nanny, or seamstress. Fauset worked as a high school French and Latin language teacher partly because it was one of the few career opportunities available for her, despite graduating Phi Beta Kappa from Cornell University. In *Plum Bun,* Fauset highlights the dilemma of the black female artist who desires to express herself artistically yet must also find a means of financial support.

Although Angela earns an adequate income as a teacher, she finds the role stifling and boring. After her parents' deaths, she feels no longer connected to Philadelphia or her racial identity. She decides to begin a new life as a white woman and heads to New York in search of fame, fortune, and a wealthy white husband. Nevertheless, she remains connected to her black folk roots via her art while studying at Cooper Union in New York. Fauset convincingly suggests that the folk functions as the root of African American art and culture in *Plum Bun*: "In showing again implicitly that Black Art is best based partly on Black folk materials, Fauset makes Angela the painter do her best work with portraits of Hettie [sic] Daniels, an old Black servant, and 'Fourteenth Street Types,' whom she observes upon her arrival in New York" (Sylvander 1981: 170). Despite her bourgeois aspirations, Angela's art stems from the folk. By using the lower-class Hetty as the subject matter of Angela's art, Fauset highlights the beauty of black women in America and challenges the traditional ideas about valid subjects for art.

Angela's use of the black woman as subject for visual art mirrors that of Harlem Renaissance artists like Laura Wheeler Waring, who was well known for her portraits of black women. In fact, Waring provided sketches for one of Fauset's travel pieces, "Dark Algiers the White," which appeared in the *Crisis* in April–May 1925. Her collaboration with Waring illustrates Fauset's awareness of the presence and talent of African American women artists. Fauset's depiction of the folk as the source of African American art echoes *There Is Confusion* as exemplified by Joanna's choice of the street song for the Dance of Nations.

Angela's bourgeois aspirations and her desire to pass for white in order to succeed as an artist and gain access to centers of status, power, and wealth stem from an incident in the art academy in Philadelphia that underscored the precarious position of the black female artist. A former model and high school classmate reveals her true ethnicity, and Angela can no longer pass for white. Frustrated by the racism she encounters once people realize her real racial identity, Angela makes the decision to move to New York and pass for white to further her social and economic opportunities. Angela rationalizes the decision to her sister, in a way that reflects her bourgeois aspirations, as she asks, "'Why should I shut myself off from all the things I want most,—clever people, people who do things, Art,—' her voice spelt it with a capital,—'travel and a lot of things which are in the world for everybody really but which only white people, as far as I can see, get their hands on. I mean scholarships and special funds, patronage'" (*Plum Bun*: 78). Angela's decision to pass for white reveals the bourgeois aesthetic that guides her actions. In contrast, Virginia believes that aligning oneself with other blacks represents the best way to counter racism in the world of art.

Fauset underscores this difference in aesthetics through the titling of the sections of the novel. The first section, "Home," signifies the folk in the valorization of Junius and Mattie as working-class individuals with bourgeois aspirations for their children. The sections "Market" and "Plum Bun," which reveal Angela's bourgeois ambitions, depict her passing for white and her willingness to deny her race and self-respect in order to secure a wealthy husband. The final sections, "Home Again" and "Market Is Done," signify the proletarian aesthetic and the folk aesthetic, since they present the revelation of Angela's true racial heritage when a black classmate faces discrimination and Angela's acceptance of her ethnicity and abandonment of materialism. Fauset's appropriation of the nursery rhyme "Plum Bun" signifies her subversion of children's literature to comment on race, class, and gender in America as well as her appropriation of the kunstlerroman to depict the female artist's coming of age.

Despite Angela's bourgeois aspirations, the folk still serve as inspiration for her art. Enthralled by the "down and out" near the hotel in which she resides, Angela decides that she will use the setting of 14th Street as the subject for her art. Angela's *Fourteenth Street Types* suggests a vitality, a richness, and beauty in the experience of what might be termed the lower classes in American society. In fact, Angela's *Fourteenth Street Types* and Miss Powell's *Street in Harlem* both elevate the ordinary and common when both women win art awards at Cooper Union, again reinforcing Fauset's valorization of the folk in art. Fauset's conceptualization of Miss Powell represents a fictionalization of real-life artist Augusta Savage and the discrimination she encountered as a black female artist (Wall 1995). *Plum Bun* was published about five years after this highly publicized incident. Through the fictionalization of Savage's plight, Fauset calls attention to the way racism militates against the black female artist. As an African American literary artist, Fauset too had faced discrimination in her education. Although she desired to attend Bryn Mawr after graduation from high school, officials at the private women's college helped Fauset to obtain a scholarship from Cornell University (Sylvander 1981). Later, when Fauset joined the NAACP she became involved in a number of cases of discrimination against blacks by universities, including the case of a black Smith College student denied on-campus housing just as Fauset had been while an undergraduate student at Cornell (Wall 1995).

Unlike Miss Powell and her sister Virginia, Angela views art as a way of gaining access to the finer things in life and fulfillment of her bourgeois desires. As a result of her entry into the world of intellectuals and arts via her friend Martha Burden, Angela meets Roger Fielding, a young millionaire—a man she hopes will eventually marry her and provide her with all the material comforts of life. She does not have the same connection or commitment to art as her classmate Miss Powell, who cannot suppress her color or art to marry white and wealthy. As in *There Is Confusion* and *Comedy: American Style*, bourgeois aspirations and class consciousness influence Angela's choice of a potential mate, yet Fauset belittles this attitude by illustrating that heterosexual relationships based upon material gain only lead to spiritual emptiness and loss of self-identity and self-worth. Determined to achieve wealth and social status, she initially rejects fellow artist Anthony Cross as a potential mate because of his commitment to being an artist even if it means being poor, which runs counter to her bourgeois aesthetic: "She wanted none of Anthony's poverty and private and secret vows,—he meant, she supposed, some promise to devote himself to REAL ART,—her visual mind saw it in capitals. Well, she was sick of tragedy, she belonged to a tragic race" (*Plum Bun*: 143). In Angela's mind, money and marriage to Roger Fielding take precedence over artistic expression. In the portrayal of Angela and Roger's relationship, Fauset reveals how class distinctions and bourgeois attitudes influence the choice of a suitable mate even when race is not a factor. Class prejudice interferes with Angela's desire to marry Roger, who would rather have her as his mistress than as his wife because she is not of the proper class or social background. Fauset's portrayal of the factors that complicate Angela and Roger's courtship reveal that class often militates against women as much as race. When Angela realizes that marriage without love and respect represents no marriage at all (even if it means money and status), Angela becomes recommitted to being an artist and later even rejects Fielding's marriage proposal to her.

Fauset presents the maturation of Angela as she reconnects with her folk roots and racial heritage and renews her relationship with her sister Virginia and Anthony Cross (the two have become engaged). Angela's hard work toward developing her artistic skills pays off as she and Miss Powell both receive rewards from Cooper Union for *Fourteenth Street Types* and *A Street in Harlem*, renderings of the folk in New York. Their decision to portray the lives of ordinary people living in the city reflects an important aspect of black female art—using nontraditional subjects as art. Miss Powell's desire for artistic expression reveals a proletarian aesthetic as she attempts to connect with the urban masses in her art and function as a voice for the oppressed. As a visibly black woman who cannot pass, she has to struggle even harder than Angela for the sake of her art just like many real-life black female artists during the Harlem Renaissance. Nevertheless, Miss Powell's happiness is short-lived, since the racist Americans on the selection committee at the Fontainebleau School of Fine Arts return to Miss Powell the passage money she was to use for sailing to France. They claim that her presence aboard the ship will make the white students uncomfortable. Prejudice against blacks prevents her from realizing her potential as an artist. Fauset's depiction of Angela's reaction, which includes the revelation of her true racial identity to a group of reporters who have gathered at Miss Powell's apartment, reflects the proletarian aesthetic and protest element in the novel. Angela realizes that in suppressing her racial identity, she hides her ethnicity and reinforces a racial hierarchy that perpetuates rather than eradicates the problem. The depiction of Miss Powell's plight and the white reporters' attitudes reflects the struggle of black female artists in the early twentieth century. To be black, female, and an artist means to face racism, sexism, and class prejudice.

*Plum Bun* depicts a black female artist's coming of age and her journey toward self-understanding and self-definition. Angela goes to France with money she had saved while working as a fashion illustrator. When Angela gives up pursuing an artistic career and passing for white as a means to acquire the bourgeois trappings of wealth, fame, and social status, she finds peace and sense of self. More importantly, she regains her close relationship with Virginia, whom she had rejected after moving to New York, and also regains Anthony Cross's love. In abandoning the greed and materialism (like Joanna Marshall and Vera Manning in *There Is Confusion* and Amy in "The Sleeper Wakes"), she undergoes a significant change: "Racial and sexual and monetary conventions and rules and deceits were the bonds that bound young Angela Murray. During the course of *Plum Bun* they unobtrusively disintegrate to be replaced by hard work, independence of thought, honesty in human relationships" (Sylvander 1981: 189). Angela's quest for self proves successful as she comes to terms with her art, her family, and herself. She successfully negotiates the folk, bourgeois, and proletarians strains in herself.

In *There Is Confusion* and *Plum Bun*, Fauset presents the foundations for an aesthetic of African American art and culture. The folk represents the source of African American visual and literary expression. Fauset valorizes bourgeois aspiration and attitudes when they contribute to racial uplift and advancement, but criticizes class elitism and color consciousness. The proletarian aesthetic manifests itself in the insistence on the equality of all individuals despite race, class, and gender. As Jacqueline McLendon (1995) rightly notes, "Indeed, the novel itself resists closure, disrupting accepted practice to allow the simultaneous expression of 'black' textuality and an emerging black woman's voice" (49). Fauset presents an insightful view of race, class, and gender, anticipating the works of later African American female writers such as Alice Walker, Gloria Naylor, and Toni Morrison.

Despite Fauset's notable achievements as an editor, novelist, essayist, and short story writer, she continued to face challenges in finding a market for her literary expression and investigation into the racial consciousness of America. In fact, Zona Gale (one of the guests at the 1924 Civic Club dinner honoring Fauset's first novel, *There Is Confusion*) would be instrumental in helping Fauset earn a contract for her third novel, *The Chinaberry Tree*. On 21 March 1924, novelist Zona Gale sat at a dinner table in New York's swanky Civic Club surrounded by other poets, novelists, short-story writers, impresarios, editors, and publishers to celebrate the publication of Jessie Fauset's *There Is Confusion*. The event embodied what Gale and others hoped would be the forging of new relationships among the black and white intelligentsia who sought to revise and reconstitute the treatment of race, class, and gender in art and life. Organizers of the event hoped that the Civic Club dinner would set the foundation for the New Negro Movement in American arts and letters. Unfortunately, the Civic Club dinner did not quite fulfill the expectations of the attendees and participants in reconfiguring the politics of artistic production and reception for African American writers. In 1931, seven years after the Civic Club dinner to celebrate the publication of *There Is Confusion*, the lives of Jessie Fauset and Zona Gale would intertwine again as Fauset composed a letter to Zona Gale asking her assistance in getting her third novel, *The Chinaberry Tree*, published by the Frederick A. Stokes Company.

Jessie Fauset initially had difficulty in finding a publisher for her third novel *The Chinaberry Tree* because readers at the Frederick A. Stokes publishing company viewed the novel as an inaccurate portrayal of African Americans due to the absence of primitivistic and exotic images as signified by best-selling novels such as Carl Van Vechten's *Nigger Heaven* (1926) and Claude McKay's *Home to Harlem* (1928). Fauset's *Chinaberry Tree*, which meditated on race, class, and gender in a middle-class black family, seemed to go against the current (at least on the surface) of the popular texts of the period. As a consequence, Fauset found herself in the ironic position of asking a critically and commercially successful white female writer from the Midwest known for her realistic exploration of race, class, and gender in America in novels such as *Birth* (1918) and *Miss Lulu Bett* (1920) (which garnered a Pulitzer Prize in 1921 when she adapted it into a play) to authenticate her novel by writing an introduction. Gale responded affirmatively to the request by telegram, and Fauset, in return, sent her thanks and invited Gale to a tea that would be held on 3 January 1932, in honor of *The Chinaberry Tree*'s publication (Sylvander 1981). Fauset's predicament calls attention to obstacles African American female and male writers faced in having their voices heard in the literary arena.

The need for Gale to endorse Fauset's submission, and in effect authenticate the realism of *The Chinaberry Tree*, is reminiscent of the eighteenth-century practice of authenticating authorship of African American works by presumably illiterate slaves—as happened with Phillis Wheatley's poems, which were authenticated by John Hancock, her owner John Wheatley, the governor of Massachusetts, and other distinguished residents of Boston. In the nineteenth century, prominent white abolitionist and novelist Lydia Maria Child wrote a preface for Harriet Jacobs's *Incidents in the Life of a Slave Girl* (1861) verifying the authenticity of the narrative and Jacobs's role as the author of the account of her enslavement and escape. Similarly, abolitionist William Lloyd Garrison authenticated the truthfulness of Frederick Douglass's *Narrative of the Life of Frederick Douglass* (1845), noting that Douglass did indeed write the account of his bondage and freedom. Fauset's experiences call attention to underlying prejudices against the African American individual's status as a literate and creative individual as well as assumptions about the definition of authentic African American life, culture, and experience. Despite the misgivings of the Frederick A. Stokes Company, *The Chinaberry Tree* proved to be a critical, if not a commercial, success. Critics such as Gerald Sykes of the *Nation* praised the book, lamenting the publishing company's failure to promote the book adequately (Sylvander 1981). In a 1932 *Opportunity* article, Alain Locke emphasized the connections between Fauset's novel and the classic literary tradition (Sylvander 1981).

As in *Plum Bun*, the themes and characterizations apparent in *The Chinaberry Tree* bear affinity to earlier short fiction written by Fauset that arguably served as a model for this novel. Fauset's 1920 short story "Double Trouble" (the *Crisis*) serves as a prototype for her fascinating study of family ties and genealogical relationships in *The Chinaberry Tree*. She features similar characters and a story line of tangled family histories. While Fauset does not employ a fairytale motif as in "The Sleeper Wakes," she does borrow from the refrain "Double, double toil and trouble" from Shakespeare's *Macbeth*. The story features Angelique, a seventeen-year-old girl on the brink of womanhood. Like many heroines of Jessie Fauset stories, Angelique has mixed racial heritage. At the story's onset, the reader learns that mysteries surround Angelique's parentage and the whereabouts of her mother and her father. This serves to foreshadow Angelique's stark realization later in the story that she and Malory Fordham, her beau, are indeed brother and sister and involved in an unwittingly illicit relationship. Malory disapproves of Angelique's friend Asshur Judson, one of the few males who treats her well, due to the young man's folk interests, including farming. Asshur's folk background marginalizes him in the mind of Malory Fordham, who considers himself to be superior to Asshur as a consequence. Although enchanted by Angelique's beauty, Malory recognizes that the black bourgeoisie in Edendale view her as being from a lower socioeconomic class. A variation of her name reappears in *Plum Bun*, for the protagonist is named Angela Murray or Angele Mory.

Fauset's story deals convincingly with the history of miscegenation and the blending of black folk and white bourgeois status through family ties and history. Angelique lives with her cousin Laurentine and her Aunt Sal. Two white sisters visit them frequently. From their clothing and behavior, Angelique can perceive their affluence and social status. The Courtney sisters travel to Europe, know French, and possess an air of sophistication. They embody the idea of the bourgeois white American immersed in Western culture and civilization. In contrast, Laurentine has spent time in the West Indies and knows how to speak Spanish. Her travels and linguistic skills suggest a different type of worldliness. Ironically, Angelique views Laurentine as someone with a shameful past due to the sexual relationship between Aunt Sal and Ralph Courtney, which ultimately produced Laurentine. The Courtney sisters are the half sisters of Laurentine. For Angelique, the miscegenation in Laurentine's family tree represents the past, and she smugly prides herself on not possessing such a troubled family legacy. She views the Strange family's multiracial background as a remnant of slavery. Fauset's inclusion of this aspect of the story reminds her readers that the legacy of slavery still exists for her twentieth-century audience, many of whom would have been descendents of unions between slaves and slaveowners.

The relationship between Asshur and Angelique represents the tension between the folk and the bourgeois. Laurentine dislikes Asshur Judson because of his background, and despite her attraction to him, Angelique holds ambivalent feelings toward the young man who studies agriculture. She views him as someone with very narrow interests because of his desire to learn to become a better farmer. The story highlights the Du Bois–Washington debate over higher education for African Americans. For Du Bois, higher education meant a focus on the liberal arts and cultivating the Talented Tenth of black professionals and intellectuals who would lead African Americans to social and economic equality. In contrast, Booker T. Washington emphasized a vocational, hands-on education for African Americans. The bourgeois nationalism of Du Bois and the utilitarianism of Washington echo throughout "Double Trouble" in the depiction of Asshur Judson and the opposition other African Americans express to his chosen field of study. Malory, who represents the black bourgeoisie in his attitudes and actions, seems a more suitable match from Angelique's perspective, yet Fauset foreshadows the negative implications of a relationship between the two in her literary allusions. After a street encounter with Malory, Angelique recites lines from Macbeth—"Double, double, toil and trouble"—and later she goes home to memorize the witches' speech in Macbeth and to read a chapter on Greek tragedy. The lines from Macbeth and the reading assignment on Greek tragedy foreshadow the tragic ending of the story. Furthermore, the readings stimulate her imagination, and in her dream she pursues Malory, whose face transforms into a Greek mask, like those that characters would wear in a tragic Greek play. Not only does the dream foreshadow the tragic consequences of her desire for Malory when the two discover they are sister and brother, but the dream also suggests the negative consequences of pursuing someone out of a desire for social status and ambition rather than love.

While the fairytale motif may not be as apparent in "Double Trouble," Angelique bears affinity to Amy in "The Sleeper Wakes." Like Amy, she holds romantic ideas about love, relationships, and marriage. She hopes a dashing, wealthy man will lead her to riches, happiness, and romantic love. She considers herself to be superior to her cousin Laurentine, who doesn't appear to have such great prospects as a result of the stigma of illegitimacy surrounding her birth. Angelique thinks she will be the first lady of African American society and prepares herself for that role. When Malory invites her to the Methodist Sunday School picnic, she cannot wait to descend upon the picnic as the companion of Malory Fordham. Unfortunately, she is whisked off by Mrs. Thompson, who accidentally cuts her hand when she's helping the woman to prepare food for the picnic. The couple are disappointed, assuming again that Malory's social standing prevents Angelique from gaining full acceptance. However, when Malory attempts to introduce Angelique to his family the next day, one of the sisters refuses to allow her in. The following day Malory admits to her that they are relatives (brother and sister) after being pursued down a street by Angelique, whom he had been trying to avoid. Symbolically, he falls over a tree root while trying to elude her. The tree symbolizes the tangled family tree of his family. The reference to the tree also anticipates the title of the novel that "Double Trouble" serves as a prototype for—The Chinaberry Tree. Fauset writes, "He tripped over a tree root, fell, reeled to his feet, and, breathless, found her upon him. She knew that this was her dream but even so she was unprepared for the face he turned upon her, a face with horrid staring eyes, with awful gaping lips, the face of a Greek tragic mask!" ("Double Trouble": 37). The story becomes like a Greek tragedy of incest and lies. The news shocks and upsets Angelique, who always assumed that her own family history held no secrets. From Laurentine, she finds out that her mother had an affair with Malory's father and fled Edendale with him. The name of the city belies the secrets and lies that lead to unhappiness and tragedy. Laurentine feels triumphant knowing that her cousin now realizes that her family background marginalizes her as well. In fact, Laurentine blames

Angelique for the dearth of prospects for marriage. The ash constructor's son desires to marry her, but he comes from a working-class background. She could not attract someone like Mr. Deaver, the pastor at the African Methodist Episcopal Church, an occupation socially acceptable to someone who has bourgeois aspirations. Despite her own mother's actions, Laurentine claims that townspeople view Angelique as having "bad blood," and the taint of that blood affects her (Laurentine) as well ("The Sleeper Wakes": 38). Laurentine's blunt remarks reveal to Angelique that the dreams of marrying a wealthy and prosperous man like Malory will not come true. She then sets her sights on Asshur Judson, the farmer, upon receiving a letter from him. Unlike the other men in the story, he treats her with respect despite her parentage. As a farmer, he remains closer to the folk heritage of African Americans and seems to embody a spirit of goodwill and fairness, more than Malory Fordham does.

While the story's plot line seems reminiscent of Greek tragedy, the ending conveys the possibility of Angelique finding happiness one day if she allows herself to abandon her idea that marriage represents the key to social standing. The story has shortcomings, its melodramatic story line being a prominent one, but it serves as the basis and foundation for *The Chinaberry Tree*. Similarities abound between the story and the novel in characterization. Laurentine and Aunt Sal appear in *The Chinaberry Tree*, as do Malory and Asshur. Angelique becomes Melissa in *The Chinaberry Tree* (Sylvander 1981). The story remains essential to an understanding of Fauset's fiction and of *The Chinaberry Tree*. "Double Trouble" reflects Fauset's desire to deal with weighty themes in a short-story form, yet at times her stories cannot sustain the tension of these serious issues she attempts to present, and her short fiction seems incomplete and overly melodramatic. Still, by placing intense stories like "Double Trouble" in the *Crisis*, Fauset exposes her readers to key issues regarding the politics of race, class, and gender through her reworkings of fairytales and her appropriation of allusions from other literary texts.

Like *There Is Confusion* and *Plum Bun*, *The Chinaberry Tree* follows the structure of the kunstlerroman in its depiction of the coming of age of a female artist, Laurentine Strange, an expert seamstress. Fauset chronicles the young woman's attempt to be a creative artist and negotiate the socially prescribed roles for women as wives and/or mothers. The novel features middle-class blacks with bourgeois aspirations. Fauset presents the folk as the root of African American life, history, and culture as well by offering a proletarian aesthetic in the pleas for racial, sexual, and class equality in the same manner as in *There Is Confusion* and *Plum Bun*. Arguably, *The Chinaberry Tree* emphasizes the folk aesthetic more than her first two novels do. The tree functions as the controlling metaphor for the entire novel. As Lupton (1984) notes, "The chinaberry tree, given to Sal Strange by her rich, white lover, Colonel Halloway, represents, at various times in the novel, freedom, protection, secrecy, exposure, intimacy, openness, and endurance. It is, also, of course, the family tree, the family consisting of Sal, her illegitimate daughter, Laurentine, a visiting cousin, Melissa, whose mysterious roots are finally revealed toward the end of the novel, as she is about to elope with her half brother" (384). The chinaberry tree symbolizes the southern folk background of Aunt Sal Strange, who was given the tree as a reminder of her Alabama girlhood by Colonel Halloway, when he relocated to New Jersey and brought her with him. Fauset's use of a tree as a controlling metaphor as well as the secret siblinghood and use of pastoral imagery hearken back to "Double Trouble." Fauset's use of pastoral imagery to convey theme, imagery, and symbolism anticipates the pear tree and mulberry tree as a symbol of sexual awakening in Hurston's *Their Eyes Were Watching God* (1937) and *Seraph on the Suwanee* (1948), respectively.

In *The Chinaberry Tree*, Fauset centers her kunstlerroman around Laurentine Strange and her relationship with her family, friends, clients, and art. Laurentine's perception of herself and her place in the world manifests itself in her response to her family heritage and antecedents as she attempts to negotiate the multiple folk, bourgeois, and proletarian aspects of her personality and background. When Laurentine's Aunt Judy first comes to live with Sal and Laurentine after the colonel's death, Laurentine initially dislikes her southern folkways. However, her resistance changes as Judy's sociability enables her to participate in the community. Judy also introduces her to the art of sewing, from which she is able to earn a livelihood. Despite the folk roots of her training in sewing, Laurentine employs her skill to realize her bourgeois aspirations: "Laurentine, a seamstress, refuses to sew for African American women, but her reputation as a designer for wealthy whites finally earns her social acceptance among them" (Lewis 1992: 382).

Fauset's portrayal of Laurentine hearkens back to the black female artist figures with bourgeois ambitions in her other kunstlerroman novels: Joanna Marshall in *There Is Confusion* and Angela Murray in *Plum Bun*. However, Laurentine contrasts with Joanna and Angela as a female artist in her lack of formal training, for she learns her craft at home through female relatives and not in a special school. Art for Laurentine is her livelihood. Unlike Joanna, she cannot rely on her father's money to subsidize her when she does not derive income from her artistic production. While Angela and Joanna's artistic endeavors as painter and dancer, respectively, may be considered high arts, Laurentine's clothing design may be viewed as a low art in the sense that her artistic productions are not displayed in galleries or viewed on stage, and she does not win awards for her clothing designs. Of the female artist figures, Laurentine resembles Amy Boldin from "The Sleeper Wakes," a clothing designer of dubious racial ancestry who is illegitimate as well.

In *The Chinaberry Tree*, black bourgeois Red Brook society expresses rigid moral and sexual codes, which serve to marginalize Laurentine with her illegitimate background. Like Joanna Marshall in *There Is Confusion* and Angela Murray in *Plum Bun*, Laurentine Strange views marriage as an avenue into bourgeois society. For her, Phil Hackett, the son of a wealthy black ash contractor, represents an entrée into respectability, stability, and affluence for her. Like Angela Murray of *Plum*

*Bun* and Maggie Ellersley of *There Is Confusion*, Laurentine equates marriage to a man from the bourgeois class with success and happiness.

Fauset parallels Laurentine's bourgeois pretensions with those of her cousin Melissa Paul, who comes to live with them after her mother marries and moves to Chicago. Melissa, like Laurentine, desires to be a part of the middle-class black community of Red Brook, but her desire seems overshadowed by the chinaberry tree, symbolizing the relationship between Sal and Colonel Halloway. Aware of the scandal surrounding the Stranges, Melissa feels superior to Laurentine because she is unaware of the circumstances surrounding her own birth. She fails to realize that her mother had an affair with Mr. Forten, a prominent man in Red Brook. Similarly, Laurentine views herself as superior to Melissa because of her successful business as a seamstress, her homeownership, and her upper-class southern white father (Lewis 1992: 383). Marriage functions as a primary goal and means of achieving respectability and bourgeois status for the two young women. Sal views marriage as a means of legitimizing the life of her daughter and niece. She sees Asshur Lane as a symbol of peace, stability, and calm in Melissa's life: "As for Asshur Lane, young man as he was, she could picture him already as the rock he might be to a woman in the weary land called life" (*The Chinaberry Tree*: 32). Because Sal and Colonel Halloway could never join as husband and wife because of the racial prejudices of the era, she especially desires for her daughter and niece to have the opportunity for marriage.

Fauset's presentation of the two cousins' suitors, Phil and Asshur, exemplifies the bourgeois and folk aesthetics resonating throughout the novel. Asshur desires to be a farmer, which tempers Melissa's feeling toward him. Although Asshur can provide Melissa with a home, an automobile, and financial security, she dismisses the possibility of a serious relationship with him because she views his intended vocation of farmer as lowly. She would prefer to marry an African American man who is entering a profession such as teaching, medicine, or law. In her depiction of Melissa's conflicting attitudes toward her two suitors, Fauset calls attention to the dilemma of black women at the beginning of the twentieth century (not that the issues differ greatly today) in resolving issues of love with the concerns of economic and social security. In her portrayal of Asshur's acceptance of Melissa's illegitimate background (revealed to her shortly before she and Malory intend to elope) and his undying devotion to her, to the black community, and to racial progress, Fauset valorizes love, community, and acceptance as the basis for African American heterosexual unions. Asshur represents a resolution of the folk and bourgeois in his quest for racial uplift, material acquisitions, and his devotion and respect for the land and other individuals.

Social class and rank play an important role in Red Brook society, a world which represents respectability and social status. Laurentine fails in her first attempt to enter that society when Hackett rebuffs her for fear that association with an illegitimate individual will detrimentally affect his budding political career. Laurentine then successfully develops a friendship with Mrs. Ismay, the wife of a respected doctor and a member of her church. The Ismays represent

the elite segment of Red Brook society as revealed in their affluent neighborhood: "This section of Red Brook had by tacit consent been handed over to the
better class of colored people" (*The Chinaberry Tree*: 85). Through the Ismays,
Laurentine meets Dr. Denleigh, a young African American doctor who takes a
romantic interest in her. Her relationship with Dr. Denleigh represents a new
beginning for Laurentine, for not only does he possess social status but he reflects an open-minded attitude toward her parentage. He stands in opposition to
the class consciousness that Phil Hackett manifests.

Like Dr. Denleigh, Asshur values an individual's inner qualities rather than
their wealth, social station, or parentage. As the son of a southern minister in
Alabama, Asshur has been taught the importance of racial uplift and valorization of the folk. He exemplifies the philosophy of serving the community. As a
result, he plans to spend the summer in the South teaching the folk, echoing
Philip Marshall of *There Is Confusion*. Later, he plans to attend an agricultural
college and run his uncle's farm. Asshur represents the bridge between the bourgeois and folk classes. Although he has formal education and has spent a good
deal of time in the North, he feels a connection with the South through his family, the church, and the land.

While Melissa distances herself emotionally from Asshur in favor of Malory,
Laurentine draws closer to Dr. Denleigh. Like Asshur, Dr. Denleigh has a southern folk background. His family comes from Charleston, South Carolina, where
his father owned a store that supported a wife and eleven children until his death.
Later, his mother turned the family home into a boardinghouse and earned
enough money to send him to Washington, D.C., where he received a high school
education and attended Howard University. Later he married a woman from an
upwardly mobile and genteel family, but she was unfaithful to him and the union
proved disastrous. Because of Dr. Denleigh's poor childhood and the economic
struggles he has endured, he has not forgotten his folk roots and as a consequence refuses to be judgmental or elitist despite his hard-won social status, unlike Phil Hackett.

The valorization of the folk as embodied by Dr. Denleigh bears affinities with
Frances E. W. Harper's landmark text *Iola Leroy* (1892). Iola, a light-skinned
African American woman and daughter of a white plantation owner and slave
mother, prefers to live as a black woman in the South and work toward racial
uplift among the southern folk at the end of the Civil War rather than live the
life of a bourgeois white or black woman in the North. Her husband, Dr. Latimer, also prefers to align himself with the folk and attend to their physical and
spiritual needs although he could lead the life of a member of the emerging black
bourgeoisie in the North. Harper's novel too functions as a meditation on folk,
bourgeois, and proletarian aesthetics in her valorization of Iola and her husband's embracing of racial uplift, love for the folk, and bourgeois educational
backgrounds.

The proletarian aesthetic, which appears to a lesser degree in *The Chinaberry
Tree* than in *Plum Bun* and *There Is Confusion*, manifests itself in Dr. Denleigh's

earlier ambitions to be like black colonial hero Crispus Attucks and fight for independence. He even desires to have been alive during the Reconstruction period so that he could have shaped the direction of the African American history, enabling African Americans to achieve social and economic equality. Dr. Denleigh's comments reveal a proletarian sensibility similar to the ideology espoused by Philip Marshall in *There Is Confusion* and espoused by the NAACP in the 1920s and 1930s.[5] Dr. Denleigh also bears affinities with A. Philip Randolph, who cofounded the *Messenger* with Chandler Owen and the Brotherhood of Sleeping Car Porters. An embodiment of folk, bourgeois, and proletarian aesthetics, Randolph was a black southerner and Anglophile who adopted a British accent to appear more refined and cultured, yet through the establishment of his periodical and the organization to benefit porters he displayed proletarian interests (Hutchinson 1995). Randolph and Owen viewed the *Messenger* as more radical than other publications of the era, such as the *Crisis* and *Opportunity*, and their publication functioned as an organ for the Brotherhood of Sleeping Car Porters (Huggins 1971). Fauset's Dr. Denleigh appears to be a fictionalization of Du Bois and Randolph in relation to their social and political activism.

Fauset presents history, both public and private, as it impinges upon the present and the future lives of the Strange family. For Fauset, history functions as a way to meditate on race, class, and gender in the United States at the beginning of the twentieth century. When townspeople learn of the mutual attraction between Melissa and Malory, Gertrude Brown, the daughter of a wealthy doctor from a respectable family, sets out to acquire Malory's attentions for herself. Later, when Mr. Stede, a friend of Aunt Sal's, spots the two lovers out one day, Melissa becomes concerned that the entire town will learn of their relationship. The thought of someone telling him and revealing the scandalous family history involving Aunt Sal and Colonel Halloway frightens her because of Malory's conservatism and sense of social propriety. Malory reveals his elitism in his response to Melissa's revelation of Laurentine's parentage and how they acquired the white house in Red Brook. Appalled and judgmental, he initially criticizes Aunt Sal's behavior. Although he eventually apologizes for his reaction, it creates a chasm in their relationship by revealing that in some ways the two have opposing outlooks on life. Malory's class consciousness echoes Phil's attitudes on color, class, and society.

The past, present, and future mesh into one as the consequences of Sal, Colonel Halloway, Judy, and Mr. Forten's actions affect their offspring. Fauset's presentation of the consequences of miscegenation reflect the tradition of tragic mulatto novels such as William Wells Brown's *Clotel* (1853), Charles Chesnutt's *Wife of His Youth and Other Stories of the Color Line* (1899), and Frances E. W. Harper's *Iola Leroy* (1892). By presenting the plight of light-skinned African Americans with black and white racial heritage as the products of unions between aristocratic wealthy white men (the bourgeois) and black female slaves (the folk), the authors illustrate the problematics of negotiating race, class, and gender in the nineteenth century. In these novels and stories, the authors call attention to the absurdity of racial, class, and gender prejudice by pointing out that blacks and whites in America often stem from the same family tree as a result of the racial and sexual politics of life in the antebellum and postbellum South. Just as the intergenerational race and class mixtures depicted in the families of the tragic mulatto novels serve as a microcosm of American society as a whole, Fauset uses the Stranges' complex family history as a means of analyzing and criticizing racial, class, and gender prejudice. When Gertrude Brown's mother reveals to Dr. Denleigh the relationship between Malory and Melissa, Dr. Denleigh tells Laurentine. Their relationship reaches its climax and culmination when Melissa meets the stares of the townspeople at a picnic she attends with Malory and later when Malory attempts to take her to his home. On the day she and Malory planned to marry, she encounters him and he reveals their brother–sister relationship. Shocked and horrified, she faints in disbelief at the turn of events. Through the depiction of entangled family histories, Fauset emphasizes how past actions affect future lives.

Fauset illustrates that individuals must face history, regardless of the pain that ensues, in order to achieve autonomy. The consequences of history bring the Strange family even closer. Laurentine, Dr. Denleigh, and Aunt Sal take especial care in watching over Melissa, who suffers from physical and emotional shock at the news. Fittingly, Asshur's love, understanding, and patience save the Strange family. As a symbol of reconciliation between the bourgeois and the folk, both Dr. Denleigh and Asshur share an affinity with one another's values and beliefs because of their connections with the South, the folk, service, uplift, and a belief in communalism over elitism. Asshur's love and concern transforms Melissa, who once scoffed at the idea of marrying a farmer. When he tells her he still has one year before he graduates from Tuskegee Institute in Alabama and asks if she would mind living in the South in Rising Sun, she agrees to marry him and live there.

Like Joanna Marshall in *There Is Confusion* and Angela Murray in *Plum Bun*, Melissa represents a successful negotiation of folk and bourgeois aesthetics in her valorization of bourgeois goals and appreciation of folk culture and heritage. In her maturity, she also does not balk at the ideal of later moving back to New Jersey so Asshur can manage his uncle's farm—revealing an abandonment of her bourgeois attitudes on the meaning of success. In fact, Asshur's plans represent a reconciliation between the bourgeois and the folk, in that he plans to apply the science he learned at Tuskegee Institute to tending the land. Dr. Denleigh and Asshur provide spiritual and emotional healing to the Strange household. The unions between Melissa and Asshur as well as that between Dr. Denleigh and Laurentine transform the sign of the chinaberry tree from a symbol of shame, illicit sex, and transgression to one of love, endurance, and strength. Like Melissa, Laurentine evolves as an individual as well in her realization that bourgeois aspirations need not overshadow romantic love. Denleigh teaches her the values of honesty, companionship, integrity, and respect for all individuals regardless of background or socioeconomic status.

Through Dr. Denleigh, Laurentine learns to integrate the folk and bourgeois strains within herself. He also represents an awakening of her social and racial consciousness, forcing her to face the folk (which she had suppressed) during a visit to Harlem early in their courtship: "They went to the Lafayette Theatre where Laurentine looked at the audience more than at the stage sensing that oneness which colored people feel in a colored crowd, even though so many of its members are people whom one does not want ever to know" (*The Chinaberry Tree*: 307). Like Helga Crane in Nella Larsen's *Quicksand*, Laurentine feels both drawn to and repelled by her immersion in the black world of Harlem due to her own divided consciousness over her mixed racial heritage. When she sees blues singers and erotic dancers, she evinces a mixture of attraction and repulsion as if the folk music and the dancing evoke aspects of her self, heritage, and history that she once suppressed in her bourgeois aspirations. Lewis (1992) contends that "Laurentine's uneasiness with an animated black folk culture in Harlem cabarets indicates Fauset's own rejection of it, as well as that of Du Bois, her mentor" (383). However, Laurentine's ambivalence could also be read as Fauset's attempt to promote the resolution of folk and bourgeois cultures.

The negotiation of folk and bourgeois cultures also manifests itself in Fauset's symbolic use of the color red in the novel: for example, the chinaberry's red berries and the name of the town Red Brook. Dr. Denleigh, unlike other members of the Red Brook community, does not view the Stranges as having bad blood from the illegitimacy in the family line. A doctor, he is aware that certain traits are more social than biological. The chinaberry tree, and its red berries, signify the blood in the Strange family, which has come to be viewed by the Red Bank community as tainted by illegitimacy and later by incest from the relationship between Melissa Paul and Malory Forten, her half-brother. The name Red Bank signifies blood and the importance of family lines in the community. Blood serves as a link between classes when members of the folk and bourgeois unite in sexual union and produce offspring as well as the connection between blacks and whites in the event of miscegenation. Fauset posits that individuals must come to terms with their bloodlines in order to reconcile the folk and bourgeois aspects of their background and culture.

The proletarian aesthetic manifests itself also in Laurentine's relationship with Dr. Denleigh. When the couple face racial discrimination at a New York restaurant, Laurentine begins to more fully understand the impact of race in America. While living in Red Brook, she leads a life fairly insulated from racism, although it exists there as well. The poor service the couple receives, the irony of racial discrimination in a democracy, taints the atmosphere. The scene serves an important function in underscoring the impact of race on the lives of African Americans of all classes at the turn of the century. Fauset's depiction of the incident echoes the racial incidents in which blacks are denied equal access to education, jobs, and establishments in *There Is Confusion* and *Plum Bun*.

The novel's ending resolves the folk, bourgeois, and proletarian aesthetics through the prospective marriages of Asshur and Melissa and Dr. Denleigh and

Laurentine. Fauset deconstructs conventional notions about legitimacy/illegitimacy, chastity/sexual experience, and sin/atonement in her characterizations of the Strange women and their heterosexual relationships. Fauset criticizes society's definitions of right and wrong, suggesting morality exists on a continuum. Sal and Halloway's relationship is not presented as one of exploitation or abuse, but one of love that racial taboos prevented from flourishing. Fauset presents the community's ostracism of Laurentine and Melissa because of their parentage as negative and hypocritical. Phil Hackett and Malory Forten, members of a black middle class in Red Brook characterized by bourgeois aspirations, represent self-righteousness, while Dr. Denleigh and Asshur Lane, as products of southern black folk communities, exemplify spirituality, morality, acceptance, and communality. Through her depictions of Asshur and Dr. Denleigh, Fauset merges the most positive aspects of folk and bourgeois culture into two figures. The novel's proletarian criticism of racism, class prejudice, and sexism may not be as strong as in Fauset's other novels but nevertheless manifests itself. Fauset again presents a multilayered account of the African American experience as she reveals how the folk, bourgeois, and proletarian aesthetics complement rather than compete with one another.

Like her three other novels, Fauset's *Comedy: American Style* addresses race, class, and gender issues in a provocative and compelling manner. The novel blends the bourgeois, folk, and proletarian aesthetics in its exploration of how colorism affects an African American family. In her presentation of intraracial and interracial color prejudice in the novel, Fauset explores the complex history of race, class, and gender in the United States. In order to understand Fauset's treatment of colorism, it is necessary to address the history of the "one-drop rule" and the "brown bag tests" in American society. In the seventeenth century, slaveholders advocated the one-drop rule (one drop of black blood or one black ancestor makes the individual black) in order to claim the offspring of black female slaves and white slaveholders as black and in effect slaves. Virginia adopted the policy in 1662, and other colonies quickly followed suit (Russell et al. 1992). Brown bag tests were in reference to the shade of a person's skin; someone whose complexion was darker than a paper bag was denied admission to clubs, organizations, and institutions that were color conscious. The history of miscegenation in the United States led to a color and class stratification within the African American community as lighter-skinned blacks sometimes received privileges their darker skin counterparts did not receive in the seventeenth, eighteenth, and nineteenth centuries as having their masters (often their fathers) provide them with freedom, land, money, and/or educational opportunities (Russell et al. 1992).

To understand the focus on color consciousness in *Comedy: American Style*, one must understand the history of color, power, and privilege in its social and historical context. In antebellum America, white slaveowners and overseers fathered children with black female slaves: "Rape was a fact of life on the plantations. At any time and in any place, female slaves were subject to the drunken or abusive sexual advances of a master, an overseer, a neighbor, or a master's son" (Russell et al. 1992). Hurston testifies to this fact in *Their Eyes Were Watching God* through Nanny's narrative of her life in pre-Emancipation Georgia, when she was raped by her slave master before he went off to fight in the Civil War. As a result, her daughter Leafy is born. Leafy later bears Janie, whose heritage is part of this aspect of sexual violence in the plantation system. Many of the offspring of these forced unions became house slaves: "Masters considered mulattoes more intelligent and capable than pure Africans, who in turn were thought to be stronger and better able to tolerate the hot sun. As color increasingly divided the slave community, frictions developed in the cabins. Light skinned slaves returning home from their days in the 'big house' imitated the genteel ways of upper-class white families, and the mulatto offspring of the master often flaunted their education" (Russell et al. 1992: 18). A two-tier class system developed as a consequence, with some of the mulatto offspring receiving opportunities to read and write from their masters or mistresses, and in some cases they were manumitted or received more formal education and training than dark-skinned blacks. As E. Franklin Frazier notes, "'Society' among Negroes had its roots among the house servants who enjoyed a certain prestige among the other slaves on the plantation during their social gatherings" (162). Even after slavery was abolished, the pre-Emancipation free blacks viewed themselves separately from the post-Emancipation free blacks. As a consequence, "Many of them boasted of their 'blood,' which generally referred to their white ancestry" (Frazier 1957). Since their white ancestors represented the southern aristocracy, they considered themselves to be from genteel family backgrounds. Some actually lost the capital they had accumulated prior to the Civil War, and as a means of trying to maintain their roles in society as more upper-class and privileged, they created their own separate social spheres (Russell et al. 1992). Ironically, despite the fact that whites discriminated against them, they discriminated against darker-skinned blacks, whom they considered in many cases to be inferior. By assimilating these ideas of color consciousness and class consciousness in larger American society, they perpetuated a power and class gap among African Americans. Granted, these attitudes originated in and were reinforced by the color/class dichotomy in the larger society.

As a means of self-preservation and protection, this elite group formed organizations and clubs, such as the Blue Vein Society in Nashville and the Bon Ton Society in Washington, D.C. (Russell et al. 1992). African American writers of the Reconstruction and Harlem Renaissance era chronicled the color and class consciousness. Charles Chesnutt writes about the Blue Vein Society in "The Wife of His Youth" (1899), a story that deals with color and class consciousness of blacks in reconstruction era America. In *Their Eyes Were Watching God*, Mrs. Turner counsels Janie that light-skinned blacks should form a separate racial and social class. Wallace Thurman's book *The Blacker the Berry* (1929) explores intraracial and interracial class and color consciousness. *The Wedding* (1995) by Dorothy West explores the color and class prejudice in Washington, D.C., when the dark-skinned Sabina has difficulty attracting a mate at the historically black college in D.C. she attends because of the intraracial color prejudice. The preoccupation with this subject may stem from the personal experiences of these writers and their exposure to the upper echelons of the African American community from their status as writers, artists, and former students at historically black colleges (Hurston attended Morgan College and Howard University, and Fauset taught at the prestigious M Street High School in Washington, D.C., where upper-class black students attended, and she was a member of the NAACP). The legacy of color and class consciousness continued even after the Harlem Renaissance in the proliferation of organizations such as Jack and Jill or the Links, where membership is largely light-skinned blacks (Russell et al. 1992). The legacy has persisted long enough for young contemporary filmmakers, such as Spike Lee in his film *School Daze* (1988), to treat color and class consciousness among African Americans as a well-known commonplace. *School Daze* has a scene in a beauty parlor where dark-skinned black women with "natural" and unprocessed hair and light-skinned black women with chemically straightened hair or hair extensions sing and dance in a humorous, yet disturbing sequence. The light-skinned women praise the virtues of being light, genteel, and bourgeois, while the dark-skinned black women portray an Afrocentric message in the celebration of their dark complexions and "natural" hair. Lee's film highlights the tensions of color and class consciousness on the campus of a historically black college in the late twentieth century.

During the period of the Harlem Renaissance, Harlem also served as a microcosm of the African American community at large. A definite color and class caste system existed in the layout of the area. Neighborhoods in Harlem like Strivers Row and Sugar Hill represent the areas of Harlem where the upper-class African Americans lived (Russell et al. 1992). Churches played an important role in the African American community, yet the churches succumb to the color/class gap as well. A number of tests designed to exclude dark-skinned blacks predominated in some churches, including policies that allowed membership only to blacks whose skin tone was lighter than a paper bag or lighter than the color of a door, or whose hair could flow freely through a fine-tooth comb (Russell et al. 1992). Schools promoted these ideas as well, including historically black private schools as well as colleges and universities. They perpetuated a system wherein lighter-skinned blacks gained easier access to churches, schools, and other organizations that could foster social and economic development, thereby leading to an exclusivity that handicapped darker-skinned blacks. A study of the activities, politicians, ministers, and professionals of the period reveals that many of the members of the Duboisian Talented Tenth had a lighter skin color. This stems from social, cultural, and historical factors that privilege light-skinned blacks (Russell et al. 1992). Not surprisingly, light-skinned blacks such as Du Bois rose to the forefront during the Harlem Renaissance. Many of the Harlem Renaissance texts feature light-skinned protagonists, often light enough to pass for white. The upper class or the protagonists who aspire to be upper class tend to be the products of a mixed-race parentage or the offspring of light-skinned blacks. The light-skinned blacks represent the bourgeoisie, whereas the darker-skinned blacks represent the folk. These protagonists usually reclaim their black heritage by the end of the stories or novels, recognizing the importance of unity with other black Americans. Such texts suggest that race is a social construct rather than a biologically determined fixed construct. In *Plum Bun*, Angela Murray, able to pass for white, has bourgeois aspirations and separates herself temporarily from the black community. Her sister, Virginia, has dark skin and remains with the black community. The housekeeper, Hetty, has dark skin and represents one of the few instances of the folk in the novel. Miss Powell, a fellow art student and classmate of Angela Murray's, cannot pass, and her identifiably dark skin color militates against her achieving the success as an artist she deserves. In *Comedy: American Style*, Fauset's most sustained study of color and class prejudice, Olivia Cary's color/class prejudice brings harmful social and psychological effects upon her and her family members. Thus Fauset disparages color and class prejudice among her African American characters and illustrates the relationship between the color, class, and gender gaps in America as a whole.

Commentary on *Comedy: American Style* focuses on Fauset's criticism of color and class consciousness. Reviews contemporaneous with the 1933 publication of the novel by Hugh Gloster and Sterling Brown note Fauset's analysis of colorism in the United States (Sylvander 1981). Robert Bone (1958) categorizes the novel as one that presents a black woman striving for a white identity. Later assessments also concentrate on the treatment of color and class prejudice. Lewis (1992) notes that "In this work, Fauset alerts the reader to the tragedy that results from complete denial of one's African ancestry and to the cruel nature of color/class hegemony that can exist in black families" (384).[6] Bernard Bell (1987) characterizes *Comedy: American Style* as Fauset's analysis of black bourgeois females. Jacqueline McLendon (1995) argues, "Thus, Fauset leaves us with the thought that in an ideal world origins might not matter, but in the completely racialized world in which we live what is important is a 'wholesome respect for family' and love and pride" (70). Most studies of this novel tend to focus on Olivia Cary's color complex and bourgeois aspirations and the detrimental effects her actions have upon her family. In *Comedy: American Style*, Fauset deconstructs the politics of race, class, and gender in her exposition of the folk, bourgeois, and proletarian aesthetics in this powerful morality tale.

Although the bildungsroman and kunstlerroman still appear as narrative forms in *Comedy: American Style*, they are not the central narrative technique, nor is Phebe Grant, a clothing designer, or Marise Davies, a dancer, presented as the main character. The novel follows the conventions of drama as signified by the chapter titles—"The Plot," "The Characters," "Teresa's Act," "Oliver's Act," "Phebe's Act," and "Curtain," which highlight the tragic consequences of color consciousness. The narrative form of drama heightens the tragedy of Olivia Cary's color complex and the havoc it wreaks upon the psychological, spiritual,

emotional, and physical well-being of all those in her family and circle of ac-
quaintances. As Fauset was an aficionado of plays, it is not surprising that she
would employ the dramatic form for a novel.

Fauset presents the bourgeois aesthetic through the characterization of Olivia
Cary, whose antecedents include Amy in "The Sleeper Wakes" and Angela Murray of *Plum Bun*. As a child, Olivia feels greater affinity with her light-com-
plexion black mother than her darker-skinned father. Her early awareness that
whites receive more privileges has an indelible effect upon Olivia's perception
of race in America, much as the early experiences of Angela Murray shape her
views on ethnicity in *Plum Bun*. Like Angela, Olivia perceives whiteness as an
avenue to personal and material success in a racist society. Olivia's desire for
whiteness informs decisions she makes on marriage and childbirth. Because she
desires to be white, Olivia vicariously experiences whiteness through her choice
of husband and the complexion of her children. Her mania mirrors the protagonist in Eloise Bibb Thompson's "Masks," which features a light-skinned black
woman who marries a black male with a light complexion in order to produce
"white" children, but to no avail, for her child has brown skin.[7] Similarly, Olivia's
third child, Oliver, stands in stark contrast to his light-skinned siblings, Teresa
and Christopher, Jr.

Fauset presents marriage as an avenue to bourgeois desires in *Comedy: American Style* and as a means of moving up the social ladder through the characterization of Olivia, yet she presents marriages based upon social and economic
gain rather than love as shallow and empty. In the end, Olivia's marriage proves
a disaster; her greed, materialism, and racism ruin her marriage and her children's lives. As a young woman, Olivia weds Christopher Cary, a medical student who will provide her with a bourgeois style of life—social status and affluence. A product of a bourgeois "Old Philadelphian" mother who is two
generations away from the Charleston, S.C., folk experience, his suitability rests
in his social background and his light complexion: "She knew now that it was
highly unlikely that she would meet with and marry a white man of Cary's education, standing and popularity. Certainly not in this section of the country
where her affiliations could be so easily traceable" (*Comedy: American Style*
28). Dr. Cary functions as her consolation prize. Unlike Angela Murray, she does
not leave home in an attempt to escape her identity.

Olivia Blanchard Cary represents the detrimental effects of color and class
consciousness. Olivia disapproves of her daughter's friend Marise Davies because of her dark skin while she encourages her daughter to befriend Phebe
Grant because she looks white. She does not want visibly black people in the
house because Olivia fears their neighbors might suspect their true ethnicity.
Olivia stands in stark contrast to other light-skinned blacks in the novel. Her
husband Christopher has pride in being African American despite the racism he
encounters as a black man at the turn of the century. He tries to instill knowledge of black history and achievements in his children. Phebe stands in contrast
to Olivia as well. Unlike Olivia, light-skinned Phebe functions as a representa-

tive of the folk. When her high school friend Nicholas Campbell tells her she could pass for white to achieve her goals, Phebe tells him she would not want to pass for white, contending that individuals should be proud of their heritage. Fauset also depicts opposing viewpoints on color and class consciousness through the characterizations of Teresa and Christopher, Jr., in opposition to Olivia. When Olivia requests that Teresa and Christopher be sent off away from home to further their education, Teresa realizes her mother wants Oliver to stay at home because she does not feel he deserves a good education since he has darker skin. Teresa recognizes her mother's desire to live vicariously through her as manifested in her enrollment at Christie's Academy, an exclusive private school for girls that will produce genteel and cultured young women, reflecting Olivia's own bourgeois ambitions. Olivia views Christie's Academy, in New Hampshire, as the appropriate school for her daughter because of its exclusivity: "Most of the students were the children of people belonging to the upper middle-class; people whose names never appeared in the papers, who took themselves and their positions seriously and sensibly. The men of this group were probably pillars in their respective communities, thoroughly American and for the most part New England American" (*Comedy: American Style* 70). The white Anglo-Saxon Protestant backgrounds of the student body make it an attractive school to Olivia Blanchard. The school had few black or Jewish applicants in its history, and Olivia hopes it will remain that way. She views blackness as a taint. As a consequence, she wants her daughter educated in that white and affluent setting.

Teresa lacks the social ambition that drives Olivia. She feels that she already comes from a long line of distinguished individuals. Teresa recognizes that whiteness does not necessarily mean refinement. Fauset emphasizes this point through her characterization of Alicia Barrett, an educated, cultured, and articulate black student in Teresa's school. Fauset's depiction of Alicia Barrett as in many ways surpassing her white classmates in culture and studiousness at the posh private school functions as a criticism of color consciousness and racial stereotypes of brown-skinned blacks. The relationship between the two girls has a bold impact upon Teresa and her identity. When she goes home to Chicago with Alicia, she reveals her racial heritage to her friend and admits to the lie she has been living. Her double life in a sense has left her estranged from both the black and white race as she soon discovers while in Chicago with Alicia. Alicia brings Teresa into a whole new world of affluent, cultivated, and politically active blacks proud of their ethnicity, and Teresa meets Henry Bates, an ambitious dark-skinned black man and a friend of Barrett's family. The Barretts and their circle of friends exemplify the proletarian aesthetic in their embracing of social protest, political activism, and promotion of racial uplift.

For Teresa, Henry represents freedom from her mother's goals and a means of saving her brother Oliver by incorporating him in her new family. When Teresa visits home for a few weeks before beginning her studies at Smith after graduating from prep school, she learns that Olivia makes Oliver work as a butler during her civic club meetings. Teresa's promise to him that she will marry

Henry and let Oliver live with them reflects her desire to counteract the legacy of racial self-hatred. She pities her brother because he has not received the care and attention that she and her brother have received from their mother. Teresa's studies in college serve as an interlude to her hoped-for marriage. However, Olivia discovers Teresa's plot to elope after her boyfriend's commencement at the Massachusetts Institute of Technology, and she prohibits Teresa from marrying Henry, a brown-skinned man. Much to Henry's dismay, his fiancée has been so influenced by her mother's teachings that she proposes that he pretend to be a Mexican rather than an African American to make their life easier.

In an affirmation of his African American identity, Henry refuses to pass for another race. Disgusted, he leaves Teresa, for he cannot live a lie. Fauset's depiction of Olivia and Teresa's color complex and desire to pass to achieve their bourgeois aspiration and middle-class respectability functions as a criticism of individuals denying their blackness. As a result of her inability to challenge her mother by leaving with Henry, Teresa is doomed to a life of loneliness, alienation, and suffering. The quest for whiteness and affluence causes Teresa's, and indirectly Olivia's and Oliver's, downfall. After her failed attempt to marry Henry, Teresa obtains a job tutoring her brother's college friends in French back in Philadelphia, which gives her new direction. She decides to go to France to improve her skills in the language. For Teresa, it signifies the furthering of her education, while Olivia views it as a way to break free from her husband and sons. The class and color consciousness Olivia expresses in the United States worsens in Europe.

When Teresa enrolls at the University of Toulouse and becomes close to a professor named Aristide Pailleron, Olivia encourages the match: "Ultimately, Olivia forces the daughter to pass for white and to marry a Frenchman, who mistreats her, and she denounces the oldest son's friendship with a young lady who does not meet her requirements of color and class" (Lewis 1992: 385). Olivia views her daughter's marriage to a European as a prize and the culmination of all her desires for her daughter and herself as well. For Olivia, France represents culture, affluence, prestige, and whiteness, which she craves for herself and daughter. In a desire for respectability, Teresa marries Aristide although she does not love him. The absurdity of the arrangement stems from her mother's desire for whiteness and social respectability with the poor Frenchman. Her marriage to Aristide leaves her lonely and conflicted. In Olivia's quest to have her daughter marry well and white, she ironically places her daughter in a lower socioeconomic level, for Aristide cannot support the three in the lifestyle that Olivia strives for. Fauset's presentation of Teresa's plight in France functions as an ironic comment on race and culture. Olivia's love of France stems from her Eurocentrism and love of whiteness as preferable to Afrocentrism and blackness. Since France historically has been the birthplace of leading literary, artistic, and political figures in the Western cultural canon, it has been viewed as the pinnacle of European and white civilization. As a former student at the Sorbonne in 1925 (an institution she wrote about in "The Enigma of the Sorbonne" for the *Crisis* in 1925) and the possessor of an M.A. in French from the University of Pennsylvania, Fauset would well have been acquainted with perceptions of French art, culture, and tradition. By presenting Teresa's life in France and her husband as spiritually, morally, culturally, and psychically deprived, Fauset exposes the error of Eurocentric beliefs and attitudes about Western Europe and whiteness as the ultimate fulfillment of an individual's needs.

Elitism and color prejudice negatively affect characters in *Comedy: American Style*. Of all the characters, Oliver's plight presents the most tragedy and pathos. Oliver functions as a sign and symbol of Olivia's inability to be white and a manifestation of her worst fears: "To her Oliver meant shame. He meant more than that; he meant the expression of her failure to be truly white. There was some taint in her, she told herself once, not long after Oliver's birth.... For she belonged to that group of Americans which thinks that God or Nature created only one perfect race—the Caucasians" (*Comedy: American Style*: 205–6). She views Oliver as a curse on her and cannot accept him as a son despite his devotion to her. Like Mrs. Turner in *Their Eyes Were Watching God*, Olivia worships whiteness. Filled with racial self-hatred, her racism colors her perception of others.

Oliver experiences two rejections that influence his sense of identity and self-worth. The first rejection comes at the hand of his mother, experienced when he discovers a letter she wrote to his father about him from France. Olivia views his visible blackness as a hindrance to her plans for the family. Although Teresa represents his last chance at happiness and acceptance into a family unit, she reneges on her promise of letting him come live with her one day in a letter she writes him after marrying Aristide. She fears that her brother's complexion will reveal that he is black. Feeling like an outsider in his own family and a displaced person rejected by his mother and sister, Oliver commits suicide out of lack of love and acceptance. Olivia's legacy of colorism and elitism in effect kill her son, setting the stage for more tragic consequences later. Teresa's betrayal of her brother Oliver indicates the far-reaching effects of color consciousness and the desire to pass for an easier life. Even Phebe, who once vowed she would never pass, succumbs to the temptation as well in much the same way as Amy in "The Sleeper Wakes" and Angela Murray in *Plum Bun*. Her desire to pass encompasses her bourgeois desires and attitudes. She views being perceived as white as an asset, enabling her to build a larger customer base for her sewing and meet wealthy, upwardly mobile men. Her passing results in a relationship with Llewellyn Nash, a young wealthy white man reminiscent of Roger Fielding in *Plum Bun*: "He was a great believer in class-distinctions; he was firmly convinced that certain people in the world were born to serve; others as definitely born to rule" (*Comedy: American Style*: 229). Nash contrasts with her childhood friend Nicholas Campbell, a young black medical student who constantly has to battle against racism and class prejudice just to succeed, like Peter Bye in *There Is Confusion*.

Fauset presents intraracial racial color tensions and conflicts in depicting the relationship between Christopher Cary and Marise Davies, who leaves Philadelphia to become a successful actress and dancer in New York despite the racism black women artists face at the turn of the century. In a scene reminiscent of *There Is Confusion* (when Joanna Marshall sends a letter to Maggie Ellersley warning her to stay away from her brother because of their different social standings), Olivia Cary sends a note to Marise requesting a meeting. Olivia's disdain for the young woman results from her color and from class prejudice. As a result, when Christopher asks Marise to join him in marriage, she indicates that marriage with him might be dull and pedestrian in comparison to her exciting stage life. Olivia has succeeded in thwarting potential marriages for two of her children because their chosen mates are of a darker hue.

Olivia's insistence on a color code facilitates the relationship between Christopher Cary and Phebe Grant in a sense. The two rekindle a friendship at a dance sponsored by a social club, and as a consequence, Phebe ends her relationship with Llewellyn Nash, who had proposed to her in a scene reminiscent of Angela Murray's rejection of Roger Fielding in *Plum Bun*. When Phebe reveals to Nash her ethnicity, he reacts in shock. After overcoming his shock at her true race, Nash proposes that the two live together in Europe as lovers. Similarly, Amy's ex-husband Wynne in "The Sleeper Wakes" proposes that she be his mistress after he divorces her when he learns of her black heritage. Fauset in these scenes connects back to the slave narrative tradition of Jacobs's *Incidents in the Life of a Slave Girl* (1861) and Frederick Douglass's 1845 autobiography. In Jacobs's narrative, Mr. Flint, her owner, desires her as his concubine. She, in turn, engages in a relationship with a white man named Mr. Sands as a means of choosing her own sexual mate and father of her children hoping he will assist her in obtaining her freedom from Mr. Flint. Similarly, in Douglass's narrative, he calls attention to his white ancestry and the sexual abuse black female slaves endured from white masters.

Fauset presents the union between the folk and bourgeois classes through the marriage of Phebe and Christopher, Jr. Due to the tensions in his family caused by Oliver's suicide, the Cary family experiences downward mobility as Christopher, Sr.'s interest in the medical practice wanes. The tensions amplify when Phebe becomes Olivia's daughter-in-law. Olivia's extreme class prejudice affects her treatment of Phebe and her mother. It also causes Olivia's disdain for the neighborhood where the young couple reside, which has a large number of blacks. In these sentiments, Olivia anticipates Cleo Judson from Dorothy West's novel *The Living Is Easy*, who disdains all-black neighborhoods due to her bourgeois aspirations and her equating whiteness and status.

As a representative of the folk, Phebe contrasts with Olivia in her background and her sensibilities. When her father-in-law's finances are ruined by the Great Depression and by his apathy toward his practice after the death of his son, Phebe becomes the primary breadwinner for them. In fact, she invites his parents and her mother to move in with them despite the cold way Olivia has treated her after the Carys can no longer maintain their home and servants. She stands in contrast to the bourgeois pretensions and prejudices of Olivia Cary. She functions as a symbol of healing and renewal for the Carys in the same manner as Asshur Lane of *The Chinaberry Tree.* Elitism and color consciousness bring discord to Christopher and Phebe's new home. In a scene echoing her treatment of Oliver, Olivia demands that Phebe's mother Sarah serve her white civic club members. Olivia views herself as superior to Phebe's mother Sarah because of her background and the fact that Sarah has worked as a seamstress much of her life. The elitism, class prejudice, and racism prove worrisome for Phebe, driving a wedge between her and her husband, almost prompting the young wife to engage in an affair with Nicholas Campbell, who now lives in New York as a doctor and husband of Marise Davies.

In *Comedy: American Style,* Fauset criticizes class and color prejudice through the portrayal of Olivia's downfall. After having left her family to go to France and live with Teresa, she encounters a cold greeting in France from her son-in-law. Despite her dreams of wealth and grandeur for her daughter, she finds Teresa unhappily married, shabbily dressed, and despondent. Ironically, the very forces that drove Olivia to press her daughter to marry the Frenchman have resulted in her daughter's dissipation and sadness. Unable to acquire financial assistance from her daughter and son-in-law, she appeals to her husband, who can give her few funds. Alone and living in a *pension* in France, Olivia has alienated everyone who once cared about her due to greed, materialism, snobbery, and racism: "By the end of the novel, she is psychologically broken and spends her days sitting by the window of her lonely Paris room, watching and waiting for an Anglo Saxon woman and her son, who sit in a courtyard reading and laughing together. The scene reminds the reader, if not Olivia, of the past—of the lost years when Olivia's dark-skinned son had sought out his mother to confide in, and when he desperately needed her attention" (Lewis 1992: 385). Fauset's depiction of the rise and fall of Olivia Blanchard Cary serves as a warning against racial and class prejudice within and outside the African American community. *Comedy: American Style* serves as a culmination of the themes and issues introduced in *There Is Confusion, Plum Bun,* and *The Chinaberry Tree* and the short stories in the *Crisis.* Fauset's last published novel functions as her bleakest and most scathing in its criticism of racism and class prejudice in American society. The comedy in the title functions ironically in its commentary on the absurdity of racism and class prejudice in American society, which leads to destruction for all.

In her novels and short stories, Fauset challenges the reader's assumptions about race, gender, and class, suggesting that the lines drawn between black and white, rich and poor, the folk, proletarian, and bourgeois separate and cause dissension with the African American community. Through her blending of various aesthetics, she reveals the nonmonolithic nature of African American life. Far from being a writer removed from the masses or lacking a political and social criticism, Jessie Fauset expertly deconstructs the black bourgeoisie to subvert misconceptions regarding race, class, and gender. Of the three (Fauset, Hurston, and West) her work most prominently, at first glance, displays the lives of the black middle class, but she also portrays characters from lower socioeconomic levels and valorizes the folk as the source of African American culture and artistic expression. The criticisms of race, class, and gender prejudice express the proletarian aesthetic ingrained in her novels and short stories. Fauset's novels and short stories provide a provocative commentary on American life and culture, setting the foundation for writers such as Hurston and West, who would continue to explore similar issues in their novels and short fiction.

## NOTES

1. Sylvander (1981) provides an overview of the critical response to *There Is Confusion* in 1924 from leading newspapers and magazines. Sylvander includes reviews from black periodicals such as the *Messenger* and *Opportunity* as well as publications such as the *New York Times Book Review*, the *Times Literary Supplement*, and the *Literary Digest International*. Her account of the reviews suggests that early reviewers focused on Fauset's depiction of black middle-class values and mores and compared her with Edith Wharton, obscuring her depiction of blacks from lower socioeconomic levels.

2. Lewis (1989) stresses that African American writers of the Harlem Renaissance often sought to revise what they considered as one-dimensional and stereotypical portrayals of black life in America. Noting Jessie Fauset's distress at the success of T. S. Stribling's *Birthright*, he writes:

> Both excited and disappointed by the flaws in white T. S. Stribling's race novel, the best-selling *Birthright*, she sensed clearly that the moment was ideal for a New Negro Novel by a New Negro, pressing the idea on Walter White and others in her select circle of acquaintances: "We reasoned, 'Here is an audience waiting to hear the truth about us. Let us who are better qualified to present that truth than any white writer, try to do so.'"
> (123)

3. *Maggie: A Girl of the Streets* (1893), by Stephen Crane, chronicles the life of a white female whose socioeconomic class, gender, and environment militate against her in the quest for financial and personal success and fulfillment. The similar names of the two characters in *Maggie: A Girl of the Streets* and *There Is Confusion*, coupled with their common low socioeconomic levels, and the fact that each possesses a beauty that "blooms" amid their poor and bleak surroundings as young women, suggests the parallel between the two.

4. Fauset was literary editor from 1919 to 1926 under the direction of W. E. B. Du Bois, according to Sylvander (1987). Her professional and personal relationship with Du Bois, her mentor, leads me to assert the possibility that Philip Marshall and the *Spur* from *There Is Confusion* may be a fictionalized account of Du Bois and his relationship with the NAACP and the *Crisis*, its official publication.

5. Fauset's work on the *Crisis* from 1919 to 1926 and her involvement in the early stages of the NAACP's development suggests that she may have modeled characters in her novels on people she knew.

6. It is Lewis's contention that Fauset created light-skinned, educated, and middle-class heroines to counter stereotypical treatments of black women in fiction.

7. "Masks" was first published in *Opportunity* 5 (1927): 300–302 but was reprinted in *The Sleeper Wakes*, an anthology edited by Marcy Knopf.

# REFERENCES

Bell, Bernard. 1987. *The Afro-American Novel and Its Tradition.* Amherst: University of Massachusetts Press.

Bone, Robert. 1958. *The Negro Novel in America.* New Haven, Conn.: Yale University Press.

Brawley, Benjamin. 2000. "The Negro in American Fiction." Pp. 959–65 in *The Prentice Hall Anthology of African American Literature,* eds. Rochelle Smith and Sharon L. Jones. Upper Saddle River, N.J.: Prentice Hall.

DuPlessis, Rachel Blau. 1985. *Writing Beyond the Ending: Narrative Strategies of Twentieth-Century Women Writers.* Bloomington: Indiana University Press.

Fauset, Jessie Redmon. 1993. "The Sleeper Wakes." In *The Sleeper Wakes: Harlem Renaissance Stories by Women,* ed. Marcy Knopf. New Brunswick, N.J.: Rutgers University Press.

Frazier, E. Franklin. 1957. *Black Bourgeoisie: The Rise of a New Middle Class in the United States.* New York: Macmillan.

Holman, C. Hugh, and William Harmon. *A Handbook to Literature.* 1992. New York: Macmillan.

Huggins, Nathan. 1971. *Harlem Renaissance.* New York: Oxford University Press.

Hutchinson, George. 1995. *The Harlem Renaissance in Black and White.* Cambridge, Mass.: Harvard University Press.

Jenkins, Wilbert. 1986. "Jessie Fauset: A Modern Apostle of Black Racial Pride." *Zora Neale Hurston Forum* 1, no. 1: 14–24.

Lewis, David Levering. 1989. *When Harlem Was in Vogue.* New York: Oxford University Press.

Lewis, Vashti Crutcher. 1992. "Mulatto Hegemony in the Novels of Jessie Redmon Fauset." *College Language Association* 35, no. 4: 375–86.

Lupton, Mary Jane. 1984. "Bad Blood in Jersey: Jessie Fauset's *The Chinaberry Tree.*" *College Language Association* 27, no. 4: 383–92.

McDowell, Deborah. 1990. Introduction to *Plum Bun* by Jessie Fauset. Boston: Beacon Press.

McLendon, Jacquelyn Y. 1995. *The Politics of Color in the Fiction of Jessie Fauset and Nella Larsen.* Charlottesville: University Press of Virginia.

Miller, Nina A. 1996. "Femininity, Publicity, and the Class Division of Cultural Labor: Jessie Redmon Fauset's *There Is Confusion.*" *African American Review* 30, no. 2: 205–20.

Sylvander, Carolyn Wedin. 1987. "Jessie Fauset." *Dictionary of Literary Biography: Afro-American Women Writers from the Harlem Renaissance to the Present,* ed. Trudier Harris and Thadious Davis. Detroit: Gale.

———. 1981. *Jessie Redmon Fauset, Black American Writer.* Troy, N.Y.: Whitston.

Wall, Cheryl. 1995. *Women of the Harlem Renaissance.* Bloomington: Indiana University Press.

Wintz, Cary D. 1988. *Black Culture and the Harlem Renaissance.* Houston: Rice University Press.

# 2

# "How It Feels to Be Colored Me": Social Protest in the Fiction of Zora Neale Hurston

In 1927, Zora Neale Hurston sped down the backwoods of rural Florida in a $300 used gray Chevrolet dubbed "Sassy Susie" in search of stories, rituals, and customs indigenous to southern black folk as part of a folklore-collecting expedition. Sponsored by Columbia University and the Association for the Study of Negro Life and History, the expedition represented one of several trips Hurston would take to preserve and valorize African American artistic, historic, and cultural traditions.[1] Adopting critical methods and strategies learned at northern elite institutions for the study of southern black folk culture, Hurston merged the bourgeois and the folk as she analyzed, celebrated, and valorized the cultural contributions of African Americans. Hurston promoted a proletarian aesthetic in her insistence on the value of African American customs, stories, and art. The 1927 field expedition exemplifies the folk, bourgeois, and proletarian aesthetics in Hurston's personal life and anthropological studies.

When Hurston traveled to Florida in 1927, she initially experienced problems in negotiating these strains as she related to the folk of Florida in her research: "She later admitted in *Dust Tracks* that her early difficulties arose because 'the glamour of Barnard College was still upon me. I dwelt in Marble halls. I knew where the material was, all right. But I went about asking, in carefully accented Barnardese, "Pardon me, but do you know any folk-tales or folk-songs?"'" (Hemenway 1977: 90). Her experience reveals that she remained a part of yet separate from both the folk communities of Florida and the bourgeois circles of New York, Baltimore, and Washington, D.C. Nevertheless, her dedication to bringing these two worlds together suggests a proletarian aesthetic, arguing for the respect and valorization of all socioeconomic levels, races, and cultures.

Her folklore expeditions also reveal the politics of race, class, and gender behind the relationships between writers and patrons during the Harlem Renaissance. During the 1927 expedition, Hurston and fellow Harlem Renaissance writers Langston Hughes and Jessie Fauset traveled to Booker T. Washington's gravesite in Tuskegee, Alabama. Despite the fact that Zora Neale Hurston and Jessie Fauset were often viewed as polar opposites (Hurston as folk and Fauset as bourgeois), this event reveals common ground between the two women in their appreciation of African American history and culture. After returning to New York, Hurston began a relationship with Charlotte Osgood Mason in an effort to finance artistic projects related to black folklore (*Novels and Stories:* 1017). Hurston's connection with Mason reveals the relationships between black artistic production, self-representation, and white patronage in African American literary production. From 1927 to 1931, Mason controlled Hurston financially through the stipends she allocated the author and artistically by designating when, where, and how Hurston would disseminate her findings on "primitive" African American folklore and customs. African American artists of the period often had to negotiate their vision of the African American experience alongside the stereotypical assumptions of individuals like Mason in order to write and survive financially. Hurston's desire to find an authentic voice free from the constraints of others (such as Mason and white publishers) manifests itself in her novels, short stories, and essays.

In essays such as "How It Feels to Be Colored Me" (*The World Tomorrow* 1928), Hurston articulates the complexities of her life in pre–Civil Rights Movement America. She writes, "Sometimes I feel discriminated against, but it does not make me angry. It merely astonishes me. How can any deny themselves the pleasure of my company! It's beyond me" (*Folklore, Memoirs, and Other Writings:* 829). By suggesting that racial discrimination lies beyond her comprehension, she suggests the irrationality of oppressing others for the color of their skin. She also defiantly suggests that she will not allow racist individuals to confine or control her. The title of her essays suggests that she asserts the "Me," meaning her own voice and conceptualizations about her experiences as a black woman. Her essay serves as a meditation on the politics of race, class, and gender, which she also articulated in her short stories and in her four novels.

As an astute individual often exposed to patronizing attitudes toward African Americans, Hurston employed the genre of nonfiction essay to expand upon the politics of race and class in publishing. In her essay "What White Publishers Won't Print" (*Negro Digest* 1950) Hurston lambasted the one-dimensional portrayal of blacks, calling for a deeper and more realistic rendering of African American life in fiction that would explode the either-or dichotomy of blacks as solely bourgeois or solely folk. Instead, she calls for the depiction of the average African American individual—that is, the masses. Hurston's essay evokes a proletarian aesthetic in its protestation of biased depictions of black life and its assertion of the need to connect with the common, ordinary African American. She notes, "Literature and other arts are supposed to hold up the mirror to nature. With only the fractional 'exceptional' [bourgeois] and the 'quaint' [folk] portrayed, a true picture of Negro life in America cannot be. A great principle of national art has been violated" (*Folk-*

From left to right: Jessie Fauset, Langston Hughes, and Zora
Neale Hurston in Tuskegee, Alabama, standing in front of
Booker T. Washington's gravesite. The photograph is from the
Yale Collection of American Literature, Beinecke Rare Book
and Manuscript Library.

*lore, Memoirs, and Other Writings:* 955). Hurston's commentary reveals a writer
who attempted to merge the folk, bourgeois and proletarian in an effort to render
a more accurate and sophisticated depiction of African American life and culture.

Hurston's development of her aesthetic voice can be traced by examining the
triangle of folk, bourgeois, and proletarian aesthetics in relation to her use of
narrative strategies in "Spunk" (1925), "Sweat" (1926), "The Bone of Contention" (1930–35, unpublished during her lifetime), "The Gilded Six Bits"
(1933), *Jonah's Gourd Vine* (1934), *Their Eyes Were Watching God* (1937),
*Moses, Man of the Mountain* (1939), and *Seraph on the Suwanee* (1948).[2] The
bildungsroman, a narrative form depicting an individual's emotional, physical,
mental, sexual, and spiritual development, offers Hurston a medium for exploring race, class, and gender. The kunstlerroman, a special form of the bil-

dungsroman, captures the growth and the development of the artist. As an African American female writer, Hurston used the kunstlerroman as an effective tool for presenting the social, political, and economic forces that shape the growth and the development of the artist. This examination of Hurston's fiction will examine how Hurston connects the narrative techniques of the bildungsroman and the kunstlerroman with formal elements such as theme, character, plot, and symbolism to meditate on folk, bourgeois, and proletarian aesthetics. Through her complex portrait of African American life, she challenges stereotypical notions of blacks as primitive or exotic, providing a more truthful and authentic representation of black art, culture, and tradition.

This study runs counter to previous critical assessments of Hurston's work. Critics have categorized her fiction as folk realism and obscured the bourgeois and proletarian aesthetics in her work because of her perceived social, economic, and cultural background. Part of the reason may be Hurston's own role in constructing a public persona. Although Hurston was born in Notasulga, Alabama, she claimed Eatonville, Florida, an all-black town steeped in African American folkways and tradition, as her birthplace in her 1942 autobiography *Dust Tracks on a Road (Folklore, Memoirs, and Other Writings)*. Her family roots in Notasulga date back two generations. Alf Hurston, her father's father, established several Baptist churches in Notasulga. Not surprisingly, her father became a Baptist preacher, and Hurston's four published novels carry biblical allusions in their titles, which suggests the impact of coming from an outwardly highly religious family. Hurston's family relocated to Florida between 1893 and 1895, and they ultimately settled in Eatonville (Wall 1995). Her insistence upon Eatonville as her hometown may lie in Hurston's desire to counteract stereotypical images of blacks as dependent, unassertive, uncreative, and imitative. By celebrating an all-black town as her birthplace, she and Eatonville merge into an entity autonomous from the Anglo-American culture and one with rich and vital artistic traditions steeped in African American culture. Eatonville served an important function for the residents of the community. The town stood as a symbol of black self-sufficiency and pride in the Jim Crow South (Wall 1995). As a black writer of the New Negro movement, idealizing Eatonville as her birthplace enabled Hurston to identity herself and her hometown as the epitome of the black self-definition, autonomy, and pride that characterized the Harlem Renaissance.

Hurston's life represents an attempt to reconcile folk, bourgeois, and proletarian aesthetics personally and artistically. Although Zora Neale Hurston fashioned herself as a folk icon, a study of her biographical roots illustrates both bourgeois and proletarian identities. The actuality of her birthplace runs counter to her representation in *Dust Tracks on a Road*. In her first chapter ("My Birthplace,"), she boldly claims Eatonville, Florida, as her birthplace. Hurston writes, "I was born in a Negro town" (*Folklore, Memoirs, and Other Writings*: 561). Of course, Hurston knew her true birthplace to be Notasulga, Alabama, but as a part of the New Negro Movement or Harlem Renaissance, Hurston must have felt the need to affirm her blackness, and to promote the New Negro ideas of black self-sufficiency and independence. By creating a persona for herself as the daughter of an all-black town, she attempted to contextualize her work as springing from a decidedly black, and in particular all-black, wellspring of creativity. Not surprisingly, Eatonville and Florida serve as the settings for much of her long and short fiction as well as her folklore-collecting expeditions. Like many of her characters such as Janie Mae Crawford, Nanny, Jody Starks, and Tea Cake in *Their Eyes Were Watching God*, Hurston was a migrant, someone who continued to move socially, economically, artistically, and geographically throughout her life while retaining her connection to the place where she spent much of her youth. In fact, one could make the argument that Eatonville did indeed serve as her birthplace, for the stories, the sermons, and the interactions she had in this environment formed and developed her artistic sensibilities.

In her autobiography, she points out that her parents were from a small community near Notasulga, Alabama. Her father, John Hurston, came from a working-class black family that made a living through farm labor. A poor young man with aspirations, he began courting Hurston's mother, Lucy Ann Potts, whose family owned land, which placed her in a more bourgeois class among the African Americans in rural Alabama. Because John Hurston's family did not own land, others with more material resources looked down upon him. He lived "over the creek" with the other blacks who lived on plantations owned by wealthy whites (*Folklore, Memoirs, and Other Writings:* 567). Nevertheless, love prevailed, and the marriage of the bourgeois and the folk produced Zora Neale Hurston.

After their marriage, the young couple lived on a plantation in a small cabin, yet her father, dissatisfied with his life and his meager resources and lack of opportunity, relocated to Eatonville, a town where he felt he would have more opportunities, since it was an all-black area. Later, Lucy joined him in Florida, where he moved up socially and economically to become mayor of Eatonville. By Eatonville standards, the family led a bourgeois style of life. They owned their own land, built a large home, and cultivated a farm. Unlike many black women of the time, Lucy Potts never had to work outside the home, which indeed placed her in a very privileged position for a black woman of that era and illustrates John Hurston's stature in the town. Hurston openly admits her father's infidelities in her autobiography, which she later explores in her novel *Jonah's Gourd Vine*. (She models the book's protagonist, Reverend John Pearson, after her own father.) Her parents remained together despite her father's infidelities. The couple produced eight children, and John Hurston managed to support his large family with the assistance of a garden. As a child, Hurston read voraciously, including *The Swiss Family Robinson*, *Scribner's Magazine*, fairytales, *Gulliver's Travels*, Greek and Roman mythology, Norse tales, the Bible, and Rudyard Kipling stories. Much of her reading consisted of fantasy and romantic tales, which fueled her imagination, allowing her to travel mentally and spiritually beyond Eatonville, Florida. Yet she remained immersed in the rich African American oral tradition and culture through her interactions with townspeople. According to her autobiography, one of her most vivid early memories is of the porch in front of Joe Clarke's store, where people told tales, played the dozens (verbal jousting), and commented on everyday life. According to Hurston, "There were no discreet nuances of life on Joe Clarke's porch. There was open kindnesses, anger, hate, love, envy, and its kinfolks, but all emotions were naked, and nakedly arrived at" (*Folklore, Memoirs, and Other Writings:* 599).

Although Hurston as a young girl was not allowed to sit on the porch to hear the stories because of her age, gender, and status as the daughter of the mayor, she would often wander in and out of the store in order to hear the stories, the tales, and the commentary, much of it of a sexual nature. Her exposure to the porch talk and its folktales later inspired her writing in novels such as *Their Eyes Were Watching God*, where Jody Stark's store porch becomes the center of the town's activities and fueled her interest in folklore and ethnology as a college and university student. In this sense, Eatonville and the porch of Joe Clarke's store served as the center of her apprenticeship as a writer, storyteller, and thinker. While Hurston's father also played an important role in her life, her mother played a notable role in her development as a writer and artist. Hurston's mother encouraged her to read the Bible, which serves as the basis for much of her fiction, directly or indirectly. Furthermore, her mother always encouraged her to be ambitious and to never give up on her dreams and aspirations. This spirit infiltrated Hurston's mind, spurring her on to a constant quest throughout her life. Curiously, Hurston's best-known, and arguably best written, novel, *Their Eyes Were Watching God*, is a "motherless" novel. Janie Mae Crawford, despite three husbands, bears no children, and her mother flees when she is an infant, leaving her to be reared by Nanny, her grandmother. As Carol P. Marsh-Lockett (1999) points out, "Study of her novels reveals that motherhood is a presence therein but that it exists in a marginalized, politically powerless form, the mothers themselves lacking communities of women and rarely finding their own voices except to uphold a patriarchal superstructure" (100). Why is this pattern prevalent in Hurston's fiction when her own mother played such an important role in her life? Although Hurston chronicles the marriage of her parents in her highly autobiographical novel *Jonah's Gourd Vine*, her fiction in general does, as Lockett asserts, marginalize mothers. This may stem from her truncated relationship with her mother, who died in 1904, when Zora was thirteen years old. Later her father remarried a woman whom Hurston disliked, which later resulted in her leaving home. Her mother's death at such a young age, when a female finds herself at the brink of womanhood, may be a factor in the decentering of mothers in her texts, except for the elegiac representations of her mother in *Jonah's Gourd Vine*. The only other novel by Hurston with a mother as a central character is *Seraph on the Suwanee*, a portrait of a white southern mother who weds a man with bourgeois aspirations. In addition, Hurston, despite two marriages, never had children of her own, which may be due to the tensions she faced between the role of wife and that of a writer with a migratory style of life. Those two roles proved incompatible for Hurston. Many other women writers of the Harlem Renaissance, including Fauset and West, had no children.

Even though mothers do not play the significant role one might expect, given Hurston's predilection for domestic fiction, her mother's memory lives on in her writings. Cheryl Wall notes, "Although one could argue that Zora Hurston set out to honor her father's art and that of the Eatonville storytellers, the history of her career is, to a considerable degree, the history of her effort to recover her mother's voice" (Wall 1995: 145). Upon her mother's death, Hurston moved to Jacksonville to attend school with her sister Sarah, where she remained until 1905. From 1906 to 1911, Hurston lived with relatives and friends of her mother in Florida. In 1912 she relocated to Sanford, Florida. A tumultuous relationship with her stepmother after she returns to her father's house necessitated Hurston's migration again. After living with one of her brothers in Memphis from 1914 to 1915, Hurston's dissatisfaction led her to travel as a maid for a singer with a Gilbert and Sullivan theatrical group along the East Coast. Settling in Baltimore after becoming ill, Hurston went to high school and began taking classes at Morgan College in Baltimore (now Morgan State University) and later began taking classes at Howard University in Washington, D.C., in 1919. From 1919 to 1920, Hurston attended Howard, where she would receive an associates degree. An English major, she joined a literary club sponsored by Alain Locke, a Howard University professor of philosophy who also happened to be the first African American Rhodes scholar. Her story "John Redding Goes to Sea" and a poem "O Night" were published in *Stylus*. Washington was a center of black intellectual and artistic activity and Howard University was an important site for the black bourgeoisie, and Hurston was able to attend a literary salon sponsored by Georgia Douglas Johnson. Other individuals who attended the salon were Jean Toomer, Marita Bonner, Jessie Fauset, May Miller, Alain Locke, and W. E. B. Du Bois (*Folklore, Memoirs, and Other Writings*: 962–63). Hurston's relationship with Locke helped to sanction and solidify her role in the New Negro Movement, for he included her story "Spunk" in his anthology *The New Negro*, which was published in 1925. This exposure helped to place her work among those of the notable Harlem Renaissance writers Countee Cullen, Langston Hughes, and Jessie Fauset.

Hurston relocated to New York City to pursue a literary career, promptly winning writing prizes in a contest sponsored by *Opportunity* magazine in 1925. At the awards dinner she met Countee Cullen, Carl Van Vechten, Langston Hughes, and Fannie Hurst, whom she would later work for as a companion and driver. Later that year, Hurston enrolled at Barnard, an elite women's college, to pursue a degree in anthropology, and in 1926, she engaged in anthropological fieldwork in Harlem (*Folklore, Memoirs, and Other Writings*: 964). This period reveals much about the fusion of folk, bourgeois, and proletarian strains in her life. While attending bourgeois institutions, she contributed poems to proletarian and protest-oriented publications, such as *Negro World*, which was published by Marcus Garvey's Universal Negro Improvement Association. On one level, her inclusion in

*Negro World* may not be surprising, given her interest in African American culture and history, yet her selections in *Negro World* can best be described as wholly apolitical (Wall 1995). Perhaps, despite her precociousness, Hurston's efforts in *Negro World* reveal an author struggling to find her voice and place. In 1925 she also contributed the essay "The Hue and Cry About Howard University" to the *Messenger* (*Folklore, Memoirs, and Other Writings:* 964). Hurston's inclusion in the *Messenger* reveals her connections with important Harlem Renaissance publications. The other two premier journals of the period, *Opportunity* and *Crisis,* differed from the *Messenger,* as George Hutchinson (1995) notes: "*The Messenger* presented a stridently iconoclastic approach, more often than not ridiculing the notion that African American culture was distinctly different from European American culture and stressing the 'mulatto' character of U.S. culture" (289). Most of the contributors to the *Messenger* were black males, which means Hurston's inclusion represented a deviation from the norm.

Besides contributing to a number of publications, Hurston actively worked to create forums for her work. For example, 1926 proved a pivotal year for Hurston, when she began actively working with a community of African American writers in New York City to establish a journal called *Fire!!,* which produced only one issue in November of that year. Although *Fire!!* yielded only one issue, Hurston's short story "Sweat" appears in this journal, as does her play *Color Struck.* Both texts illustrate Hurston's evolution as a writer and her exploration of racial, sexual, and class politics.

In 1927 Hurston would utilize the theories she learned at Barnard and put them into practice with her folklore-collecting trip to Florida. That year also proved momentous in her personal life, as she married Herbert Sheen, a medical student. Always in quest for ways to finance her interests, Hurston made the acquaintance of Charlotte Mason in 1927 and found in the eccentric socialite a patron willing to fund her explorations. The relationship proved tumultuous, for Mason demanded ownership and rights to all the folklore that Hurston collected during her travels. Furthermore, Mason accepted as African American only the primitivistic, a narrowness that perpetuated a condescending attitude toward African American cultural expression. The collaboration between Hurston and Mason ended in 1931, as did her marriage with Sheen. Perhaps the demands of medical school and burgeoning career as a physician, coupled with Hurston's itinerant lifestyle, created a wedge in the marriage. Thereafter Hurston would have to rely on funds from book sales, teaching, giving guest lectures, fellowships, and domestic work to earn a living. In 1939, she would try marriage again, wedding Albert Price III, who was considerably younger than Hurston. He was twenty-three, and she was forty-eight years old. The couple divorced the following year (*Folklore, Memoirs, and Other Writings*). Hurston's two marriages give a sense of how the rigors of personal life and the tensions in her career avocation affected one another.

Not surprisingly, her 1937 novel *Their Eyes Were Watching God* deals with the problems of heterosexual relationships between individuals whose ages, desires, and dreams come into conflict. From the 1930s until her death in 1960, Hurston would shuttle back and forth between the Caribbean and different regions of the United States, leading a migratory existence while writing her four major novels, numerous short stories, plays, and nonfiction essays. When the heyday of the Harlem Renaissance ended with the stock market crash of 1929 and the Great Depression of the 1930s, Hurston found fewer opportunities and outlets for her work. For many women writers of the Harlem Renaissance, teaching served as a means of supplementing one's income, but Hurston could not utilize this career option to its fullest potential, because her feistiness, independence, and contentious behavior often resulted in her leaving or losing teaching positions she acquired to support herself. Furthermore, two failed marriages meant reliance on one income—her own. From the 1930s until her death in 1960, she found it increasingly difficult to support herself. She relied on fellowships, domestic work, advances from publishers, and temporary teaching positions for money throughout her life. When those opportunities ended and her health began to fail, Hurston found herself a resident at the Saint Lucie County Welfare Home in Florida, where she would die on 28 January 1960 from heart disease. In "How It Feels to Be Colored Me," Hurston wrote compellingly of her life as a black woman during a period of racial turmoil and injustice in America. She would define herself as "not tragically colored" and would assert that she excluded herself from "the sobbing school of Negrohood" as a means of articulating her independence, resilience, and defiance (*Folklore, Memoirs, and Other Writings:* 827).

While her life and literature may seem tragic at times to those who know of her impoverished final days, Hurston always evidenced in her own experiences and in the lives of her characters a sense of survival. Her texts do not feature a defeated race, class, or gender. Instead, she emphasizes the humanity of their condition and predicament that shines through in her own literary output. An examination of Hurston's novels and short stories presents the dynamism and complexity of life for blacks and whites in nineteenth- and twentieth-century America. When Hurston began her first novel, *Jonah's Gourd Vine*, in 1933, she had broken free from the artistic control of Mason. The money she had received from Mason from 1927 to 1931 had both helped and hindered her artistically (Wall 1995). After placing "The Gilded Six Bits" in *Story* (1933), the publisher inquired about a longer work of fiction and in response she managed to complete *Jonah's Gourd Vine* in two months (Hemenway 1977).[3] Contemporary reviews focus on Hurston's deftness at handling folkways and rituals. In a 1934 review that appeared in *Opportunity*, Estelle Felton wrote, "Miss Hurston's detailed understanding of the customs and tradition of her people is an invaluable aid in winning for this book the praise some critics have given it" (Felton 1993: 4). In the *New York Times Book Review* of May 1934, Margaret Wallace noted, "Not the least charm of the book, however, is its language: rich, expressive, and lacking in self-conscious artifice" (Wallace 1993: 9). Later criticism also focuses on the folk elements in the text. Bell (1987), for example, writes, "Her complete identification with folk values, her ear for language, and her lively imagination contribute to the vivid impressions and dramatic appeal of the narrative but distort its structure, characters, and mood" (120).

A close examination of *Jonah's Gourd Vine* reveals strains of folk, bourgeois, and proletarian aesthetics in her rendering of the African American experience. The incorporation of multiple aesthetics may stem from the biographical and autobiographical elements in the text inspired by Hurston's own life and experience:[4] "The novel's main characters are named John and Lucy [the names of Hurston's own parents]; their history is the Hurston family history. The plot takes John from life on an Alabama plantation to a ministerial position in Eatonville. Zora even uses the deathbed scene that she remembered as a major trauma of her youth, when her dying mother asked her to stop the neighbors from removing her pillow at the moment of passing" (Hemenway 1977: 189). Through the fictionalized portrayal of her parent's marriage, Hurston meditates on race, class, and gender in the South and the nation as a whole. She also sets the foundation for the exploration of these issues in her later novels, including *Their Eyes Were Watching God; Moses, Man of the Mountain;* and *Seraph on the Suwanee.*

Hurston adopts the bildungsroman and kunstlerroman as the narrative structure in depicting the coming of age of John Pearson, a preacher and poet. As a man who desires to be a "big voice" in the community, John signifies the oral tradition in the African American community through his role as a minister. Hurston uses third-person omniscient narration to chronicle John's physical journey from Alabama to Florida and his social, economic, and political rise from folk fieldhand in Alabama to his bourgeois status as minister and moderator of the African Methodist Episcopal (A.M.E.) Church in Eatonville. However, John's rise to social prominence is followed by a self-inflicted fall. While John has the potential to be a spiritually, physically, mentally, and emotionally well-rounded individual, he never attains it.

By framing the novel primarily around one individual, John Pearson, Hurston presents a microcosm of the African American social, political, and economic experience in the Jim Crow South of the early twentieth century. Hurston presents the folk aesthetic through her chronicle of John's youth in a rural agrarian community in the South. A light-skinned black man of mixed racial heritage, John lives with his mother Amy and his stepfather Ned, who eke out a living as sharecroppers under an exploitative system that benefits whites to the detriment of blacks. Hurston's depiction of John as a mulatto enables the author to examine the complex history of intergenerational race and class relationships in the United States in the manner of Jessie Fauset.[5] Hurston draws on the slave narrative tradition in the depiction of John's mixed racial and class background (his father may be Master Alf Pearson).

During the period of slavery, the sexual relationships between white plantation owners and black female slaves often produced children, as revealed in slave narratives such as *Narrative of the Life of Frederick Douglass* (1845), Harriet

Jacobs's *Incidents in the Life of a Slave Girl* (1861), and Frances E. W. Harper's novel *Iola Leroy* (1892). Hurston's presentation of John's biracial background allows her to illustrate the common heritage of blacks and whites in the South, offering a criticism of color and class prejudice, for racism and elitism function as self-hatred and self-estrangement. Hurston also connects to the politics of color, class, and privilege within the African American community through her depiction of Ned's negative attitudes toward John. As a consequence of Ned's prejudices against John, whom he considers favored by his wife and the community because of his light skin, Amy encourages John to go "over de Creek" to work for Master Alf Pearson (the bourgeois white landowner in Notasulga). She feels John will have better opportunities for advancement elsewhere.

The land "over de Creek" represents the contrast between the bourgeois and folk elements of rural Alabama. In "over-de-Creek" society, John obtains the tools he will employ in rising to the middle class and a position of power later in life: written and verbal communication skills. He learns to read and write and gains experience in bookkeeping and managing an estate. He also meets Lucy Potts, a young African American woman from an affluent family of "big niggers" who represent the black bourgeoisie (*Novels and Stories:* 23). Hurston employs the contrast between John and Lucy's socioeconomic status to meditate on color, class, and community. Like Nanny in *Their Eyes Were Watching God*, Emmerline Potts wants her daughter Lucy to have a financially comfortable existence. She dislikes John because of his low origins and the fact that he does not own his own home and land. She advises Lucy to marry a man like Artie Mimms, a prototype for landowner and farmer Logan Killicks of *Their Eyes Were Watching God*. Mimms owns farmland and animals. Emmerline views marriage as a social and economic transaction for women. In order to ensure the family's bourgeois status, she wants her daughter to marry an affluent man. Emmerline wants her daughter to follow the model of the genteel wife. Nevertheless, Lucy chooses love over economic security and marries John.

The marriage between Lucy and John accompanies his rise in stature and status in Notasulga as they soon move into house-servant quarters near the big house. Pearson raises his salary, and John becomes foreman on the plantation. John's ego swells, and he becomes enamored of the many single women in the area despite having a loving wife and several children. His desire for physical and sexual relationships ironically leads to his spiritual conversion, as the guilt manifests itself in a desire to reconcile his philandering with God by developing himself into a preacher or "big voice" in the community. Hurston presents John's transformation from folk fieldhand to bourgeois politician (he later becomes mayor of Eatonville and state moderator for the A.M.E. Church) as a means of meditating on the fluidity of class in the African American community as well as the role of the black preacher. John's sexual, religious, economic, and political dominance cause problems in his marriage and in the community.

The congregation thinks he considers himself unaccountable for his own actions. Hurston equates John with the biblical figure Jonah from the Bible in her depiction of his rise and fall. She appropriates the image of the gourd vine and worm from the Old Testament tale of Jonah in which God causes a worm to devour a gourd vine that protects Jonah from the sun's heat (Speisman 1991). The growth and subsequent death of the gourd vine serve as a powerful unifying metaphor in Hurston's narrative. The worm in Hurston's text appears symbolically in three central images that function in conjunction with one another— a snake, a train, and John's phallus (a sign of his promiscuity).

Of the three images, the snake is the prevailing one, for the train and John's sexual organ are configured as snakelike objects. Snakes connote evil, as exemplified by Satan's adoption of the serpent body in the Garden of Eden to seduce Eve. John encounters snakes on several occasions. Once, he and Lucy walk home from school and encounter a snake in the river. He kills it to protect her. Also, John sees a train for the first time after destroying the snake. From his vantage point of never having seen a train, it looks like a mechanized snake. The train represents mechanization as well as the means of his escape from the Jim Crow society of rural Alabama to Eatonville, Florida, the all-black community where he rises socially and economically. Later, he has recurring dreams of snakes attempting to kill Lucy. The snakes signify his sexual organ, and John's promiscuity endangers his marriage to Lucy. Before John's death, when his car collides with a train, he has another dream about a snake after having a one-night stand with a young woman despite his marriage to Sally Lovelace, his third wife. Snakes, trains, and his uninhibited sexual appetite portend danger, trouble, and ultimately death for John Pearson (Speisman 1991). Thus, through her artful rendering of the gourd vine and worm as controlling metaphors surrounding key incidents in the novel, Hurston successfully connects the bildungsroman and kunstlerroman with key formal elements such as plot, character, theme, and symbolism.

Like the biblical Jonah, John's pride and greed lead to his downfall. Egotistical, he becomes a larger-than-life individual who showers verbal abuse upon his wife Lucy and has extramarital affairs. Prior to her death, Lucy berates him for his affair with Hattie Tyson and his behavior toward her, but he strikes her. He spends the rest of his life atoning for his treatment of Lucy. When John finally recognizes the damage the marriage to Hattie wreaks on his career as minister, A.M.E. state moderator, and mayor, he accuses Hattie of being a bad mother to the children, an unfaithful wife, and an alcoholic. Claiming that he and Hattie have never had the romance that he and Lucy once shared, John laments her inability to fulfill the socially prescribed role of a pastor's wife. Through the portrayal of the problem-ridden marriage, Hurston meditates on folk and bourgeois aesthetics in African American society. As the wife of a prominent man, Hattie expects the trappings of bourgeois clothing, lodging, and spending money. Although some church members despise her, others are sympathetic toward her plight and use it as a means of retribution against John, who they feel has risen too high in the community. Deacon Harris wants to topple John Pearson from his lofty position. The "gourd vine" symbolizes John's rise as a preacher, politician, and state moderator. However, John's growth is stunted by his own actions. Using a folk remedy to conquer a member of the bourgeoisie, Deacon Harris suggests that Hattie employ a "two-headed doctor," or conjure man, against John. Conjuring in *Jonah's Gourd Vine* is an example of the folk customs, rituals, and beliefs in Hurston's depiction of the southern African American community.

John's fall in stature stems from the congregation's anger at his improprieties as well as its dwindling size from community members migrating to the North in search of jobs. In the Great Black Migration, as it is known, southern blacks left the agrarian South in large numbers for the more industrialized North in search of greater social and economic opportunities between the 1890s and the 1930s. The migrations had a variety of causes, including the rising cost of food due to World War I and an oppressive racial climate in the South (Wintz 1988). Hurston's depiction of the Great Black Migration anticipates Dorothy West's novels *The Living Is Easy* (1948) and *The Wedding* (1995), in which the migration of blacks from rural southern folk environments to the industrialized North in search of a bourgeois middle-class existence plays a vital role. The depiction of the Great Black Migration enables Fauset, Hurston, and West to meditate on folk (southern, rural) and bourgeois (northern, industrial) aesthetics.

Hurston also employs the migration as a vehicle in the text for orchestrating the transformation in John's position in the church and community. Deacon Harris sees the decreasing congregation and number of Pearson supporters as a way to topple John, for many of John's supporters have left to go north. As a result, Deacon Harris brings in a competitor, Reverend Cozy, to vie for John's position in the church. In his call for black consciousness and criticism of race, class, and gender prejudice, Cozy evokes a proletarian aesthetic. Despite his proletarian and black nationalist rhetoric, Cozy lacks John's power with words and ability to connect with the masses on an emotional level.

*Jonah's Gourd Vine* calls attention to the issues of voice and how the black preacher uses the word to influence the community in its depiction of the sermon John delivers to his church prior to resignation. Hurston figures John as a poet in his rendering of metaphor and symbolism into art to convey meaning to the audience. John bases his last sermon upon the book of Zechariah from the Bible. He appropriates its sentiments to his own predicament in the church and the community: "The climactic sermon begins with the text of Zechariah 13:6, taken to be about the wounds of Jesus received in the house of his friends. The text then becomes part of a traditional sermon topic: the story of God's creation of the world and his gift of Jesus as an agent of salvation" (Hemenway 1977: 196). Preaching the dynamic sermon, John mixes biblical text with the southern black folk vernacular. Transforming himself into a martyr figure, he protests his treatment by the congregation through equating himself with Jesus Christ. Hurston's inclusion of the sermon is the novel's most compelling moment, revealing the marriage of the folk and bourgeois, the biblical and the secular, the elite and the masses in the novel. Hurston's field explorations in search of folklore provided her with the basis of John's sermon: "It was collected from the

Reverend C. C. Lovelace of Eau Gallie, Florida, on May 3, 1929, and Hurston had published it before in her *Negro* essay" (Hemenway 1977: 197).

Hurston may also be struggling to capture the oral African American story-telling tradition in the written form to convey the power and artistry of the preacher—the premier black poet. The preacher functions as a poet through his appropriation of theme, plot, character, symbolism, and metaphor to convey the message of the Bible to his congregation. He appropriates both written and spoken discourse in conveying his message. As a central figure in the African American community, he represents the mediation of the secular and the religious, God and the congregation, as well as the mortal and the immortal. Hurston presents John's final sermon as his swan song to the congregation, and another stage in the life and death of the gourd vine. After being unable to find work in Eatonville because of the community's ostracism, John heads to Plant City in hopes of beginning a new life. He meets a wealthy landowner named Sally Lovelace, who has been in love with him ever since she saw him preach in Eatonville. John weds her because she represents the chance for a new beginning and economic security. Through Sally's real-estate holdings and his talent as a carpenter, he regains bourgeois status in Plant City. The name of the town—Plant City—signifies growth and development for the gourd vine, which was cut down by the deacons who retaliated against him when he was pastor of the church.

Hurston presents John's ascension into the bourgeois class through his marriage to Sally and her material possessions. John slowly becomes a big man again, symbolized by the Cadillac she buys him to affirm his bourgeois status in the community. When he returns to the Eatonville area to visit his friend Hambo, he succumbs to his sexual inclinations again and has a one-night stand with Ora, a woman who is impressed with his car and bourgeois status. Hurston introduces snake imagery again as his sexual inclinations (as embodied in his sexual organ) conquer his marriage vows to Sally. As he heads back home to Plant City after the liaison, John feels wracked with guilt and fails to see an oncoming train, another snakelike image. The Cadillac, a symbol of bourgeois power, affluence, and opulence, leads him to his doom. The split between his public persona as preacher and private persona as womanizer and materialistic individual merge into one, creating disastrous consequences as he runs head-on into a train. As a snakelike and phallic image, the train functions as a mechanized embodiment of his sexual appetite, which leads to his death.

In *Jonah's Gourd Vine*, Hurston uses the life story of John Pearson as a means of presenting folk, bourgeois, and proletarian aesthetics through his physical and emotional questing after self-fulfillment and self-actualization. The novel establishes Hurston's appropriation of African American folk customs, rituals, and beliefs in her fiction. Her focus on a black middle-class community presents a bourgeois aesthetic. Admittedly, the proletarian aesthetic receives the least attention in this work, but it has major importance in the sense that John leaves Notasulga for Eatonville in part to escape the exploitative system of sharecropping. Hurston's portrayal of the social, political, and economic plight of black sharecroppers functions as a criticism of an agrarian-based economy. The portrayal of the exploitative sharecropping system and "race men" such as Reverend Cozy illustrates a proletarian aesthetic as well, yet Hurston also indicates Cozy's limited power to change things without the consent of the people.

The biographical and autobiographical elements in the text suggest the novel may function as a means for Hurston to meditate on her own socioeconomic, educational, and cultural background, which contained folk, bourgeois, and proletarian elements. More importantly, the composition may have served as a personal catharsis for the author. Perhaps the production of her first novel enabled her to negotiate the past, the present, and her future in an effort to give voice to the African American community and experience. Similarly, Hurston's 1937 classic *Their Eyes Were Watching God* continues to explore the complexities of race, class, and gender in the United States through the appropriation of kunstlerroman and bildungsroman techniques. While *Jonah's Gourd Vine* depicts John Pearson's coming of age as a preacher-poet, *Their Eyes Were Watching God* features the female artist and storyteller Janie Crawford. The novel continues the concern with voice and silence that have derived in part from stories such as "Spunk" (*Opportunity* 1925), "Sweat" (*Fire!!* 1926), "The Gilded Six Bits" (*Story* 1933), *Jonah's Gourd Vine* (1934), *Mules and Men* (1935), and later texts such as *Moses, Man of the Mountain* (1939), and *Seraph on the Suwanee* (1948). Hurston may have incorporated and fictionalized her own experience as a black female artist attempting to express her own voice in a racist, sexist, and class-conscious society. The inspiration stems from the emotional turmoil surrounding her love life and her failed attempt to negotiate a relationship with a graduate student she met in 1931 who wanted Hurston to give up her career (Hemenway 1977). The depiction of Janie's three marriages and struggle for voice, empowerment, freedom, and autonomy may stem from Hurston's own attempt to negotiate her role as artist with a desire for a heterosexual relationship.

Although Hurston's short fiction reveals a talented writer adept at presenting complex themes and imagery in the form of a short story, surprisingly little critical attention focuses on her contributions to African American magazines of the Harlem Renaissance period. In fact, an analysis of her earlier works reveals her evolving literary voice and exploration of racial, gender, and class politics. In stories such as "Spunk," "Sweat," "The Gilded Six Bits," and "The Bone of Contention" (the last unpublished during Hurston's lifetime), Hurston presents characters and plotlines that would later serve as models or prototypes for her best-known novel, *Their Eyes Were Watching God*, and to a lesser extent, her other novels. "Spunk," which was awarded second place in the *Opportunity* magazine contest in 1925, reveals Hurston's deft incorporation of folklore, dialect, and power relations within heterosexual relationships. The main characters anticipate protagonists in her novels, including *Their Eyes Were Watching God* and *Seraph on the Suwanee*, in the portrayal of domineering and abusive males. The story centers on Spunk Banks and his lover Lena Kanty, the wife of Joe Kanty. Strong and mean-spirited, the sawmill hand Spunk Banks functions through sheer intimidation of others, including Lena. An intimidating man in size, he creates an aura of invulnerability and fortitude. Oppressive, violent, and chauvinistic, he objectifies women and serves as a predecessor to Joe Starks in *Their Eyes Were Watching God* and Jim Meserve, the white male protagonist of *Seraph on the Suwanee*. His name signifies his personality. He is a man full of spunk and vigor, an outlawlike figure with his own set of rules that contradict those of the rest of society. Few people seem willing to stand up to Spunk, except for Joe Kanty, who finally tires of being cuckolded. Spunk may represent excitement, adventure, and reckless abandon for Lena, which might seem an appealing contrast to the mundane aspects of her life. In this respect, she may mirror Janie and Missie May, the wife in "The Gilded Six Bits," who represent married women attracted to other men because of their swaggering sexuality, zest for life, and strong sense of self.

The climax of the story is the fight between Joe and Spunk, and Joe dies from a gunshot wound. Despite her feelings for Spunk, Lena feels saddened by her husband's death. Spunk prevails in the trial and is found innocent because he argues that he killed Joe in self-defense. He surprises the townspeople by his desire to marry Lena. He approaches both women and work with a reckless abandon. However, Hurston employs elements of the supernatural in their exposition of the consequences and retribution for Spunk's behavior. A black bobcat, rumored to be the incarnation of Joe Kanty, circles the house after Spunk moves into it with Lena. Later, the bobcat reappears while Spunk works at the sawmill, and the bobcat shoves Spunk onto the saw. The story becomes part of the folklore of the community as members speculate on who will be Lena's next lover now that Spunk has died, ultimately killed by Joe Kanty in the end.

Spunk represents the embodiment of the male folk spirit, a freewheeling man determined to live, love, and work hard with wild abandon. Hurston's portrayal of Lena suggests a woman who desires adventure and excitement as a relief from her humdrum existence, and her relationship with Spunk seems to represent a convenient escape from her marriage. Her tears for her dead husband at the hands of Spunk suggest guilt, and perhaps a realization that she does not truly love Spunk but finds herself cowered and terrified by his power, which at one point seemed appealing but later seems menacing. The depiction of the black bobcat as the embodiment of Joe Kanty evokes folk imagery: The underdog proves triumphant in his return from the grave to wreak havoc and revenge upon Spunk, his nemesis. The story functions then as a proletarian statement criticizing the abuse and misuse of power. Ultimately and ironically, Lena finds herself free to find another lover upon the death of both Spunk and Joe Kanty. After the funeral, the community gathers to commemorate the loss of Spunk. The townspeople consume food and alcohol in the same greedy fashion in which they consumed the lives of Joe, Lena, and Spunk in their fascination with the love triangle that played out before them. Although the story is titled after the character Spunk, the hero of the story appears to be the black bobcat who exacts vengeance for Joe Kanty. The moral of Hurston's story is that consequences arise for one's actions, at least for the male characters of Joe and Spunk. Lena lives on, possibly to perpetuate the cycle of men sacrificing their lives for her.

Zora Neale Hurston's "Sweat" (1926) originally appeared in *Fire!!*, the short-lived magazine that Hurston and other writers hoped would fuel the flames of the Harlem Renaissance. The story serves as a model for the novel *Their Eyes Were Watching God* in its depiction of racial, gender, and class politics and *Jonah's Gourd Vine* in its utilization of snake imagery to signify sexuality. The story explores the multiplicity of folk, bourgeois, and proletarian aesthetics in its depiction of a married couple in a small southern community. The protagonist, Delia Jones, works as a washwoman for prominent white families. The principal breadwinner for the family, she labors hard to provide food, shelter, and comfort for herself and her husband.

Hurston's depiction of Delia as a washwoman reflects the reality of limited job opportunities for black women during the early twentieth century in addition to showing the harsh economic realities of life for blacks in the rural South. As Angela Davis (1981) notes, African American women historically have worked as domestic help for low wages. By 1910 more than 50 percent of African American women held jobs, and about a third of these women worked as domestic servants. During the heyday of the Harlem Renaissance in the 1920s, more than 50 percent worked as domestics, and by 1930, three-fifths of the African American female workforce was employed as domestic help. The number of African American women employed as domestics decreased during World War II, but in 1960 one out of every three African American women in the workforce still worked as a domestic servant (Davis 1981). Hurston's characterization of Delia as a domestic worker reflects the reality of limited job opportunities for black women. This reality had interesting implications for racial, sexual, and class politics. African American women performed the majority of domestic work in their own homes as well as the homes of white bourgeois women who could afford domestic help. As a consequence, strength, resilience, and fortitude remained character traits of women employed in these positions who, like the protagonist of Hurston's novel, shoulder a huge responsibility in their households. The source of black female power resides in the folk experience born out of slavery and carried on into postslavery American society. Davis (1981) rightly asserts that "Black women could hardly strive for weakness; they had to become strong, for their families and their community needed their strength to survive" (231).

The very qualities that ensured their survival and that of their families sometimes left them open to vilification. During the nineteenth century, the "cult of true womanhood" prevailed. The ideal women was weak, delicate, submissive, unable to do hard labor, white, chaste, and passive. Slave women did not have the luxury of subscribing to this idea, for they were forced to work in order to survive. Even after slavery ended, black women worked outside the home to provide economically for the family. The representation of Delia in "Sweat" illustrates Hurston's deft portrayal of a black woman whose sweat remains unappreciated by the ones she labors for—her husband and the whites in her community. Writing in 1903, W. E. B. Du Bois (1989) presented the gifts that African Americans have given to American society, willingly and unwillingly. He writes, "Here we have brought our three gifts and mingled them with yours: a gift of story and song—soft, stirring melody in an ill-harmonized and un-melodious land; the gift of sweat and brawn to beat back the wilderness, conquer the soil, and lay the foundations of this vast economic empire two hundred years earlier than your weak hand could have done it; the third, a gift of the Spirit" (214). Despite her sweat, Delia endures abuse, physical and emotional, at the hands of her husband, who proves in ironic ways more oppressive than the whites in the rural community in which she lives. Hurston's "Sweat" is a proletarian statement on the value of all work and an indictment of the tripartite race, class, and gender prejudice faced by working-class black women.

Through her characterization of Sykes (Delia's husband), Hurston renders a scathing criticism of misogyny and sexism. Sykes scorns her for her work, which he considers to be lowly, and he disrepects her despite the economic assistance she brings to them. Like Jody Starks in *Their Eyes Were Watching God*, he berates, patronizes, and devalues his wife, whom he considers to be a commodity. His sadistic threatening takes many forms, including one that focuses on her phobia of snakes. Sykes himself embodies the snake, for he is evil, treacherous, sneaky, and lethal. Wall (1995) notes, "The snake becomes Syke's symbol, imaging his sexuality and his evil" (150). Later Delia will utilize the qualities of a snake and reappropriate them in an assault against her husband. At the story's outset, Delia finds herself hard at work sorting clothes and singing while her husband plays a trick upon her. He takes the bullwhip he employs in managing animals, and he places it on her. The long, black, round bullwhip becomes symbolic of her husband's sexuality. The unmistakable phallic imagery reinforces Sykes's sense of himself as a sexual creature, yet the emphasis on "limp" also suggests the ineffectual nature of that sexuality in their marriage. The bullwhip represents a masculinity by which he constantly lords it over her in his mistreatment, his physical abuse, and his philandering with other women—in front of his wife. Not surprisingly, Delia fears snakes and by extension the whip.

As noted earlier, Sykes criticizes every aspect of Delia's life that remains important to her: her work and her church. Church represents an important part of her life and a sanctuary and retreat from the oppression she faces at home from her husband, yet he mocks her religious devotion and accuses her of hypocrisy for washing clothes on Sunday, a day of rest. The abuse proves too much for Delia, and she stands up to her husband, complaining about all the sweat she generates for the family as a hard worker and breadwinner. In a moment of desperation she poises her iron skillet to hit him. Fearful, he refuses to retaliate physically.

Like Janie Crawford of *Their Eyes Were Watching God*, Delia cherishes romantic dreams of love and romantic relationships only to have them ended by the reality of married life. Sykes spends money on other women and redirects his anger over his own inadequacies toward Delia and beats her sometimes as a consequence. His brutality toward Delia factors into all their interactions. The townspeople, a representative of the folk, play a major part in this story and represent the voice of the community. They recognize that he abuses his wife and that she provides the income for the family. Joe Clarke, who owns the store in the town, serves as a prototype for Jody Starks in his representation as a member of the black bourgeoisie. He compares women to a sugar cane, which men grind and wring until the cane dries out. Joe Clarke deconstructs the politics of race, class, and gender in heterosexual relationships and astutely examines the roots of Sykes's misdirected and projected anger toward Delia. One day when Delia walks past the store with the laundry and her pony, she sees her husband buying something for Bertha (his girlfriend), and her husband proudly flaunts his new woman before Delia, with no regard for her feelings. Consequently, he insists on maintaining the adulterous relationship and the tension between the two rises as he and his lover make no pretense about their relationship.

Sykes actively tries to get Delia to leave the home she paid for by playing on her worst fears of snakes. One day after coming home from work, she discovers that he has placed a rattlesnake in a box. Sykes invades his wife's domestic safe space, to unsettle her. The snake becomes a metaphor for Sykes's vicious and violent nature. His sexism and sadism prevent him from apologizing to his wife for frightening her, and he orders her out of the home that her income maintains. She utilizes her role as a washwoman and her connections with the upper-class whites to threaten consequences if he tries to make her leave her own home. She recognizes the prominence of the whites and the social hierarchy in her community. She, as a black woman, may not have the power to fight back against him without some assistance—that is, from the powerful whites whom she works for, yet ironically she does through her own cunning and intelligence discover a way of counteracting him on her own. The following day, when she returns from church, she finds the snake residing in a basket in her bedroom; presumably her husband left it in there for her. Fearfully, she runs for safety to the kitchen and then out the door up to the hay barn, where she goes to sleep. When she awakes, she hears her husband destroying the box the snake used to live in, and later she heads to the bedroom window and peers in from outside. The snake, by the story's end, becomes the metaphor for Delia's self. Hurston writes, "Sometimes he [the snake] strikes without rattling at all" (*Novels and Stories*: 965).

Like the snake, Delia "strikes without rattling at all." She does not announce her presence to her husband, but allows nature to take control. While in the house, Sykes hears the snake and mistakenly think it is under the stove in the kitchen, and he flees to the bedroom for safety. When he gets into the bed, the snake, which had been hiding there, attacks him. Sykes has been bitten by the very snake he used to terrify his wife. His own vengeful, evil nature bites back at him. Her husband calls her name, but Delia will not assist him. The following morning, she continues to hear him moan, and after she awakens, she comes into the house, and Sykes crawls on the floor toward her, submitting to his wife finally. Now Delia remains powerful, and he finds himself powerless. He dies, and she lives on, strengthened and emboldened by the promise of a new stage in her life, free from the oppression and hatred of her husband. Hurston's "Sweat" hearkens back to W. E. B. Du Bois's *Souls of Black Folk*, in which he writes of the three gifts African Americans have given to America—spirit, sweat, and song. Delia represents the black folk for her sweat and her struggle to maintain her dignity. Sykes beats her, but he does not conquer Delia, and ultimately, she wins the battle of wills. Hurston's keen analysis of racial, sexual, and gender politics in "Sweat" foreshadows her treatment of these themes in her novels and shows the possibility of female emancipation. As in *Their Eyes Were Watching God*, female emancipation can be achieved only through the death of the male heterosexual partner—whether figurative or literal.

Of all her stories, Hurston's 1933 story "The Gilded Six Bits," best explores the issue of power, money, gender, and class. Thematically, the explorations of heterosexual relationships and the complex power relations mirror Hurston's other fiction. The character of Otis D. Slemmons serves as a prototype for Jody Starks of *Their Eyes Were Watching God*, and the theme of female dissatisfaction in a boring, mundane marriage also permeates the tale. The title refers to money as a commodity of exchange, and the term "gilded" suggests the illusion of prosperity and the precarious nature of the aspiring black bourgeoisie. The story's power resides in its Afrocentric storyline, which develops three characters in a rural southern town—Missie May, her husband Joe, and Otis D. Slemmons. The men in the story use money as a means of enticing and entrapping women in the small community. Missie May and her husband share a weekly ritual after his return from work. Unlike Delia in "Sweat," the primary breadwinner in the family is Joe, the husband, and not the wife. He always throws silver dollars in the doorway when he comes home, and she dutifully picks them up and places them next to her plate during their meal on Saturday afternoon. The two, like actors, reenact this ritual, with each person having his or her appointed role. After he throws the money in the doorway, Missie May and Joe engage in foreplay. The money serves as a type of foreplay, which anticipates Missie May's act of infidelity with Otis D. Slemmons, who also uses money to acquire power and affection from her.

Otis represents the black bourgeoisie in his flashy clothing and his big dreams and aspirations. He establishes an ice-cream parlor in the town, which the townspeople associate with upward mobility and advancement. The townspeople with disposable income to spend on sweets go there to show off their wealth. The ice cream becomes a metaphor for Otis D. Slemmons. Ice cream, like Otis, seems hearty and filling, yet as time passes, it melts away and lacks substance and gives no sustenance. The townspeople, like Joe, admire him for his experience in big cities like Chicago, Philadelphia, Jacksonville, Memphis, and Philadelphia and for his clothing and physical appearance. Overweight, his physical stature matches his larger-than-life personality and the persona he presents to everyone else. In fact, Joe admires Otis's stature and reputation and his business acumen. Joe covets Otis's possessions, especially the five-dollar gold piece that serves as his stick pin as well as the gold charm on Otis's watch chain. He also admires his sexual prowess with women.

Initially, Missie May proves to be the skeptic, suggesting that Otis's ostentatious display of wealth has no place in their small community. One night after coming home from work, Joe returns home to find Missie May and Otis in the bedroom. Dumbstruck, he reacts with laughter, but later he punches Otis and manages to obtain the golden charm and the watch chain while hitting him. Although Joe did not intentionally try to take the charm and the chain, the incident proves symbolic. In one punch, he manages to topple down the bourgeois man who came to the folk town. Through his brawn, he conquers the man who sought to conquer his wife. The charm and chain symbolize Otis's bourgeois notions of the community and how precarious those ambitions ultimately prove to be. The broken chain also symbolizes the end of Missie May's relationship with Otis and serves as a constant reminder to her of the marriage vows she broke. Joe also uses it to remind his wife that her love and affection represent a commodity that can be bought and sold to the highest bidder. The incident transforms their relationship. Hurston shows the destructive nature of the bourgeoisie on the folk by illustrating how gross materialism can lead to destruction and ultimately self-hatred. Joe reminds Missie May of her gross materialism and her infidelity by placing the chain and charm under her pillow, which she finds one morning, only to discover to her horror that the charm is not really gold, but rather "a gilded half dollar" (*Novels and Stories*: 994).

She realizes that she worshiped a false prophet and sold herself to the highest bidder, one who paid her with false currency. The guilt and shame make a powerful impression upon her as she longs for her marriage to return to its earlier basis. The couple finally reaches a type of reconciliation when Missie May discovers that she is pregnant and she has a child, who looks just like Joe. In fact, he later buys supplies at the store with the gilded money and decides to buy his wife and new son some molasses candy kisses. When he returns home, he throws money in the doorway, just like he did before the arrival of Otis, signifying a return to the old days. Now, however, Missie May, after her recent childbirth, cannot race to the door. Instead, she crawls toward him. Missie May bears affinity to Janie of *Their Eyes Were Watching God*, who also found herself attracted to a bourgeois man more appealing than her spouse. However, Missie May's husband (unlike Logan Killicks) fights back against the intruder into their relationship, and Missie May discovers before it is too late that her lover's artificiality lacks substance and true merit, like his gilded money.

Hurston dissects the politics of sex, money, race, and class in a proletarian story that preaches against materialism. On the surface, the story may appear to be apolitical, particularly with its focus on the domestic life of its characters, yet this very aspect becomes a site of political commentary for Hurston. Hurston's short fiction and novels use the home as a microcosm for larger society. Marriage and relationships between men and women become a metaphor for the politics of race, class, and gender. Because much of her fiction focuses on small, rural, southern, all-black communities and the dynamics of heterosexual relationships, Hurston has been misread as a writer who failed to address the social, political, and economic issues of her time. In contrast, this reading suggests that Hurston criticizes injustice in a subtler way through her handling of the domestic arena and the "women's sphere" in her work.

As a precursor to her play *Mule Bone: A Comedy of Negro Life* (co-authored with Langston Hughes) and to *Their Eyes Were Watching God,* "The Bone of Contention" (unpublished during Hurston's lifetime, but written between 1930 and 1935) represents an excellent example of Hurston's use of animal metaphors for the folk experience. Ironically, the protagonist of the story, Joe Clarke, utilizes the mule as a means of cementing his bourgeois standing in society and reinstating the hierarchy. The mule also reflects the social, political, and economic disparities amongst the main characters in this story set in Eatonville, the all-black town in which Hurston grew up. The story focuses on Brazzle's yellow mule, which in the novel becomes Matt Bonner's mule. The narrator describes the mule as "His Yaller Highness" (*Novels and Stories:* 968). Hurston's terminology here plays on the color consciousness among African Americans, particularly during the early part of the twentieth century. The term "high yellow" was often used to refer to light-skinned African Americans, who were part of the mulatto elite and descendents of slaves and slave masters. Sometimes they had more opportunities for education and social advancement than darker-skinned blacks because of their heritage. After the end of the Civil War and during the Reconstruction Period and even afterward, light-skinned racially mixed individuals often assumed leadership positions in African American churches, historically black colleges, and civil-rights organizations. As a consequence, the color line within the African American community often reflected a class line or caste system as well. In *Their Eyes Were Watching God,* Hurston deconstructs color consciousness through the characterization of Mrs. Turner, who approves of Janie because of her light skin but disapproves of her husband Tea Cake because of his dark skin and folk background.

"The Bone of Contention" uses this imagery to describe the mule, which represents the lowest rung of the society but through the oral storytelling of humans becomes elevated to mythic proportions. The mule signifies the folk and by extension the rural agrarian community. The mule becomes a pawn for Joe Clarke to establish himself as the most prominent man in the community. More importantly, the mule becomes a metaphor for the identity of the town and a frame of reference for their understanding of themselves and their environment. Although Brazzle owns the mule, the community owns the mule as well, for the animal's status becomes legendary and the center of a court battle that pits Baptists against Methodists. When the mule dies, Brazzle takes the mule to the swamp and leaves its body for any scavenging animals. Nevertheless, the townspeople go to the swamp to see the body laid to rest. The mule serves as a symbol for the politics of race and class in the story.

Joe Clarke's store functions as the central lifeline of the community where people congregate to tell stories, usually romantic tales of their heroic feats and deeds. They become types of wish fulfillment. Joe Clarke represents the bourgeois black entrepreneur who prides himself on having created the town of Eatonville through his drive and ambition in commercial and business expansion. He becomes mayor of the town, the main political and judicial leader. Like Jody Starks in *Their Eyes Were Watching God*, Joe Clarke owns the store, runs the post office, and serves as mayor. In contrast, Reverend Simms, a Methodist minister, has more stature than actual political and economic power in the town, and he resents Joe Clarke. "The bone of contention" occurs when Dave Carter complains that Jim Weston, a Methodist, hit him with a mule bone left belonging to Brazzle's mule during a fight, and he claims that Jim later took a turkey that rightfully belonged to him. He wants Jim banished from the town. Although Clarke is a Methodist, he decides there should be a trial over the incident at the Baptist Church, knowing that he (Clarke) will support Dave, and that Simms will support Jim, a fellow Methodist. He feels that Jim will lose the trial and subsequently will suffer a loss of reputation in the community. As a consequence, he will cement his own place in the society.

During the trial, Jim claims that he did hit Dave with the mule bone and that the turkey rightfully belonged to him and not to Dave. Reverend Simms claims that a mule bone is no weapon according to the Bible or contemporary laws in the United States. In contrast, Elder Long, a Baptist, invokes the Bible to suggest that the mule bone can be a weapon. He notes that in Judges 15:16, Samson killed many Philistines with an ass's jawbone. Consequently, he argues that since donkeys or asses father mules, a mule bone is equivalent to an ass's bone. Joe Clarke concedes that the mule bone is a weapon, and he banishes Jim from town for two years, knowing that Simms's association with Jim will stigmatize the Methodist minister as well. "The Bone of Contention "employs the mule to signify power dynamics within a small close-knit community. Little critical attention has been devoted to this story, which serves as a significant precursor to the classic *Their Eyes Were Watching God*, in which a mule also functions as a metaphor for power relations.

Despite Hurston's prolific output of novels, short stories, essays, and plays, *Their Eyes Were Watching God* has generated the most critical attention. Contemporary reviews stressed Hurston's simplistic treatment of the black masses or the lack of social criticism in the novel. In a 1937 review, Richard Wright (1993: 17) asserts, "Miss Hurston can write; but her prose is cloaked in that facile sensuality that has dogged Negro expression since the days of Phillis Wheatley." Similarly, in a 1938 *Opportunity* review Alain Locke (1993: 18) writes, "Her gift for poetic phrase, for rare dialect, and folk humor keep her flashing on the surface of her community and her characters and from diving down deep either to the inner psychology of characterization or to sharp analysis of the social background." Later criticism focuses on Hurston's depiction of a black female folk hero. As Mary Helen Washington (1993: 98) notes, "Most contemporary critics contend that Janie is the articulate voice in the tradition, that the novel celebrates a woman coming to self-discovery and that this self-discovery leads her ultimately to a meaningful participation in black folk traditions." The present study is concerned with the use of bildungsroman form and class aesthetics in Hurston's work. Hurston also effectively uses setting as a means of presenting the triangle of aesthetics, as the folk "muck" supplants the bourgeois house and the proletarian farm as the site of African American culture. Appropriating the kunstlerroman narrative form, Hurston presents the growth and development of Janie Crawford as a storyteller and agent of female empowerment. The novel begins with a third-person omniscient narrator documenting the community's reaction to Janie's return to Eatonville after leaving with her third husband Vergible Tea Cake Woods, then switches to Janie's first-person explanation of her life experiences to her friend Pheoby and her growth as an artist and an individual. The third-person omniscient narrator returns at the end of the novel to reveal the effect the story (Janie's work of art) has on Janie and her listener. This complex narrative structure allows Hurston to more fully explore the psychological, spiritual, and emotional development of the protagonist and her relationship with the community.

In *Their Eyes Were Watching God,* Hurston focuses on the life of Janie Crawford via flashbacks that reveal where she has come from and the direction in which she is headed in her quest for selfhood and voice—the two resources she needs to express her art as a storyteller. When Janie returns to Eatonville in her overalls, after burying her third husband, Vergible Tea Cake Woods, it shocks the residents. Because of her status as widow of mayor and real-estate entrepreneur Joe Starks, the community expects her to act and dress in a way befitting her class and age. For the women in the community, her overalls signify the folk and belie her bourgeois status as the wife of the ex-mayor of the town. Her insistence on marrying Tea Cake and ignoring the censure of the community represents rebellion and immaturity in their eyes. In their talk, they attempt to declass her, taking her down from her level. While they use words to condemn her, Janie uses language to convey her experiences to Pheoby and empower her friend as an African American female.

Hurston represents the contrast between the folk and bourgeois aesthetics through Janie's account of her adolescence. The most significant event in Janie's coming of age centers on sexual awakening, which becomes significant for her later romantic quests. When Janie kisses Johnny Taylor as a teenager, after seeing the bees pollinate pear blossoms on a tree in her backyard, and becomes sexually aroused, her grandmother Nanny insists that Janie marry and find a more suitable mate. The incident, which is an important event in Janie's life, establishes a pattern for all her heterosexual relationships. Nanny does not consider Johnny a suitable mate because he lacks financial security and the ability to support Janie in a bourgeois life. Janie's emerging sexuality terrifies her grandmother, whose own experiences as a victim of rape (as well as her daughter Leafy's) make her intent on protecting her granddaughter from any sexual exploitation or abuse. As a consequence, Nanny recoils at seeing Janie kiss Johnny. To Nanny, Logan Killicks's socioeconomic status make him a suitable mate. He owns a home, animals, and land. In her depiction of Nanny's life and experiences, Hurston connects to the slave narrative tradition, keying into texts such as Harriet Jacobs's *Incidents in the Life of a Slave Girl* (1861) and the fictionalized slave narrative by Frances E. W. Harper, *Iola Leroy* (1892).[6] Both Jacobs and Harper call attention to the sexual exploitation African American females endured at the hands of white plantation owners. Nanny's fear of Janie's sexual exploitation and her desire for her granddaughter to lead a middle-class bourgeois life stems from her wish to see her granddaughter have new opportunities Nanny was denied as a slave in the nineteenth century. While elitist, Nanny's attitudes stem from her own experiences and perceptions of the plight of the black woman in America. Her white master had raped her and she bore Leafy, Janie's mother, before fleeing Georgia during the Civil War. Her daughter Leafy was raped by her teacher, bore Janie, and then left rural Florida, where Nanny worked as a maid for a white family after the war ended. The novel calls attention to the sexual abuse black women endure from both black and white men, which connects to the racial and sexual "double bind" that black women have faced historically.

Nanny wants Janie to wed a landowning black man so that she will not be sexual or economic chattel for any man. Nanny's wish for her granddaughter's security embodies a bourgeois aesthetic grounded in the history of black women in America. Nanny's comparison of the black woman in America with the mule connects back to Hurston's *Mules and Men (Folklore, Memoirs, and Other Writings)*, which treated the issue of male/female relationships and the black woman's ability to assert her voice—a key theme in *Their Eyes Were Watching God*. Although Nanny may appear materialistic, her awareness of racial, sexual, and class inequities in America actually reveals a proletarian aesthetic in the text. While the marriage proves unhappy and unsuccessful, Nanny's attitudes are grounded in her realistic and compelling personal history of the black woman's plight in America at the turn of the century. When she advises Janie to marry Logan Killicks, it actually reflects her love for her granddaughter and desire that she not become sexual chattel.

Hurston's depiction of the passionless and oppressive marriage between Janie and Logan Killicks represents Janie's entry into the bourgeois level of West Florida society. Unlike many of the other black men in the area, Killicks owns his own home, land, and livestock. The organ he keeps in his parlor distinguishes him from the other African Americans in the community, for a parlor and an organ represent gentility. The parlor in his home reflects the bourgeois aspirations. Nevertheless, his marriage to Janie lacks passion and equality. He views Janie as a possession no better than his livestock. A defining moment of their marriage occurs when Logan notes his impending journey to buy a mule, and Janie equates her position in the household with the purchase of a mule. Thus, the mule becomes the metaphor of self, her acquisition of voice. As Nanny points out, black women are "de mule of de world."

Through her articulation of her plight to her husband, Hurston presents a continuation of power dynamics in relationships explored in her short fiction prior to *Their Eyes Were Watching God*. In "Sweat," Delia Jones, a washwoman, raises her voice to her husband about the mistreatment she endures as a commodity in the marriage. Like Delia, Janie feels oppressed and unappreciated. However, Delia must work outside the home as a washerwoman to support the family, while Janie's work is confined primarily to the farm because Logan is financially successful. Hurston suggests the confining and often oppressive circumstances for black women in marriage at the turn of the century whether the family has folk or bourgeois status.

Janie's second marriage, to Jody Starks, follows the pattern of the first regarding her mate's bourgeois aspirations and the sense of confinement fulfilling her socially prescribed role as the wife of a prominent man. Janie initially meets Jody while unhappily married to Logan, who has gone away to buy a mule. He and Killicks bear an affinity, for each man embodies on the surface bourgeois trappings. Clothing reflects his bourgeois ambitions and separates him from the rest of the community: "It was a citified, stylish dressed man with his hat set at an angle that didn't belong in these parts. His coat was over his arm, but he didn't need it to represent his clothes. The shirt with the silk sleeveholders was dazzling enough for the world" (*Novels and Stories:* 196). Starks's clothing reveals that he, like John Pearson in *Jonah's Gourd Vine*, desires to be a "big man" of power, status, and wealth. Janie's relationship with Jody represents a further immersion into the life of the bourgeois class when he relocates to Eatonville, Florida, an all-black community.

As an aspiring entrepreneur and politician, Jody acquires status and wealth from his real-estate holdings. Like Nanny, he feels that a wife should lead a privileged life and scoffs at the very notion of Janie behind a plow. He places her on a pedestal, reflecting a bourgeois ethos of middle-class womanhood in which the wife inhabits the domestic sphere. For Jody, women who work in the fields represent the folk, and in his desire to move away from that life, he wants a wife who stands in opposition to other women. Ironically, the marriage between Janie and Jody proves even more oppressive than her first one to Killicks. Being part of the elite has its price, as she soon discovers as his wife. On the surface, her relationship with him represents Nanny's dream of a bourgeois middle-class marriage for her granddaughter. Nevertheless, Hurston criticizes Jody's obsession with commerce just as Fauset criticizes marriage based on commodity and materialism rather than love. The narrative strategy of the self in conflict with the marketing of it had come to full fruition, as exemplified by Fauset's *There Is Confusion, Plum Bun, The Chinaberry Tree,* and *Comedy: American Style* and West's novels *The Living Is Easy* and *The Wedding*. In *Their Eyes Were Watching God*, Hurston portrays Jody as a larger than life. After moving to Eatonville, he acquires land and builds houses, a store, and a post office to everyone's amazement, for they did not expect to see a black man with such power, authority, and wealth.

Jody's newfound status affects the way he treats Janie. He demands that she set herself off from the rest of the women in Eatonville, which is to say, the folk.

He exhorts her to be the "bell-cow" and refers to the other black females in the community as "the gang" (*Novels and Stories:* 207). By comparing Janie to a bell cow, he reinscribes animal imagery onto her (and other women). Ironically, Janie becomes "de mule uh de world" that Nanny describes as the plight of black women even in a bourgeois middle-class marriage. A bell cow in comparison with other cows suggests a classing off between her and the other women and anticipates Janie's later affinity with Matt Bonner's mule, a neglected and abused commodity. Hurston deconstructs the idea of house and home later in the novel as she configures the Starks's dwelling as oppressive despite its grandeur. In contrast, the "muck," where she and Tea Cake own a modest cabin, functions more like a home because it houses a more egalitarian marital relationship. Jody's bourgeois aspirations and ambitions manifest themselves in the home he constructs for himself and Janie. Unlike other homes in the community, the Starks's dwelling (modeled after plantation mansions) has two stories, porches, and banisters. It dwarfs the other houses in the community. He buys furniture that suggests his bourgeois pretensions, including an expensive desk and gold spittoons for him and his wife. As Starks acquires the accouterments of the wealthy whites he has worked for in the past, he removes himself further from his constituents, the southern black folk of Eatonville who feel ambivalent about the change and progress he has brought to the community.

Hurston presents Janie's rise from folk to bourgeois status in terms of loss of identity and voice. Jody places her on a pedestal and forbids her to engage in storytelling about Matt Bonner's mule with the town residents and discourages her from asserting any individuality. Jody feels that the storytellers are low-class individuals and that Janie should not be associating with them because of her socioeconomic level. He thinks that their material possessions and status in the community make him and Janie superior to "the folk." Janie begins to dislike the elevated status she has been given and views being treated like a lady as confining. In a desire to have possession of Janie and her sexuality, Jody refuses to let her hair show at work in the store and makes her wear a head rag. Janie's quest for voice and selfhood, the basis of her art as a storyteller, continues despite Joe's domination over her. When she laments the abuse and ridicule Matt Bonner's "yellow" mule endures because of its age, she identifies with the animal as property. Jody buys it from the farmer in an attempt to impress Janie and the townspeople. When he frees the mule, she makes a speech paralleling his actions with those of George Washington and Abraham Lincoln. Janie's speech reveals her art for oratory. Her allusions to the mule and the two presidents associated with freedom suggests a recognition of her confinement in an unhappy marriage. The bourgeois lifestyle leads to loneliness and desolation, causing a new awareness of her position. She becomes more assertive and counters Jody's criticism of her. When she cuts a plug of tobacco incorrectly and he ridicules her, she counters, "You big-bellies round here and put out a lot of brag, but 'tain't nothin' to it but yo' big voice. Humph! Talkin' bout me lookin' old! When you pull down yo' britches, you look lak de change uh life" (*Novels and Stories:* 238).

Janie proves to be the "big voice" of Eatonville as she exposes his pretensions. Her speech limits Jody's status and power as a leader in Eatonville, enabling the townspeople to witness her verbal prowess and skill.

Hurston draws a parallel between Jody's physical demise by kidney failure and the end of their marriage. The growth of Janie's voice signifies resistance to his mistreatment. Fearful that Janie has conjured against him, he does not realize that her only tools of power are her words. Angry and resentful on the eve of his death, he refuses to acknowledge his mistreatment of her. To her, however, Jody is a selfish individual who, in exerting his voice, tried to devalue and limit the voice of others. When Jody dies, Janie feels a newfound sense of relief and freedom from the oppressive atmosphere his desire for wealth, status, and power gave them. Having lived the bourgeois life that Nanny prescribed for her, Janie wants to experience a life based on love rather than on money and material objects. Jody's death signals an important stage in Janie's development as an artist and her budding awareness in finding her voice and reading the text of her life.

Hurston presents Janie's third marriage to Vergible Tea Cake Woods as a reimmersion into the folk. As a member of the folk without the bourgeois aspirations of Jody, Tea Cake initially appears to fulfill Janie's quest for "the bee" for her blossom in his exuberance and swaggering sexuality. Although she is forty years old and he is twenty-five, Tea Cake's exuberance and quest for life appeals to her. A gambler and a blues man, Tea Cake wins her over through his spontaneity, passion, and wit. He stands in stark contrast to Jody's character. In Hurston's characterization of Tea Cake, she signifies on Big Sweet (in name and attitude), the tough-talking African American woman Hurston encounters and depicts in *Mules and Men*. Big Sweet functions as her guide into the work camps and juke joints of rural Florida on the folklore expedition narrated in the text. Like Big Sweet, Tea Cake reimmerses Janie into the life of the folk in "the muck." Because Tea Cake does not possess the wealth, power, and status of Jody, the citizens of the Eatonville community view him as an opportunist. They take a dim view on the couple's activities, such as playing checkers and cards, because Jody had forbidden them. He had associated those pastimes with the folk or low-class individuals. Hurston uses the relationship to meditate on folk and bourgeois conceptions of courtship, mating, and relationships.

Hurston presents African American color consciousness in the relationship of Janie and Tea Cake. Historically, blacks who were the products of unions between the white slaveholder and black female slaves often had greater privileges than darker-skinned blacks. Even after the end of slavery, the gap in power and privilege persisted, leading to elitism on the part of some light-skinned blacks and resentment from some darker-skinned blacks (Russell et al. 1992). The class and complexion difference between Tea Cake and Janie appears early on in their relationship through his actions toward her. When the couple heads to Jacksonville, Florida, so that Tea Cake can look for a job on the railroad, he takes the money she had pinned to her clothes and has a fish fry with friends without inviting her. He alleges that he viewed her as too high-class for the individuals he associated with at the fish fry. Just as the Eatonville community views Janie as high-class and above the folk, Tea Cake senses a class difference as well, using that as a reason for excluding her from the gathering. Janie does not want to be placed on a pedestal, preferring to be on a more egalitarian level with her new husband. For Janie, being "classed off" by her husbands has hurt her and prevented her from fully participating in the community.

While Killicks's milieu is the farm and Starks's is Eatonville, Tea Cake's is the muck, the Florida Everglades where sugarcane, tomatoes, and beans are harvested by migrant workers. Janie's delight on the muck contrasts with her depression on Killicks's farm and in Eatonville. Here, the muck opposes and subverts the farm. Janie no longer feels separated from the other black women, for she works alongside her husband in the fields. Furthermore, the muck functions as a microcosm of the African disapora featuring blacks from the Caribbean and the South (Wall 1995). As a result, the muck functions as Janie's first exposure to blacks from other parts of the diaspora as well as to artistic traditions. For the first time in her life, Janie marvels at her reimmersion into the folk. She can be an integral part of the environment and tell stories, expressing the creative abilities that Joe Starks attempted to stifle. The muck, however, is no utopia. Mrs. Turner, a light-skinned black woman who owns a restaurant on the muck, represents bourgeois pretensions. Hurston's characterization of her bears resemblance to color-conscious characters in the novels of Jessie Fauset and Nella Larsen.[7] Janie appeals to her because of her light complexion, but she disdains a dark-skinned black man like Tea Cake. Mrs. Turner worships whiteness as a god and idolizes anyone who has Caucasian features. Obsession with whiteness has dire consequences when Turner attempts to match up Janie with her light-skinned brother, whom she views as a better mate than dark-skinned Tea Cake. As a result, Tea Cake beats Janie to reaffirm his territorial prerogatives.

Hurston's text suggests that the inability to negotiate the folk and bourgeois aesthetics leads to class consciousness, which has a detrimental effect upon the characters in *Their Eyes Were Watching God* when the hurricane appears. Perhaps it is the inability to reconcile the folk and bourgeois elements that assumes in the novel the terrible form of the hurricane and creates Tea Cake's death. Because the elite Janie has intruded upon the muck landscape, she nearly loses her life in the hurricane. But the Indians, the noble savage folk, had already gone away. The storm indirectly causes Tea Cake's death when a rabid dog bites him while he tries to save Janie from drowning during the hurricane. As a consequence, she shoots her lover in self-defense when he later attempts to kill her in a rage precipitated by rabies. Therefore, Janie must kill Tea Cake in order to live and successfully become a self-actualized individual.

While the novel focuses primarily on intraracial rather than interracial relationships, Hurston presents the racism pervading America under the Jim Crow system when Tea Cake is pressed into the service of digging graves for those who have died in the hurricane. While not overtly a protest or proletarian novel, her work contains incidents that reveal that Hurston does not avoid criticism of racism in the United States. Janie's acquittal for shooting Tea Cake in self-defense results from the sympathy the whites feel toward her as a result of her light complexion, including their stereotypical views of black men as violent, aggressive, and bestial. Contrary to Wright and Locke's assessments, Hurston does criticize inequities in the United States. When Janie returns to Eatonville after Tea Cake's funeral, she recognizes the importance of self-reliance and self-definition. Her storytelling transforms and converts Pheoby, who, empowered by Janie's words, decides to become more assertive. More importantly, the return signifies a successful quest for self. It marks a return of the first-person narrative and omniscient narration of the original frame. The folk spirit had come back to the bourgeois town, especially with Janie as the agent of transformation and restoration. The narrative techniques and formal text elements function in tandem to reveal the folk, bourgeois, and proletarian aesthetics. In *Jonah's Gourd Vine* and *Their Eyes Were Watching God*, Hurston takes the reader on a mythical and spiritual journey. She explores the diversity and vitality of African American life, art, and culture by reconfiguring the triangle of aesthetics. *Moses, Man of the Mountain* and *Seraph on the Suwanee* lead the reader on similar journeys through the racial, class, and genderized landscapes of her imaginary worlds. Sadly, these later two novels receive far less commentary. Both novels present a compelling and sophisticated criticism of social, political, and economic injustices.

Not surprisingly, *Moses, Man of the Mountain* draws thematically from the Bible, one of Hurston's sources of inspiration as a young avid reader. When Hurston needed a publisher for her story "The Fire and the Cloud," based upon the Moses/Exodus story from the Bible, she submitted it to *Challenge*, edited and founded by Dorothy West. The story later spawned Hurston's 1939 novel, *Moses, Man of the Mountain*, in which she meditates on race, class, and gender during biblical times as a means of commenting on the pressing social, political, and economic problems that remained in twentieth-century America and the world. West published the story in the September 1934 edition of *Challenge*, which, in the tradition of *Fire!!*, sought to use art and literature as a means of uniting the folk, bourgeois, and proletarian aesthetics and classes in an effort to renew the artistic and social vigor of the Harlem Renaissance. Hurston and West's relationship began nearly a decade earlier on 1 May 1926, when the two attended *Opportunity* magazine's second annual literary contest award dinner in New York City. Both African American women writers won second prizes in the fiction category. Hurston received a prize for her short story "Muttsy," and Dorothy West garnered an award for "The Typewriter." Published by the Urban League, *Opportunity*, like its NAACP counterpart the *Crisis*, served as a forum for the promotion of African American artistic, political, and social ideas, activism, and achievements. Over the next decade, their paths would cross again on several occasions under both personal and professional circumstances.

The Harlem Renaissance signified a community of writers, artists, and promoters of African American art, culture, and traditions during the 1920s and

1930s. During the summer of 1926, Zora Neale Hurston, Langston Hughes, Wallace Thurman, Gwendolyn Bennett, Bruce Nugent, and Aaron Douglass met to establish *Fire!!*, a journal devoted to promoting the works of African American writers and artists (*Novels and Stories:* 1016). *Fire!!* signified the vibrant and thriving intellectual community among the black writers involved in establishing the publication, who referred to themselves as the Niggerati. The first and only issue of *Fire!!* (November 1926) appeared as a response to the *New Negro*, an anthology that Hughes, Thurman, and Hurston believed privileged the middle-class African American experience and ideology (Hemenway 1977). They sought to produce a magazine that would bridge the gap between the folk, the bourgeois, and the proletarian aesthetics in its valorization of African American art, life, and culture. A year later, West and Hurston's lives intertwined again when Hurston sublet her Harlem apartment to West (who had been living at the YWCA with her cousin Helene Johnson) while on a folklore expedition in the South arranged by Columbia University anthropology professor Franz Boas (Ferguson 1987). The meeting and subsequent relationship between the two women bears significance in establishing a community of writers and the melding of aesthetics during the Harlem Renaissance. Hurston being a product of Notasulga, Alabama, and Eatonville, Florida and West being a native of Boston, Massachusetts, the two women may have seemed antithetical in character and purposes. Hurston embodies the southern folk aesthetic with her interest in folklore, black dialect, the oral storytelling tradition, and her interest in anthropology. West seems to reflect the bourgeois aesthetic in her financially privileged background as the daughter of a successful fruit importer and her ownership of a summer home on Martha's Vineyard. These differences proved to be superficial. The "folksy" Hurston attended elite institutions of higher learning such as Howard University and Barnard College, which reflects her exposure to a bourgeois environment. The "privileged" West was the daughter of an ex-slave from Virginia and her family roots manifest themselves in her fiction and her biographical reminiscences. When West founded *Challenge* in 1934, it seemed only natural that Hurston would contribute to the periodical, for both women symbolized the blending of folk, bourgeois, and proletarian aesthetics within their own work and lives.

Although *Their Eyes Were Watching God* and *Jonah's Gourd Vine*, which have been heralded as exemplars of African American folk culture, rituals, and customs, have received a considerable amount of critical attention in recent years, Hurston's last two published novels are underdiscussed and underevaluated. This examination of Hurston's work contends that the scarcity of criticism on *Moses, Man of the Mountain* and *Seraph on the Suwanee* compared to Hurston's first two novels may stem more from preconceived notions and stereotypical definitions of authentic African American and female texts than from the artistic merits of the works. Because scholars of women's and African American studies have revived the literature of Zora Neale Hurston by emphasizing the portrayal of female empowerment and elements of black folk culture in her work, a novel set in Biblical times and another about white southerners in the Florida Everglades may not appear to have relevance to black life or the female experience in a patriarchal society. However, both novels present the complex blend of folk, bourgeois, and proletarian aesthetics in the treatment of character, plot, theme, and symbolism so prevalent in Hurston's first two novels. Hurston covertly and often overtly comments on a number of social, political, and economic problems facing the African American community or women through her reinterpretation of the Exodus story in *Moses, Man of the Mountain* and her meditation on the lives of Florida's rising middle class in *Seraph on the Suwanee*. By appropriating the bildungsroman as the primary narrative form in the theme, plot, symbolism, and characterization in her last two novels, Hurston presents the physical, emotional, mental, and spiritual development of her protagonists Moses (*Moses, Man of the Mountain*) and Arvay Henson (*Seraph on the Suwanee*) as a means of presenting race relations, sexual politics, and class stratification. This clever strategy enables Hurston to present fictive worlds that on the surface may seem different from those of her middle- and upper-middle-class reading audience (Egypt during biblical times and rural Floridians), yet upon closer inspection the texts reveal the universality of human experience.

In *Moses, Man of the Mountain*, Hurston employs elements of both bildungsroman and biblical allegory. Despite the novel's setting in biblical times, *Moses, Man of the Mountain* speaks to pressing social, political, and economic issues that the United States faced in the 1930s when the novel was published and still is relevant today. *Seraph on the Suwanee* also utilizes elements of both bildungsroman and biblical allegory, but unlike *Moses, Man of the Mountain*, it is not a retelling of a particular biblical event or episode. While *Moses, Man of the Mountain* comments on the social, political, and economic contexts of American and world history, *Seraph on the Suwanee* functions more as a meditation on the Old versus the New South and agrarianism versus industrialism and commercial development. *Seraph on the Suwanee*, by focusing on the life of a female protagonist from a lower socioeconomic background, addresses gender issues to a greater extent than does *Moses, Man of the Mountain*.

The novels share a focus on race, class, and gender in Hurston's exploration of folk, bourgeois, and proletarian aesthetics, revealing her concern with presenting a more complex view of the human condition. Hurston's continued exploration of these themes suggests her increasing concern as an African American woman of the 1930s and 1940s about pressing social, political, and economic issues of the period, including the Great Depression of the 1930s, increasing political tensions in Western Europe that affected the United States as a world power, and a growing dissatisfaction in the United States with sexual and racial discrimination. *Moses, Man on the Mountain* and *Seraph on the Suwanee* reveal Hurston's artistry in addressing complex social, political, and economic issues through the employment of formal elements of the bildungsroman.

When *Moses, Man of the Mountain* first appeared in 1939, it received mixed reviews from critics. Untermeyer (1993), writing in 1939, examined Hurston's appropriation of the biblical figure of Moses and the Exodus saga and laments the use of folk speech in her retelling of the event. In contrast, Hutchinson (1993) viewed the folkways in the novel more favorably, noting that "It is warm with friendly personality and pulsating with homely and profound eloquence and religious fervor" (29). Later critical assessments tend to focus on Hurston's incorporation of folklore and dialect as well. Bell (1987) notes that "Because the style relies more on black idiom than on slang, quaint spelling, and folk sayings, the dialogue here, unlike earlier books, does not attract attention to itself but complements Hurston's adaptation of biblical language and standard English" (127). *Moses, Man of the Mountain* centers on the life of Moses, the grandson of the Egyptian pharaoh. Moses, in the novel, is rumored to be the son of a Hebrew couple who defied the pharaoh's edict that all male offspring of Hebrew couples be killed. He exemplifies physical, intellectual, and spiritual strength in his affinity with the Hebrew slaves (the folk) and disdain for the Egyptian ruling class (the bourgeoisie). He leads the Hebrews to freedom from Egyptian tyranny only to discover that they desire to replicate the hierarchical nature of Egyptian society. Hurston's novel, a retelling of the Moses and Exodus story in the form of the bildungsroman, explores the race, class, and gender politics of the biblical period in relation to nineteenth- and twentieth-century America through her treatment of theme, characterizations, symbolism, and plot. By adopting the bildungsroman narrative form, Hurston meditates on the physical, emotional, spiritual, sexual, and intellectual awakening of the protagonist. Moses' growth, development, and experiences as well as his role as a leader among men and women enable Hurston to explore issues of race, class, and gender through the medium of biblical allegory, narrative, and allusion. The social, political, and economic structures of Egyptian and later the more egalitarian Midianite society serve as a microcosm of the world and an allegory of the racial, sexual, and class oppression blacks and women face. By equating the experience of Moses and the Hebrews in biblical times with that of African Americans during slavery in the United States and afterward, Hurston launches a powerful protest against oppression. The novel then functions as more than a biblical revision or retelling, but as an example of protest or proletarian literature anticipating later works by other writers such as Richard Wright's *Native Son* (1940) and Ann Petry's *Street* (1946).[8]

Hurston artfully equates the experiences of the Hebrews under Egyptian rule and tyranny with that of African Americans under slavery in eighteenth- and nineteenth-century America. Her appropriation of the Bible derives from African American history and literary tradition. In fact, "Black Americans, from the seventeenth century until today, have constantly translated the Scriptures into their own versions of truth, frequently melding them with Afrocentric traditions; the spirituals and folktales dealing with God, angels, and the Devil are only two obvious results" (Lowe 1994: 208). As the daughter of a Baptist minister who was expected to attend church every Sunday and through her folklore collecting expeditions and research on African American life and culture,

Hurston was well acquainted with the Old and New Testaments of the Bible, Negro spirituals, and sermons. From a personal and professional standpoint, the Bible seems only natural as a source for Hurston's fiction and commentary on race, class, and gender.

The appropriation of the Exodus story in particular represents a longstanding tradition in African American oral and written literature, including Frances E. W. Harper's "Moses: A Story of the Nile," Martin Luther King's "I See the Promised Land," and Richard Wright's *Fire and the Cloud.* In fact, Hurston may have been acquainted with Harper's long poem, which was published in 1869. The two works parallel one another in the use of allegory, references to conjuring, and the use of several voices in the text. It is possible that Hurston may have been introduced to Harper's work by one of her professors at Howard University or perhaps by another academic. Besides, Hurston was a friend of James Weldon Johnson, who refers to Harper's poem in his introductory remarks to *The Book of American Negro Poetry* (Lowe 1994).

Hurston's *Moses, Man of the Mountain* also bears affinity to Wright's *Fire and the Cloud.* Wright's work focuses on a community leader and Moses figure who views religion as ineffective in fighting discrimination and leads a demonstration of blacks and whites to protest oppressive conditions. In fact, Hurston's short story "The Fire and the Cloud," which appeared in Dorothy West's *Challenge* in 1934, serves as the basis for the novel and shares the same title as Wright's novella. In the story, Moses sits on Mt. Nebo and contemplates the future of the Hebrews and their readiness to be responsible, empowered, and productive individuals.

In African American literature, the story of Moses and the Exodus takes on metaphoric, historic, allegorical, and symbolic implications in relation to the history of blacks in the United States and the legacy of slavery. For black slaves, Moses served as a source of inspiration, empowerment, and supernatural powers as he led his people (the Hebrews) to freedom: "Moses's heroic stance appealed to African born slaves, for the African epic hero often has an unusual birth, becomes endangered or exiled during childhood, and has rigorous testing before gaining power " (Lowe 1994: 209). For the slaves, Moses embodied the folk and the power of conjure through his special relationship with God, and he represented the promise of emancipation. Through her appropriation of the Bible and its depiction of the Moses/Exodus narrative, Hurston translates into written form the importance of the Moses figure to African American religion, history, and culture.

In addition to the precedent set for Hurston by African American literary and oral traditions, Hurston's appropriation of the Bible may have other reasons and sources as well. Her willingness to replace biblical language with black folk dialect, rituals, and customs emphasize the issue of racial heritage rather than religion, and her willingness to utilize humor in her multicultural rendering of Moses' life and experience may be the result of her exposure to Louis Untermeyer's *Moses,* published in 1928 (Lowe 1994). While there is no conclusive proof that Hurston knew Untermeyer or read his novel, he and Hurston might have encountered each other at the home of Carl Van Vechten (Lowe 1994). Also, Van Vechten may have mentioned Untermeyer's novel to Hurston when she was working on *Moses, Man of the Mountain* (Lowe 1994). Economics may also have played a role in Hurston's decision to present the Moses/Exodus story in novel form. The novel might have served for her as an entrée into the cinema world, which could provide fame and financial security as well as a wider forum for an author's ideas. From 1908 until the year *Moses, Man of the Mountain* appeared, more than forty films inspired by the Bible were made in Hollywood, including *Intolerance* (1916), *The Ten Commandments* (1923), and *Noah's Ark* (1928), including at least one with a New Testament theme, *The King of Kings* (1927) (Lowe 1994). A number of twentieth-century American writers, including William Faulkner, Carson McCullers, and Ernest Hemingway either wrote for the movies or had their novels dramatized in film, which could be a highly lucrative venture and stimulate sales of the author's fiction. Hurston viewed film as a possible medium for her work (Lowe 1994). The possibility of writing a novel that would be transferred to the screen and the resulting material benefits would have been especially important to Hurston since by the late 1930s she no longer received the patronage of Charlotte Osgood "Godmother" Mason.[9]

Although Hurston held a series of teaching positions at North Carolina College and Bethune-Cookman College, won fellowships, and worked for the Florida Federal Writers' Project during the mid to late 1930s, her financial situation was precarious. The fellowships provided only short-term funding and required continual reapplication. Hurston often became involved in disputes with faculty and administration at the colleges at which she was employed over the amount of time she was required to spend teaching versus writing her novels, plays, and short stories. As a consequence, her teaching stints were relatively brief in comparison with other Harlem Renaissance–era women writers like Jessie Fauset and Angelina Weld Grimke. Unlike Hurston, Fauset and Grimke worked as teachers for a large portion of their adult lives to supplement their income. In fact, teaching was one of the few professions available for an educated black woman in the early twentieth century.

Despite the demands of her professional and personal life, Hurston succeeded in completing and publishing *Moses, Man of the Mountain* five years after "The Fire and the Cloud" appeared in *Challenge*. In the novel, Hurston draws on folk, bourgeois, and proletarian aesthetics in her retelling of the biblical story of Moses and the Exodus. Adopting the narrative form of the bildungsroman, the novel focuses on Moses, who is presented as the son of Amram and Jochebed, two Hebrew slaves, who defy the pharaoh's secret police in having a son despite a royal edict banning male children.[10] Hurston's use of biblical imagery and appropriation of the bildungsroman to explore discrimination against the Hebrews in *Moses, Man of the Mountain* enables her to equate religious oppression in ancient Egypt with twentieth-century anti-Semitism in Western Europe and the Soviet Union: "The shadow of Nazism is cast from the beginning of *Moses, Man of the Mountain,* which opens on the process of marking Hebrew male babies for extinction" (McDowell 1993: 235). The contemporaneity of Hurston's biblical novel illustrates her concern with social, political, and global issues.

Hurston depicts the Hebrews or the folk as having bourgeois aspirations and desires for themselves and their children despite the tyranny they experience under the Egyptians. Amram and Jochebed want their son to achieve greatness and importance. They use Miriam, their daughter, as the agent to preserve their son's life. Although a member of the folk and scornful of the Egyptians, the Egyptians' power and affluence enchant Miriam. When she falls asleep after setting her baby brother adrift on the river in a basket at her parents' request, she concocts a story about the pharaoh's daughter discovering the son. By telling her family and friends that the Egyptian princess "found" her brother and "adopted" him, Miriam too becomes a person of status and stature in her society, which introduces the notion of class into the novel. Hurston's depiction of Miriam's rationale for concocting the story serves as a means of meditating on class and the disparity between the folk and bourgeois classes in social, political, and economic power.

Hurston successfully equates the experiences of the Hebrews with that of blacks in the United States in her depiction of racial politics in biblical times through the suggestion that Moses, the "grandson" of the pharaoh and heir to the Egyptian throne, has Hebrew blood. One of the members of the Hebrew community points out that Hebrew blood runs through the pharaoh's family, and that several of his relatives pass for Egyptians, the ruling class. Being Hebrew signifies folk status while presenting oneself as Egyptian symbolizes membership in the bourgeois class. Hurston's presentation of passing in the novel connects her with other writers of the Harlem Renaissance who reveal the ambiguities of race and color lines as a means of meditating on racism.[11] Hurston conflates the discrimination against the Hebrews by the Egyptians with American slavery and anti-Semitism in her exploration of racial and class tensions in the United States and abroad, rendering *Moses, Man of the Mountain* as a text with social, political, and economic dimensions. Her focus on pressing social problems illustrates the proletarian aesthetic in the text, negating criticism of Hurston as a nonpolitical or socially unaware writer.

Hurston presents gender oppression in Egyptian society in her portrayal of the pharaoh's household and the conditions that enable Moses and his uncle Ta-Phar to have positions of real power. In contrast, the princess has no real control over the social, political, or economic destinies of her people and herself. In Egyptian society, women function as bearers of warriors and future leaders. The princess's role is marked by confinement and rigid boundaries over her socially prescribed and acceptable role in the household. Hurston's *Moses, Man of the Mountain* comments on sexual oppression in a thoughtful and provocative manner through the depiction of the princess's "elite" position, which provides her with a life of ease and wealth but imprisonment as well. In some senses, the princess's feelings of restriction and oppression in her elite role echo Janie's experiences as the wife of Mayor Starks in *Their Eyes Were Watching God* and anticipates Arvay Meserve's plight as the wife of real-estate developer and entrepreneur Jim Meserve in *Seraph on the Suwanee*. All three women find themselves in situations, despite their social and economic affluence, in which the husbands seek to mute their voices.[12]

Hurston depicts Moses's supposed Hebrew origins as a means of meditating on folk and bourgeois ideologies as well as race. The belief that Moses is Hebrew suggests the possibility of future freedom for the folk and the vagaries of racial and political classification systems: "In sustaining the ambiguities of race throughout the text, Hurston effectively argues against a system of racial classification whose validity she disputes" (McDowell 1993: 236). Hurston emphasizes the pride and uplift the Hebrews feel in viewing Moses as the grandson of the pharaoh as the rumor spreads to the palace quarters. For the Egyptians, the rumors of his Hebrew ancestry offer an explanation for his revolutionary and proletarian beliefs as he champions the rights of the underprivileged. His wife accuses him of being a Hebrew or a slave, and as a consequence, she no longer desires to be his wife because she views him as racially, socially, and politically inferior. Furthermore, his jealous uncle Ta-Phar spreads the rumors in an effort to discredit him and depose his position as commander in chief, asserting that his racial heritage makes him unfit to be one of the elite.

Marginalized, Moses seeks power from within himself, from nature, and from the guidance of Mentu (a slave and representative of the folk) as he seeks to understand his surroundings. He would rather journey to Koptos to learn the secrets of nature and the universe than wage war with neighboring countries for land. After he kills a foreman for abusing Hebrew slaves, he becomes further marginalized and Moses must leave Egypt or suffer the consequences of the traitorous act. Moses's crossing of the Red Sea away from Egypt signifies the beginning of a new life for him as he divests himself of money and the accouterments of his former life: "Moses had crossed over. He was not in Egypt. He had crossed over and now he was not an Egyptian. He had crossed over. The short sword at his thigh had a jeweled hilt but he had crossed over and so it was no longer the sign of high birth and power" (*Novels and Stories:* 409). Hurston's depiction of Moses' crossing the Red Sea constitutes a crossing from a position of privilege to one of brotherhood with the masses, and from the bourgeois to the folk and proletarian classes.

The scene suggests that race, whether it be Hebrew or Egyptian, functions as a construct imposed by man. Race and status transcend birth and heredity. Now that he no longer considers himself as the grandson of the pharaoh, Moses can begin a new life and embark on a journey toward spiritual wholeness and renounce a focus on power and material possessions. He successfully crosses over from the bourgeois to the folk class as embodied by the trip from Egypt to Midian. Midianite society offers a sharp contrast to the social, political, and economic structure of Egypt. The Midianite king, Jethro, serves as a point of contrast with Egypt and the strict racial, sexual, and class hierarchy. The chief dresses like the folk and speaks in the common language as opposed to a formal, ornate and elite language. In contrast, in Egypt the Egyptian language signifies elitism, power, and high status. Finding the proletarian viewpoint of the Midianite leader more attractive, Moses adopts these attributes and transforms his language to conform with the masses. In fact, Jethro stresses the importance of speaking the language of the masses as a means of obtaining their understanding and respect. Hurston's depiction of Midianite society reveals a proletarian and folk aesthetic of class, power, and language.

Although the Midianite society is much more egalitarian, there are vestiges of elitism. Moses weds Jethro's daughter Zipporah, who believes marriage to him will elevate her socially. Jethro's perception of Zipporah's beliefs reflects the presence of a bourgeois aesthetic in the midst of Midianite society. Zipporah glories in wealth and finery. She treasures her status as Moses's wife in the hope that one day she will be a princess. She now views Egypt as her home rather than Midian and wants to take her proper place beside him on pharaoh's throne. Moses's antipathy toward ruling stems from his experiences as commander in chief of Egypt and his desire for an egalitarian community. He feels that absolute power corrupts the ruler and the people. He would rather use his abilities to become educated about the world, its people, and the natural environment than conquer competing armies or rule other people. Even when Moses uses his keen conjuring powers, it is not specifically to harm individuals. (One example is when he sends swarms of locusts and groups of frogs as a means of keeping Zeppo, a cousin of Jethro's, from feasting off their food and living off their household.) The people of Midian are in awe of Moses, who can turn water into blood or make manna appear from heaven. Hurston's portrayal of Moses as a conjure man reflects the infusion of folk culture into the novel and the Afrocentric appropriation of the Moses figure in the novel.[13] To the Midianites, he becomes not just an agent of God but God's voice, a role that Moses does not wish to take on because he does not want to be confused with a deity or viewed as superior to others.

Although Hurston portrays Moses as a man without the desire to be a leader or become a god in man's eyes, she depicts him as preordained to lead the Hebrews out of slavery. One day while he is on the mountain herding, communing with the animals, and contemplating men and their actions, he witnesses the burning bush and hears a voice that commands him to lead the Hebrews to the Promised Land out of Egyptian tyranny. The incident signifies a turning point in his life. Hurston's characterization of Moses's ambivalence and tension over his desire to be one of the folk and the Hebrew/Midianite desire for him as a leader evidences the tension in the novel between the folk and the bourgeois aesthetics. Hurston's characterization of Moses may represent her own ambivalence over the class divisions within the African American community among leaders, the masses, and intellectuals. While in Egypt, Moses functions as the symbol of the potential freedom for the Hebrew people and as a spiritual guide. Although Moses has unlimited conjuring powers at his disposal and the power to fell the pharaoh and the Egyptian army easily, he has pacifist beliefs and desires to reason with the pharaoh about letting the Hebrews have their freedom. However, pharaoh (now Ta-Phar) and his wife (Moses's ex) do not take him seriously. In contrast to Moses, Ta-Phar, the embodiment of the bourgeois aesthetic, suffers from a bigoted worldview and sees the world in terms of rigid race, class, and gender structures. He does not view the Hebrews as people but as slaves and refuses to allow them their freedom. As a consequence, Moses illustrates his might and power in a battle of conjuring against the Egyptian priests by turning rods into snakes, the Nile into a river of blood, and creating a plague of frogs and lice.

Hurston's depiction of the reaction of the Hebrews to their freedom further reinforces the parallel between their plight and that of black slaves in the United States as they exclaim, "Thank God Almighty I'm free at last!" (*Novels and Stories:* 501). Their phrases capture the vernacular and expressions of freed southern black slaves, revealing the connection between the plight of the Hebrews and African Americans as well as the commonality of the experience of unjust racial oppression. The newfound freedom of the ex-slaves causes tensions among them, as some begin to lament what they considered to be the security of food and shelter while they trek to the Promised Land. Tensions mount among Aaron, Moses's brother, and Miriam as the Hebrews have to fight armies they encounter on their way to the Promised Land. Despite their folk origins, Miriam and Aaron desire material compensation for helping their people gain freedom. Hurston's characterization of the two characters may be a meditation on race, class, and gender politics among the black elite and the masses during the Harlem Renaissance (Lowe 1994).

Hurston uses Moses's assessment of Miriam and her materialism to provide a statement on the legacy of slavery and its impact on women. Miriam's horrible early life as a Hebrew slave woman and her bourgeois strivings as a result of the social, economic, and political oppression she has endured mirror Nanny of *Their Eyes Were Watching God* (Lowe 1994). Hurston's presentation of Miriam's plight reveals the consequences of the folk adopting bourgeois attitudes and seeking to preserve the individual over the interests of the community. Miriam exemplifies the individual who fails in resolving folk and bourgeois aesthetics and the interests of themselves and others in their society. Hurston presents Moses's life as a series of successes and failures. On Mt. Nebo he contemplates the possibility of the Promised Land of Canaan for the Hebrews if they can maintain the course he sets out for them, a society that will be built upon racial, class, and gender equality. Hurston conflates the Promised Land of the Hebrews with the Promised Land (of the North) for the African Americans in U.S. history and their quest for civil rights. By retelling a popular and well-known story from the Bible, the center of her audience's Judeo-Christian tradition, Hurston reveals that the social, political, and economic problems of the past remain today. *Moses, Man of the Mountain* reflects the protest (proletarian) novel tradition in its call for the need to redress these problems if the nation, the world, and individuals are to achieve their potential.

Like *Moses, Man of the Mountain, Seraph on the Suwanee* has received considerably less critical attention than Hurston's first two novels. *Seraph on the Suwanee* portrays the folk or the lower socioeconomic classes in a rural southern environment but focuses primarily on whites, in contrast with her first two novels. Furthermore, Arvay Meserve, the novel's protagonist, returns to a marriage characterized by male domination and female submission. These facts may have contributed to the neglect of the novel by African American and women's studies scholars when Hurston's work was being heralded as feminist and Afrocentric. Nevertheless, the novel reveals the presence of folk aesthetic in the portrayal of lower-class whites and blacks, the bourgeois aesthetic in the portrayal of a rising middle class, and the proletarian aesthetic in its criticism of race, class, and gender hierarchies.

In 1947 Hurston acquired Scribner's as her publisher as a result of her relationship with Florida author Marjorie Kinnan Rawlings. The publisher's advance for a forthcoming novel provided her with the funds to visit Honduras, where she wanted to do anthropological research. While there, she began *Seraph on the Suwanee,* finally completing all revisions of it in 1948 after returning to the United States. Early critical response to the novel elicited mixed reviews and focused on the elements of local color in the novel. In 1948 Frank G. Slaughter wrote, "The author knows her people, the Florida cracker of the swamps and turpentine camps intimately, and knows the locale" (Slaughter 1993: 35). Similarly, Worth Tuttle Hedden, also in 1948, stated, "Miss Hurston knows her Florida Negro as she knows her Florida white and she characterizes them with the same acumen, but she gives them no more attention than the plot demands" (Hedden 1993: 36). More recent critical studies emphasize how this text deviates from Hurston's earlier novels in its marginalization of black characters. As Lillie Howard (1993) points out, "Whether *Seraph on the Suwanee* is self-defeating is debatable, but whatever Hurston's reasons for writing *Seraph on the Suwanee,* to her readers she seemed to be turning traitor, deserting the colorful black folks with whom she had hitherto aligned herself" (267). The choice of the protagonist's race may stem from the racial, sexual, and class politics of literary production and publication at the time or from her work with the Florida Federal Writers' Project from 1938 to 1939. Historically, black writers have encountered discrimination from publishers, critics, and a reading public who often view the universal as the ultimate goal for all writers, and who base their perception of universality on Eurocentric preconceptions.

A novel with black characters set in a predominantly black setting may be viewed as quaint, primitive, or exotic but not universal, and not great art. As a consequence, "A white subject matter is often offered as a remedy; the critics assume that the ultimate transcendence is not to write about black people at all, believing for some reason that white people carry no racial identity" (Hemenway 1997: 307). Facing a critical climate such as this one and desiring to have a financially successful work, Hurston may have succumbed to such pressures in the hopes that book sales would finance a future expedition to Honduras in search of an ancient civilization. From an autobiographical stance, the novel may also serve as Hurston's own attempts at negotiating female independence and heterosexual relationships in the wake of two unsuccessful marriages (Hemenway 1997). By the time the novel appeared in 1948, she had two failed marriages—one to Herbert Sheen from 1927 to 1931, and another to Albert Price III from 1939 to 1940.

Hurston's depiction of white Floridians may be based on firsthand experience from her work for the Florida Federal Writers' Project, her friendship with white Florida writer Marjorie Kinnan Rawlings (who also chronicled the lives of white Floridians in her work),[14] and her continued desire to sell a novel to the motion picture industry. Her reimmersion into the landscape and people of Florida may have stimulated her interest in writing a novel about Florida's transition from an agrarian-based economy to one of rapid commercial and industrial development. As Lowe (1994) notes, "Without a doubt, this book grew out of the eighteen months Hurston spent on the payroll of the Florida Federal Writers' Project, a time that may have been one of the happiest in her life" (264). As in the case of *Moses, Man of the Mountain,* Hurston may have had film in mind in composing the book. Prior to the publication of *Seraph on the Suwanee,* she had her agent inquire with MGM about turning the novel into a movie. The success of Marjorie Kinnan Rawlings's *The Yearling,* published in 1939, and the subsequent film titled after the novel, which was produced in 1946, may have stimulated Hurston's interest in writing a tale about white Floridians of a low socioeconomic level as well (Lowe 1994).

As in her three previous novels, Hurston adopts a variety of literary techniques, including the bildungsroman and biblical allusions in the novel's formal elements of theme, plot, characterization, and symbolism. The novel focuses on the growth of her protagonist, Arvay Henson Meserve, as a means of meditating on race, class, and gender. As a member of the folk in Sawley, Florida, Arvay Meserve is part of a close-knit community of turpentine workers, lumbermen, and farmers. While Janie of *Their Eyes Were Watching God* quests for a bee for her blossom, Arvay sublimates her sexual desires for her brother-in-law Reverend Carl Middleton—and the guilt that ensues—through devotion to her church and eschews heterosexual relationships. Her virginity marginalizes her from the community, making her a seraph or angel in their eyes, until she encounters her future husband, Jim Meserve. She replaces her servitude toward God with her devotion to, love for, and dependency on him. Hurston presents the courtship and marriage of Arvay and Jim as a microcosm of race, class, and gender in American society. She highlights the separation between the folk (poor whites) and the bourgeois (middle-class whites) through the depiction of the relationship between the young couple. Their struggle to come to terms with one another reflects the juxtaposition of folk and bourgeois aesthetics in the novel. Jim's speech, manners, and dress reflect his genteel and aristocratic background in relation to his peers. Jim's family history stands in stark contrast to that of the inhabitants of Sawley. Jim represents Arvay's introduction into the bourgeois world. The product of a family who earned its land, money, and prestige through the ownership of slaves, Jim Meserve still retains a sense of class, gender, and racial privilege despite his ability to communicate effectively with individuals he senses as being below him—in other words, the folk.

Although *Seraph on the Suwanee* depicts white protagonists, unlike her other published novels, the disparities between the folk and bourgeois classes as played out in marriage are similarly depicted in all four novels. Arvay recognizes the class disparities between her and Jim Meserve, and this causes angst in the young woman. Hurston's depiction of the class discrepancy between Arvay and Jim may represent her meditation on the socioeconomic differences between her own parents. Through her fictionalized portrayals of class discrepancies in marriage, Hurston may have been attempting to resolve the tension in her own family background and history. Hurston presents Jim as the embodiment of traditional and patriarchal views about marriage. As a husband, he tends to be domineering. Carol P. Marsh-Lockett (1999) notes, "Arvay's oppression in this new middle class existence is underscored by the symbolic surname (Me-serve) which she assumes upon marriage to Jim, for events in the marriage indicate that Arvay is to serve herself only through acquiescence and service to Jim" (102). He couches his views on women in the rhetoric of his aristocratic background. His rigid beliefs about the roles of men and women as well as wives and husbands as outlined early in their relationship tend to define all their interactions with one another, as he represents power and voice, while Arvay reflects a lack of power and voice. This concern with voice reflects a theme running throughout Hurston's fiction as revealed in Janie in *Their Eyes Were Watching God*, Lucy in *Jonah's Gourd Vine*, and Miriam in *Moses, Man of the Mountain*, and Delia Jones in "Sweat." As a female artist who endured censure from patrons, publishers, critics, and readers, the concern with voice in the fiction may have reflected Hurston's own attempts to express herself as a black female writer.

Of Hurston's four published novels, *Seraph on the Suwanee* contains the fewest representatives from the black folk community. Black folk figures do appear in the novel, primarily in the characterization of Joe Kelsey, an expert chipper for the turpentine camp that Jim is resident head of, and his wife Dessie. Despite the scarcity of black characters, they play a major role in the advancement of the plot and themes of the novel. Joe, one of the best workers at the camp as well as a singer of folk songs, discusses women, work, and alcohol with Jim. Joe advises Jim that one must "Take 'em [women] and break 'em" (*Novels and Stories:* 640). Joe's advice is ironic, given his second-class status as a black man in the Jim Crow South (Howard 1993). His viewpoint, coupled with Jim's, represents a continuation of the chauvinistic beliefs about women that Hurston depicted in Logan Killicks, Jody Starks, and Tea Cake in *Their Eyes Were Watching God* and John Pearson in *Jonah's Gourd Vine*.

On the whole, Hurston presents Joe as a positive character. An able musician, he functions as Kenny's (Kenny is the son of Arvay and Jim) teacher by turning the young man into an accomplished jazz and blues musician. Joe and the other blacks in Citrabelle provide Jim with the tools, knowledge, and methodology to become a financially successful and powerful citrus grower when he first arrives, for Jim knows very little about growing fruit initially. Blacks in the novel represent the embodiment of the folk and their vitality, dynamism, artistry, and resourcefulness. While blacks take on a minor role, they play a major one in the transformation of Jim and Arvay's socioeconomic level and prominence in the community. The presence of Joe, his wife Dessie, and the black Citrabelle workers in a novel ostensibly peopled by whites enables Hurston to meditate on the dynamics of interracial relationships in the South. The transformation from the folk to the bourgeois class for the Meserves occurs when Jim leaves the turpentine camps of Sawley in search of economic opportunity and autonomy in the burgeoning town of Citrabelle. Like Jody Starks, he acquires land, builds a lavish home towering above others in the area, and establishes himself as a developer and landowner. In a relatively short time, he transforms himself from a supervisor of farmworkers at orchards to the owner of his own orchards through hard work, business acumen, and proceeds from moonshine sales with the aid of his Sawley friend, Joe Kelsey, who moves to Citrabelle and briefly lives in a house behind Jim's.

Like Jody Starks of *Their Eyes Were Watching God,* Jim Meserve surrounds himself with the trappings of bourgeois success, renovating his home so it will match his newfound wealth and status. The house serves as the manifestation of the bourgeois aesthetic. The house and the renovations on their property reflect Jim's rise in status and affluence, causing a trickle-down effect upon those who work for him. Joe Kelsey's rise from folk to bourgeois mirrors that (but on a smaller scale) of Jim Meserve thanks to their moonshine business. Joe's rise from turpentine chipper to real-estate developer and businessman reveals his astuteness and capabilities. While Jim Meserve uses him to advance his own financial situation, Joe Kelsey also reaps the benefits by rising from the black folk to the bourgeoisie. Joe moves off Meserve's land, acquires his own home, and purchases an automobile, revealing his bourgeois aspirations. Although Arvay insists he move off the property when she finds out that Jim and Joe's money stems from the moonshine revenue, Joe and his family move, determined to start a new life in a different locale. With Joe Kelsey's departure, the folk aspect of Arvay's life diminishes, leaving her further cut off from her Sawley beginnings and origins.

Arvay's disenchantment with the bourgeois surroundings and her family's ascent compel her to feel confused, alone, and alienated, for she lacks the education and background to fulfill the role of a middle-class wife in a bourgeois household. When she sends Earl, her eldest and handicapped son, to Sawley because of his stalking of Felicia Corregio (whose family has replaced the Kelseys), she feels both relieved and guilty. However, when she brings him back to Citrabelle, there are disastrous results with him attacking Felicia and being shot when he resists capture. For Arvay, the death of Earl results in further estrangement from her folk roots, for his conception under the mulberry tree at her parent's home reflects her past life. As marginalized figures in the household, Arvay and Earl feel an affinity for one another as marginalized—she due to her folk roots and Earl from his physical and mental handicaps. When Earl dies, it signifies one more link in her folk roots disappearing because he was the most like her.

The estrangement between Arvay, the embodiment of the folk, and her two other children, representatives of the bourgeois, manifests itself in the relationship Arvay has with her two other children. Unlike Arvay, Angie has grown up in a middle-class home and has the opportunity to go to college and pursue a degree. When Angie becomes enamored of a northerner who works at a filling station and begins to renege on her plans to go to college, Arvay becomes upset. She feels that her daughter should have higher aspirations, considering the advantages she has been given. Arvay's prejudice against Howland reveals the presence of elitist attitudes despite her own lower socioeconomic origins. Like Jim Meserve, Hatton Howland is an ambitious and enterprising young man who desires to move up the socioeconomic ladder. He represents the New South in terms of his plans for financial success. After marrying Angie Meserve, he enters a financial arrangement with her father in which they will develop real estate for commercial and residential use by acquiring cheap land. Howland suggests developing the swamp land into residential lots, figuring he can mirror the success of individuals who have turned Miami Beach into a wealthy area full of prime real estate. Howland's astute business sense pays off, leaving Jim more time to pursue his new interest in shrimping and less time managing the orchards. The advancements in machinery over the years allow the swamp near Jim and Arvay's Citrabelle home to be cleared and readied for development. Hurston depicts the changing South and class divisions through her depiction of Jim and Howland's business venture.

Hurston depicts the rising middle-class or emerging bourgeois class of the New South in her portrayal of the Hatton development. Individuals from Old Money southern families live alongside those who recently acquired their money, like Howland. The children of these groups associate with another, creating a new class of bourgeois individuals made of Old and New Money. Arvay's children associate with individuals from the highest levels of society, leading a life of wealth, status, power, and pleasure. Through the depiction of the Howland Development, Hurston suggests the fluidity of class in the New South in which money enables individuals to move up the social ladder and scale. Her daughter and son-in-law's rise in Citrabelle society leaves her feeling alone and empty, for she feels that despite her husband's wealth she does not fit in, for she lacks the education and the refinement to function in this society. Hurston presents Kenny Meserve as a contrast to Angie in his rejection of a bourgeois lifestyle, as he quits school at the University of Florida to move to New York and play jazz and blues under the guidance of Joe Kelsey, his early musical teacher and mentor. Through him, Kenny learns to play jazz and blues and in time become a successful New York musician. The presentation of Joe Kelsey and the valorization of blues and jazz represents Hurston's valorization of black folk culture. Despite the novel's focus on white protagonists, Hurston's novel still promotes the black folk as the root of the American artistic tradition.

Hurston presents the internal conflicts that occur when individuals fail to negotiate the folk and bourgeois in her portrayal of Arvay's return to Sawley during her mother's illness and prior to her death. Arvay's bourgeois sensibilities have an impact upon her perception of the community, a town in transition. For Arvay, her sister-in-law and brother-in-law appear shabby, tawdry, and dissipated because Carl is barely able to make a living any more as a minister. When her mother dies, Arvay feels as if one of the last links with her folk past has disappeared. Also, she finds it extremely difficult to relate to her sister Raine and her brother-in-law Carl because of her new prosperity, outlook, and view on the world. She has returned home physically, mentally, and spiritually, but she actually feels more comfortable in Citrabelle in many ways. The diminishing of the way of life in her youth manifests itself in the dilapidated old house in which she grew up. Burning it represents a parting with that aspect of her youth and a recognition that, try as she might, she can never return to her folk roots. Her ascension to bourgeois status and exposure to material comforts renders her incapable of living in her childhood home again. Her romantic illusions about the folk past disappear as it burns down, and now she sees the house and her past differently. The burning of the house signifies an attempt to reconcile her past and present, the folk and the bourgeois, and the Old and New South. As a consequence, she becomes neither folk nor bourgeois but somewhere in between in her sensibilities.

Arvay destroys the home but refuses to get rid of the mulberry tree on the property. The protagonist may believe that the tree functions as a sacred site of her awakening as a woman and as a mother—the place in which she conceived Earl. Trees as sacred symbols of awakening are important in the Hurston canon and other Harlem Renaissance texts as well.[15] The mulberry tree becomes the sign of the sexual union between Arvay and Jim (outside the sanctity of marriage), and in turn, Earl's physical and mental handicaps functioned as the outward manifestation of the rape. Nevertheless, Arvay still holds the tree as a remembrance of her sexual awakening, the conception of her first child, and the day of her marriage to Jim, which initiated a new life for her. To destroy the tree would be to destroy her past, her child, her marriage, and her life.

Arvay's life follows a pattern of folk to bourgeois with a brief interlude back in the folk via her return to Sawley. She returns to Citrabelle and later heads to the Florida Coast in quest of Jim who is on a shrimping venture and who has immersed himself in the folk through his new vocation. When she returns to him after deciding that her role is that of wife and mother, Arvay enters a new world, one that resolves the folk and bourgeois as men of all races and socioeconomic classes work together on the shrimping boats, creating a multicultural community where class differences dissolve. While Arvay had felt stifled and confined in the spacious home with all the material and bourgeois comforts, she feels more comfortable and at ease upon the sea, which represents freedom, possibility, and expanding horizons for her. Hurston presents the sea as a utopian world, one in which class and color distinctions are blurred, presenting a proletarian environment. While the proletarian aesthetic does not exert itself as strongly in *Seraph on the Suwanee,* it exists in Hurston's depiction of racial unity on the sea.

For Arvay, the sea represents a time to contemplate the conflicting emotions and feelings about her marriage. Ultimately, she returns to Jim Meserve after deciding to accept a socially prescribed role as wife and mother. Her life has been one of self-sacrifice and self-denial. She not only gives birth to an angel (her daughter Angeline), but she becomes angelic and pure herself in her mind in the role as a wife and mother who desires to serve: "Her job was mothering. What more could any woman want and need? No matter how much money they had or learning, or high family, they couldn't do a bit more mothering and hovering than she could. Holy Mary, who had been blessed to mother Jesus, had been no better off than she was" (*Novels and Stories:* 919). Although the ending in which Arvay decides to give up her opportunity for freedom in order to serve Jim may seem the antithesis of the role of the empowered woman as seen in the end of *Their Eyes Were Watching God,* one could argue that Hurston's ending is not antifeminist in the sense that she posits the return to Jim as Arvay's choice. However, another plausible explanation of the ending is that Hurston's ambivalent portrayal of the marriage by depicting Arvay's feelings of oppression early on in the marriage yet presenting the character's decision to serve Jim as wife and mother to his children in a positive light may stem from Hurston's own conflicts about her marriages and subsequent divorces.

*Seraph on the Suwanee* perhaps best outlines the tension between the folk, the bourgeois, and the proletarian and Hurston's attempts to reconcile these aesthetics through her portrayal of the marriage between a poor white woman and a white man of aristocratic and genteel birth in the South. Hurston's depiction of the transition from an agrarian to an industrial-based society reveals changes between the Old and New South. Her novel consists of folk and bourgeois aesthetics, as she presents the rituals, customs, and cultures of black and white folk as well as the ambitions and aspirations of the bourgeois Old and New Money families of the New South. While a proletarian aesthetic may seem to be absent from the novel, the formal elements of the text, its plot, characterization, and theme, imply a proletarian viewpoint, primarily in Hurston's depiction of how the shrimpers defy the Jim Crow system by having blacks and whites on board the ship working side by side, and the novel's criticism of class, racial, and gender prejudice. Hurston's presentation of biblical figures in *Moses, Man of the Mountain* and white Floridians in *Seraph on the Suwanee* may function as a protest in the sense that she suggests that black artists, contrary to the expectations of white publishers and readers, can write novels with characters of diverse racial and class backgrounds.

The Hurston canon reflects the author's complex personal and professional life as she explored the lives of men, women, blacks, whites, the rich, the poor, and the middle class in her fiction. In comparison with Fauset and West, Hurston perhaps best stands as a sign and symbol of the interstices of folk, bourgeois, and proletarian aesthetics in the breadth and scope of her work and life. She came to symbolize the embodiment of the southern folk of Notasulga, Alabama, and Eatonville, Florida, through her valorization of folklore, dialect, and the oral storytelling tradition, but she also functioned as an esteemed anthropologist in the academic arenas of Howard University and Barnard College and managed to negotiate the bourgeois social circles in Harlem and Washington, D.C. Despite the racial, sexual, and class prejudice black women faced during the Harlem Renaissance era, Hurston and her contemporaries Fauset and West refused to mute their voices despite the constraints imposed by patrons, publishers, readers, and critics. Admittedly, Hurston has received more critical attention and fanfare than other black women writers of the Harlem Renaissance, including Fauset and West. Because of her self-representation as part of the folk and the presence of folkways in her work, Hurston can be more easily typed as a writer of the folk aesthetic than can Fauset or West. The privileging of the folk aesthetic by some critics may arise from a variety of reasons. To some, the folk aesthetic represents the authentic African American voice by connecting to the southern, rural, and agrarian heritage of blacks in America. To others, the folk aesthetic is more appealing than the bourgeois or proletarian because it enables them to avoid coping with the emergence of the black middle class or didactic literature that criticizes the establishment.

While Hurston's last two novels have not received as much critical attention as *Their Eyes Were Watching God* and *Jonah's Gourd Vine, Moses, Man of the Mountain* and *Seraph on the Suwanee* are arguably her most ambitious and experimental novels in their themes, content, narrative styles, and symbolism. In *Moses, Man of the Mountain* and *Seraph on the Suwanee*, Hurston experiments with writing about individuals across the span of time and space yet still valorizes the folk culture as the root of cultural and artistic traditions. Both novels can be viewed as one long extended protest against the cult of primitivism surrounding white reader and publisher expectations of the 1920s, 1930s, and 1940s for appropriate material for black literature. In addition, "Spunk," "Sweat," "The Gilded Six Bits," and "The Bone of Contention" represent Hurston's attempt to reconcile the folk, bourgeois, and proletarian aesthetics in the representations of race, class, and gender in her art and life. As a consequence, she bequeathed an outstanding literary legacy for future generations of readers and writers of African American literature.

## NOTES

1. See *Novels and Stories* (1995). The collection provides a chronology of Hurston's life that documents her field expeditions in the southern United States and the Caribbean.

2. All of these works appear in *Novels and Stories*, with the exception of "The Bone of Contention," which appears in *The Sleeper Wakes*, an anthology edited by Marcy Knopf.

3. Speisman (1991) offers insightful background information about the composition of *Jonah's Gourd Vine*.

4. Hemenway (1977) cautions against viewing *Jonah's Gourd Vine* as merely a fictionalized version of her family history. However, knowledge of the parallels in background of Hurston's parents and the protagonists in the novel provides insight into the author's exposition of race, class, and gender in the text.

5. In *There Is Confusion* (1924), *Plum Bun* (1929), *The Chinaberry Tree* (1932), and *Comedy: American Style* (1933), Jessie Fauset presents families of mixed black and white ancestry. In two of Fauset's novels the biracial heritage arises from the sexual union between a black female and a white male: Aaron Bye (slaveholder) and Judy Bye (slave) in *There Is Confusion* and Sal (a domestic) and Colonel Holloway (landowner) in *The Chinaberry Tree*. The light skin of Angela Murray in *Plum Bun* and of Olivia Cary in *Comedy: American Style* suggests the miscegenation in those families.

6. Harriet Jacobs comments on the sexual advances of her master, Dr. Flint, who sought to make her his mistress, following the practice of other white slaveholders in the area. Harper's *Iola Leroy* presents Iola as the product of a white slaveowning father and a black mother (light enough to pass for white). Iola is not aware of her black parentage until her father dies and her mother reveals the family secret of miscegenation.

7. Angela Murray from Jessie Fauset's *Plum Bun* (1929) and Mrs. Hayes-Rore and Irene Redfield from Nella Larsen's *Quicksand* (1928) and *Passing* (1929), respectively, call attention to class and color consciousness in the African American community. Both Angela Murray and Irene Redfield pass for white on occasions when they feel it would benefit them socially, economically, or professionally, while Mrs. Hayes-Rore, a "race woman," tends to be very elitist and associates mainly with individuals who have light skin and bourgeois backgrounds (Wall 1995).

8. Richard Wright's *Native Son* (1940) and Ann Petry's *The Street* (1946), demonstrate how outside forces militate against the protagonists because of their race, class, or gender.

9. Wall (1995) notes that Charlotte Osgood Mason funded several black writers such as Langston Hughes and Zora Neale Hurston during the Harlem Renaissance

10. *Moses, Man of the Mountain* (1939) contains references to the "secret police," a concept ordinarily associated with Russia during the early twentieth century. The reference to the secret police suggests a likening of oppression in biblical times with social, economic, and political repression in the Soviet Union.

11. McDowell (1993) notes that a number of texts from the Harlem Renaissance era, including Walter White's *Flight*, Nella Larsen's *Passing*, and Jessie Fauset's *Plum Bun*, treat "race as a cultural construct" (235).

12. A common theme appearing in all four of Hurston's published novels is the quest for voice. In *Their Eyes Were Watching God* (1937), Janie's husbands often seek to repress her voice in an effort to maintain control over her mind, soul, and body. The stories she tells to Pheoby represent a revolt against the muting of the female voice. Similarly, the pharaoh's daughter in *Moses, Man of the Mountain* has no real power despite her wealth and affluence. In *Seraph on the Suwanee* Arvay Meserve struggles to find her voice in an oppressive marriage in which her husband sees her duty as service to him at the cost of her own needs and desires.

13. One strategy Hurston employs in *Moses, Man of the Mountain* to imbue it with folk and Afrocentric elements is through the characterization of Moses as a hoodoo man (*Novels and Stories*: 443). His feats are portrayed as acts of conjure, akin to the rootsworker or two-headed doctors of folk medicine and folkways.

14. Hurston dedicates *Seraph on the Suwanee* (1948) to Majorie Kinnan Rawlings, which suggests an admiration for the work of the critically and commercially acclaimed writer, whose *Yearling* and *Cross Creek* are set in Florida and imbued with local color, much like *Seraph on the Suwanee* (1948), according to Lowe (1994).

15. Trees play a significant role in Hurston's *Their Eyes Were Watching God* as well as *Seraph on the Suwanee*. Janie's quest to find a bee for her blossom leads her into relationships with Logan Killicks, Jody Starks, and Tea Cake as she seeks ecstatic union with the opposite sex in *Their Eyes Were Watching God* (1937) after seeing bees pollinate pear tree blossoms. Jessie Fauset also utilizes the tree as an important symbol of sexual awakening in *The Chinaberry Tree* (1932), where the chinaberry symbolizes the romance between Sal and Colonel Holloway, their southern heritage, and the birth of their child Laurentine.

## REFERENCES

Bell, Bernard. 1987. *The Afro-American Novel and Its Tradition.* Amherst: University of Massachusetts Press.

Davis, Angela Y. 1981. *Women, Race and Class.* New York: Random House.

Du Bois, W. E. B. 1989. *The Souls of Black Folk.* New York: Penguin.

Felton, Estelle. 1993. "Review of Jonah's Gourd Vine, by Zora Neale Hurston." Pp. 4–5 in *Zora Neale Hurston: Critical Perspectives Past and Present*, ed. Henry Louis Gates. New York: Amistad.

Ferguson, Sally Ann. 1987. "West, Dorothy." *Dictionary of Literary Biography: Afro-American Writers from the Harlem Renaissance to 1940*, eds. Trudier Harris and Thadious Davis. Detroit: Gale.

Hedden, Worth Tuttle. 1993. "Review of Seraph on the Suwanee, by Zora Neale Hurston." Pp. 35–36 in *Zora Neale Hurston: Critical Perspectives Past and Present*, ed. Henry Louis Gates. New York: Amistad. Originally published in 1948.

Hemenway, Robert. 1977. *Zora Neale Hurston: A Literary Biography.* Urbana: University of Illinois Press.

Howard, Lillie P. 1993. "Seraph on the Suwanee." Pp. 267–79 in *Zora Neale Hurston: Critical Perspectives Past and Present*, ed. Henry Louis Gates. New York: Amistad.

Hurston, Zora Neale. 1928. "How It Feels to Be Colored Me." *World Tomorrow,* May, 215–16.

———. 1950. "What White Publishers Won't Print." *Negro Digest,* April, 85–89. Originally published in 1928.

———. 1995. *Folklore, Memoirs, and Other Writings*, ed. Cheryl Wall. New York: Library of America.

———. 1995. *Novels and Stories.* New York: Library of America.

Hutchinson, George. 1995. *The Harlem Renaissance in Black and White.* Cambridge, Mass.: Harvard University Press.

Hutchinson, Percy. 1993. "Review of Moses, Man of the Mountain, by Zora Neale Hurston." Pp. 27–28 in *Zora Neale Hurston: Critical Perspectives Past and Present*, ed. Henry Louis Gates. New York: Amistad. Originally published in 1939.

Knopf, Marcy, ed. 1993. *The Sleeper Wakes: Harlem Renaissance Stories by Women.* New Brunswick, N.J.: Rutgers University Press.

Locke, Alain. 1993. "Review of Their Eyes Were Watching God, by Zora Neale Hurston." P. 18 in *Zora Neale Hurston: Critical Perspectives Past and Present*, ed. Henry Louis Gates. New York: Amistad. Originally published in 1938.

Lowe, John. 1994. *Jump at the Sun: Zora Neale Hurston's Cosmic Comedy*. Urbana: University of Illinois Press.

Marsh-Lockett, Carol P. 1999. "Whatever Happened to Jochebed? Motherhood As Marginality in Zora Neale Hurston's Seraph on the Suwanee." Pp. 100–110 in *Southern Mothers: Fact and Fictions in Southern Women's Writing*, eds. Warren Nagueyalti and Sally Wolff. Baton Rouge: Louisiana State University Press.

McDowell, Deborah E. 1993. "Lines of Descent/Dissenting Lines." Pp. 230–40 in *Zora Neale Hurston: Critical Perspectives Past and Present*, ed. Henry Louis Gates. New York: Amistad.

Petry, Ann. 1946. *The Street*. Boston: Hougton Mifflin.

Russell, Kathy, Midge Wilson, and Ronald Hall. 1992. *The Color Complex: The Politics of Skin Color Among African Americans*. New York: Harcourt Brace Jovanovich.

Slaughter, Frank G. 1993. "Review of *Seraph on the Suwanee*." Pp. 34–35 in *Zora Neale Hurston: Critical Perspectives Past and Present*, ed. Henry Louis Gates. New York: Amistad. Originally published in 1948.

Speisman, Barbara. 1991. "Voodoo As Symbol in *Jonah's Gourd Vine*." Pp. 86–93 in *Zora in Florida*, eds. Steve Glassman and Kathryn Lee Seidel. Orlando: University of Central Florida Press.

Untermeyer, Louis. 1993. "Review of *Moses, Man of the Mountain*, by Zora Neale Hurston." Pp. 26–27 in *Zora Neale Hurston: Critical Perspectives Past and Present*, ed. Henry Louis Gates. New York: Amistad. Originally published in 1939.

Wall, Cheryl. 1995. *Women of the Harlem Renaissance*. Bloomington: Indiana University Press.

Wallace, Margaret. 1993. "Review of *Jonah's Gourd Vine*, by Zora Neale Hurston." Pp. 8–9 in *Zora Neale Hurston: Critical Perspectives Past and Present*, ed. Henry Louis Gates. New York: Amistad. Originally published in 1934.

Washington, Mary Helen. 1993. "'I Love the Way Janie Crawford Left Her Husbands': Emergent Female Hero." Pp. 98–109 in *Zora Neale Hurston: Critical Perspectives Past and Present*, ed. Henry Louis Gates. New York: Amistad.

Wintz, Cary D. 1988. *Black Culture and the Harlem Renaissance*. Houston: Rice University Press.

Wright, Richard. 1940. *Native Son*. New York: Harper and Row.

———. 1993. "Review of *Their Eyes Were Watching God*, by Zora Neale Hurston." Pp. 16–17 in *Zora Neale Hurston: Critical Perspectives Past and Present*, ed. Henry Louis Gates. New York: Amistad. Originally published in 1937.

# 3

# A Closet Revolutionary:
# The Politics of Representation
# in the Fiction of Dorothy West

In 1948, it seemed as if Dorothy West would become a household word when editors of the *Ladies Home Journal* contemplated serializing *The Living Is Easy* in the national women's magazine. However, the editorial board changed its mind, possibly because they feared that white-owned companies would pull advertising from the magazine if they featured a novel by a black woman. Furthermore, there may also have been a sense that white readers would object to the novel's focus on an African American family. Dorothy West notes, "The magazine was very enthusiastic about serializing the novel, but when their board of editors met—Blackwell's, they were powerful people—they decided against it. I have always felt that they feared the loss of advertising revenue by serializing a novel by a black woman about black people" (McDowell 1987: 276). West's interpretation of the *Ladies Home Journal's* decision not to include her novel in their magazine suggests the politics of race, class, and gender, which militated against black female writers in the twentieth century.[1]

Shortly after writing *The Living Is Easy,* West began another novel, tentatively titled *Where the Wild Grape Grows,* but the publisher, Houghton Mifflin, refused to accept it for publication. West contends that the publishing company feared the novel would have a limited audience "Because it was about middle class blacks" (McDowell 1987: 278). Later, West began a third novel about black middle-class life, incorporating part of *Where the Wild Grape Grows* into *The Wedding* (1995). Perceptions of what constitutes "authentic" black literature among white editors and publishers and readers militated against her in the late 1940s; however, conceptions of black aesthetics among blacks in the 1960s militated against the completion and submission of *The Wedding.* As Dorothy West notes, "It coincided with the Black Revolution, when many blacks believed that middle-class blacks were Uncle Toms. I feared, then, what the reviewers

Photograph of Dorothy West from the Dorothy West
Collection in the Special Collections at Boston University.

would say" (McDowell 1987: 279). Ironically, the Black Power movement, which
sought to liberate blacks from social, political, and economic oppression, created
a climate in which Dorothy West felt compelled to refrain from completing or
actively pursuing a publisher for *The Wedding*. West's nearly half-a-century
space between publication of *The Living Is Easy* (1948) and *The Wedding* (1995)
signifies the complexities of African American literature and the debate over
which aesthetics—folk, bourgeois, or proletarian—should take preeminence at
a given time.

The perception of West as a privileged middle-class Bostonian with the economic resources to own a summer home on Martha's Vineyard and her depiction of the black bourgeois class in her fiction presented obstacles to the publication, reception, and evaluation of *The Living Is Easy* and *The Wedding*. Her

experiences with publishers echo those of Jessie Fauset and Zora Neale Hurston in the 1930s.[2] The label *bourgeois* ascribed to West is incomplete, for she incorporates all aspects of the triangle in her work, which presents a variety of socioeconomic classes. Like her predecessors, Jessie Fauset and Zora Neale Hurston, West's work presents a multiplicity of voices and aesthetics. West truly functions as a closet revolutionary, for while on the surface her work and her life seem to reflect the black bourgeoisie, her novels, short stories, and essays reflect a proletarian stance.

Born in 1907 in Boston, Massachusetts, West was the daughter of Isaac Christopher West and Rachel Pease Benson. Both her parents came from folk backgrounds; her father was born a slave in Virginia. He eventually relocated to Springfield, Massachusetts, and his entrepreneurial bent prompted him to open an ice-cream parlor. After moving to Boston, he established a business as a fruit importer, where he achieved fame as the "Black Banana King." Her father would later serve as the model for the character Bart Judson in *The Living Is Easy*, who moves from rags to riches as a black businessman of folk descent and bourgeois aspirations. Her mother, too, derived from a folk experience. A native of Camden, South Carolina, she moved to Springfield at the prompting of a teacher who feared that her light complexion would make her prey to sexual predators. Although she may have visited Isaac West's ice-cream parlor while living in Springfield, the two probably did not meet until years later in Boston, where they married. Their courtship reverberates throughout the plotline of *The Living Is Easy*, where the protagonist Cleo Judson leaves her southern roots to migrate north in search for a better life. West's parents influenced her life and writing greatly, and the fusion of folk and bourgeois aspects of her background enabled her to view the world in dualistic terms. Similarly, her mother fuses folk and bourgeois elements in her background. As the daughter of an ex-slave, West's mother has the folk experience of growing up in the rural South and playing with homemade toys and wearing clothes sewn by her mother. Nevertheless, the family's bourgeois aesthetic manifests itself in sending the children to school so they could be educated (Ferguson 1987).

A bright young girl, West began attending school at the age of four and later attended both the Martin School and the Boston Girl's Latin School. According to an interview with Katrine Dalsgard, West emphasized that she was the only black student in the Boston Latin School. The other girls were "polite" to her. West notes, "All the other students were white, middle-class girls. I don't know whether they liked me or not, but they were polite" (Dalsgard 1993: 35). Nevertheless, she graduated in 1923, and later studied at Columbia University. Despite her privileged educational opportunities, West never lost sight of her roots, and her childhood continued to be a source of inspiration and meditation for her. In "Rachel,"[3] West chronicles her own childhood, which consisted of an extended family living in a large four-story home much like the Judsons in *The Living Is Easy*. West cites her relatives, who came from a variety of socioeconomic levels, dispositions, and colors, as the roots of her literary art: "The house that I grew up in was four-storied, but we were an extended family, continually adding new members, and the perpetual joke was, if we lived in the Boston Museum, we'd still need one more room. Surrounded by all these different personalities, each one wanting to be first among equals, I knew I wanted to be a writer. Living with them was like living inside a story" (*The Richer, the Poorer*: 167). West's commentary reveals a diversity in her background, which may be partly responsible for the variety of races, socioeconomic levels, and geographical spaces in her fiction. Her early childhood memories suggest that the variety in her family background may fuel the plethora of aesthetics, including the folk, bourgeois, and proletarian.

Similarly, in "Fond Memories of a Black Childhood," West notes that despite her parent's southern folk origins, they managed to acquire the wealth and status of the black northern bourgeois class, making them one of the first black families to obtain a house on Martha's Vineyard. By revealing the origins of her family, she valorizes the southern folk as the root of African American culture. West presents the diversity among the black bourgeois class in her reminiscences of her childhood on Martha's Vineyard, a location that later serves as a backdrop for *The Wedding* (1995). West presents an insider's view of the black bourgeoisie, through her recollections of important black visitors to the island such as Harry T. Burleigh, a composer. To West, Burleigh represents the bourgeois in his education and wealth. He suggests a connection to the folk through his research on spirituals. West presents Burleigh as an exemplar of the reconciliation between the elements. Other visitors include Harlem congressman Adam Clayton Powell and Judge James S. Watson, the first black judge in New York, who were a type of black aristocracy on the island. West's chronicle of her childhood reveals the folk and working-class roots of the black bourgeoisie on Martha's Vineyard, as well as providing insight into the settings, themes, and characterizations in her exploration of racial, class, and sexual politics.

West's formative years shaped her worldview, providing her with a multitude of materials and sources for her short and longer fiction. Her literary talent bloomed early; when she was fourteen years old she won a prize for best short story of the week from the *Boston Post*. When she was seventeen, she and Helene Johnson, her cousin, applied to the *Opportunity* magazine writing contest, and the two young women went to New York City for the annual awards dinner. West's story "The Typewriter" and Hurston's "Muttsy" both won a second-place award in the writing competition. "The Typewriter," her first national publication, appeared in the June 1926 issue of *Opportunity*. It blends realism, naturalism, and modernism in its depiction of an African American man who feels disenchanted with his limited opportunities. He dreams of a better life, which his daughter furnishes for him by typing letters that the protagonist dictates. In the letters, he portrays himself as a wealthy tycoon. It was not only *Opportunity* magazine's panelist of judges who recognized West's emerging talent, but her story appeared in *The Best Short Stories of 1926* (Ferguson 1987). Initially, while living in New York City, West stayed at the Harlem YWCA, but she later sublet Hurston's apartment while Hurston traveled around the South collecting folklore. West and Hurston remained on friendly terms. West recalls in a 1988 interview: "I won a little prize in *Opportunity*'s short story contest. I was seventeen and a half and Zora was twenty-five, and we split the prize. I can imagine how Zora felt: 'Who was this up-start seventeen-and-a-half with whom I split this?' But in the end she loved me. I got a beautiful letter from her once. She is writing to both of us—my cousin and me. She calls us 'dear children'" (Dalsgard 1993: 30). West's description of her relationship with Hurston suggests that Hurston could be supportive to younger female writers, even adopting a motherly tone with the younger West and Helene Johnson, her cousin. In contrast, Hurston's relationship with male writers could be described as negative and unsupportive.

West also knew Carl Van Vechten, who was quite successful in assisting many budding African American writers. Her mother's friend managed to arrange a meeting between West and Van Vechten, a prominent white critic, photographer, patron of the arts, and author of the best-selling novel *Nigger Heaven* (1926). Van Vechten provided West with advice on writing and thus proved influential in her development as a literary artist (Ferguson 1987). Hurston arranged for West to meet Fannie Hurst, whom Hurston had worked for as a personal assistant. Hurst achieved fame for her novel *Imitation of Life*, which dealt with the friendship between a black woman and a white woman. Although the relationship between West and Hurst was short-lived, Hurst aided West's career by enabling her to meet Elisabeth Marbury. Marbury would become West's agent, and after her death in 1933, George Bye would assume that role (Ferguson 1987).

West discovered the difficulties of being a black female writer in the early part of the twentieth century. Although black writers were somewhat in vogue, many magazine publishers would include only a few in each issue. She found outlets in the *Saturday Evening Quill* (Adams 2001). West placed two stories in the publication, including "An Unimportant Man" in 1928 and "Prologue to a Life" in 1929. West proved to be highly versatile. She and a friend, the novelist Wallace Thurman, won roles in the play *Porgy* (by DuBose and Dorothy Heyward, not the later Gershwin/Heyward folk opera) in 1927. The popular theatrical production moved to London in 1929, and West traveled along with the play. Unfortunately, London audiences found the play's dialect difficult to understand and the theatrical company returned to New York (Ferguson 1987).

Like Thurman in his novel *The Blacker the Berry* (1929), West explored the color and caste system, criticizing intraracial color and class prejudice and analyzing the harmful effects on the collective psyche of African Americans. The friendship with Thurman played an important role in her life and in her evolution as a writer. In "Elephant's Dance," which was first published in *Black World* (1970), West's writes a moving and compelling portrait of Thurman. Her account of Thurman's life is particularly important in light of their special relationship during the 1920s and 1930s. Ferguson (1987) notes that West saw Thurman as "the most symbolic figure of the Literary Renaissance in Harlem" (189–90). Noting how Thurman's own dark skin and awareness of color and class hierarchies within the black community influence his novel *The Blacker the Berry,* West's essay "Elephant's Dance" notes his criticism of bourgeois black society, which undoubtedly influenced her depiction of the color complex in her fiction. She writes, "He hated Negro society, and since dark skins have never been the fashion among Negro upper classes, the feeling was occasionally mutual" (*The Richer, the Poorer:* 219), She presents Thurman's life as an example of talented African American artists whose life and art reflect the realities of racism in twentieth-century America.

As many of her contemporaries sought creative freedom abroad, West traveled outside the United States for new experiences. In addition to traveling to London with *Porgy* in 1929, West also traveled to the Soviet Union in 1932 with Langston Hughes and twenty-one other African Americans. Their mission included making a film called *Black and White,* which dealt with race relations in the United States. Controversy surrounded the trip, including rumors that the Russians were trying to recruit African Americans into the Communist party. The ill-fated film project folded for a number of reasons, including a Russian-authored script that failed to capture the realities of the African American experience, and perhaps even pressure from an American who threatened to withdraw funding for a dam in Russia if the film were actually made (Ferguson 1987). West claimed in an interview: "Understandably, Russia had to have the dam, and they chose the dam" (Dalsgard 1993: 35). In her essay "An Adventure in Moscow" (which appeared in the *Vineyard Gazette* in 1985), West meditates on her experiences in Russia. She was sympathetic to the plight of the Russians who canceled the movie project because they needed the skills of the engineer for their dam. Despite the fact that the film project collapsed, West and her compatriots like Hughes remained in Russia for a while. While in Russia, West stayed nearly a year longer. Of her experiences in Russia, West noted, "That was my most carefree year. Then my father died, and I became a responsible person. But I'm very grateful that I had that happy year. I think that's why I liked Russia so much. I was carefree there. When I came back, I had the responsibility of one thing and another" (Dalsgard 1993: 36).

Upon returning to the United States, West decided to start her own magazine, called *Challenge,* with $40 (Ferguson 1987). As Ferguson notes, "This was the first little magazine of the depression that sought to bridge the divisions among the older aesthetes like Alain Locke and James Weldon Johnson, her own bohemian Renaissance circle, and the emerging social realists like the Chicago group led by Richard Wright" (192). In an interview, West stated, "The reason I started it was that in New York I had lived fast, and I thought I'd wasted time. I wanted to give the younger generation a chance. Somebody who was criticizing me said that in spite of my intentions everybody in the magazine was old.

But my contributors were the only people I knew, and I had to get the magazine out" (Dalsgard 1993: 38). Many of the early contributors included her friends and relatives like Arna Bontemps, Hurston, Helene Johnson, Claude McKay, and Langston Hughes. The magazine was intended to be a launching point for new and unknown writers, but it often featured more established individuals. The magazine, which premiered in 1934, folded by 1937 from poor sales and a lack of good-quality submissions.

The short-lived *New Challenge* had an editorial staff of West, Richard Wright, and Marian Minus. Only one issue appeared, in fall 1937, before the magazine also folded. Wright's "Blueprint for Negro Writing" appears in *New Challenge*, sounding a proletarian protest for literature that would connect with the masses and challenge the status quo (Ferguson 1987). Her foray as an editor over, West received a job as a welfare investigator in New York. Despite her bourgeois upbringing, the position gave her insight into the black working class of Harlem and the folk experience.

West worked as a welfare investigator for a year and a half and later became employed with the Works Progress Administration Federal Writers Project. Those essays remained unpublished during her lifetime, but they recently were reintroduced to the public in *A Renaissance in Harlem: Lost Voices of an African American Community*, edited by Lionel C. Bascom (1999). She wrote more than twenty short stories that appeared in the *New York Daily News* between 1940 and 1960. In 1945 West moved from New York to Martha's Vineyard, where she would live until her death in 1998. While there she would write *The Living Is Easy* and *The Wedding* (Ferguson 1987). She also regularly contributed stories and articles to the *Vineyard Gazette*. In the 1960s a more militant tone in African American writing, and her association with the black bourgeoisie, would cause some African American critics to write her off as passé and apolitical.

Contrary to the common belief, West's life actually represents a blending of the folk, the bourgeois, and the proletarian from her own family history and her experiences as a welfare investigator and her role as editor of *Challenge* and *New Challenge* . She managed to align herself with a variety of powerful voices in African American literature, forming friendships with such writers as Richard Wright, Countee Cullen, and Zora Neale Hurston. In assessing her legacy, one should note that in her life and art she bridged the gap between the triangular configuration of aesthetics, calling into question the idea that writers can easily fall into solely one category. Because of the miscategorization of West, she, of the three authors under investigation here, remains the one least written about and least recognized for her contribution to the Harlem Renaissance and to the tradition of black women's writing in America.

Surprisingly little serious critical attention has been devoted to West's short fiction. They convey powerful themes of racial, color, and gender lines, revealing her earlier explorations of folk, bourgeois, and proletarian themes. In "The Typewriter" (which appeared in *Opportunity* in 1926), West depicts the bourgeois aspirations of a working-class man with a menial job in Boston who imagines himself as a great entrepreneur via the letters he artfully composes for his daughter, who is training as a typist. Like Cleo and Bart Judson from *The Living Is Easy* and Isaac Coles from *The Wedding,* the protagonist has a southern folk background. He leaves the South for the North in search of a better life, only to find that his race and class cause the American dream to elude him. West's depiction of Jones as a transplanted southerner struggling to make a living in the industrial North stems from the history of black migration from the South to the North in search of economic opportunity. As Willis (1987) notes, "Although many forsook the rigors of sharecropping for the hope of a better life up north, not all attained Henry Ford's promise of full employment and five dollars a day. Far more black immigrants than white have discovered that the city is another name for a sporadically employed labor pool" (5).

The protagonist's current socioeconomic level as a janitor stands in opposition to his former dreams and ambition of achieving black middle-class status. His race and lack of formal education prevent him from rising socially or economically. The typewriter he rents for his daughter Millie, who wants to be a secretary or administrative assistant, functions as a vehicle by which the protagonist and his family can move from working-class to bourgeois status. On another level, the father's practice of dictating letters to his daughter in the guise of an affluent, upwardly mobile man enables the protagonist to fulfill his bourgeois desires in his imagination. He spins tales in which he transforms himself from a janitor into a successful businessman. His imagination allows him to attain his bourgeois dreams and goals. In the letters, he alters his language from rural, southern black dialect to his conception of standard American English: "He was growing very careful of his English. Occasionally—and it must be admitted, ashamedly—he made surreptitious ventures into the dictionary" (*The Richer, the Poorer:* 15). West, like Fauset and Hurston, presents dialect as the marker of the folk as opposed to the bourgeois class. For the janitor, changing his occupation and language in the letters offers him entrée into the bourgeois class. As he becomes more engrossed in the game, he carries the letters and their answers in his pocket and even mails them to herself, so that he can feel important and rise above his menial job.

As the typewriter becomes his lifeline and vehicle for bourgeois status, he becomes increasingly dependent upon the machine. When his daughter Millie receives a $12-a-week job as a secretary and returns the typewriter to the rental company, she "remains oblivious to the rewards her pretense provides for her father and does not perceive that its end causes his death" (Ferguson 1987: 188). The loss of the typewriter represents the final end of his bourgeois dreams which sustained him over the years. Miller (2000) notes, "Deprived now of his dream to live out fantasies through his daughter, robbing her of self-determination in her own life, he dies in anguish" (89). The loss of the typewriter, which symbolized his bourgeois aspirations, kills him in effect, for he no longer desires to live the life of a janitor struggling to make ends meet in America at the turn of the century. "The Typewriter" reflects the folk aesthetic in the depiction of the janitor with southern folk roots who migrates north in search of the American dream. It presents the bourgeois aesthetic in its depiction of his dreams of becoming a successful businessman and rising socioeconomic level. The proletarian aesthetic manifests itself in the outcome of the story, in which West reveals how social, economic, racial, and class discrimination harms individuals, resulting in their deaths when they cannot overcome these obstacles. In "The Typewriter," West blends various aesthetics to render the African American experience.

Whereas the typewriter signifies entrance into bourgeois society in "The Typewriter," a motion picture projector functions as the key to a family's ascension socially and economically in "The Five Dollar Bill." In this bildungsroman, West presents the folk aesthetic through the depiction of a working-class black family, the bourgeois aesthetic in the mother and daughter's quest for wealth and social status, and the proletarian aesthetic in the criticism of social and economic inequities in America. Set in an unidentified northern city, the story reveals the tensions caused by lack of money and material possessions in a working-class family. Modeling herself after a bourgeois businessman, Judy, a little girl, sets out to earn money for the family, which she plans to give to her mother to make her happy. She sees a business opportunity advertised in the newspaper. By buying and reselling reproductions of famous paintings, she can earn enough money to purchase a motion picture projector (from the firm she gets the paintings from) and charge admission to show movies. Although Judy proves successful at selling the paintings, her mother's greed, materialism, and self-interest override her daughter's interests. She claims to have sent Judy's payments for the picture reproductions, when in reality she had given them to her bourgeois college boyfriend.

In the depiction of the mother whose bourgeois concerns overshadow the love for her child and the child's best interest, West echoes Fauset's Olivia Cary in *Comedy: American Style*, whose greed and materialism override the well-being of her offspring. When Judy receives a letter from the owner of the company she acquired the paintings from informing her that he never received payment for the reproductions—which menacingly includes a newspaper clipping showing a girl who was being arrested—she reacts in fear and horror. Her suspicion of adults leads her to fear even asking if she will indeed go to jail. Judy's loss of innocence centers on the exposure to the greed of her mother. West's negative portrayal of the mother's greed is a criticism of bourgeois aspirations at the expense of others. West presents the folk through her portrayal of a working-class black family, and the proletarian aesthetic in her criticism of class prejudices. "The Five Dollar Bill," like "The Typewriter," reflects the futility of believing a machine or an object can lead to fulfillment.

In "An Unimportant Man" (which appeared in the *Saturday Evening Quill* in 1928) West blends folk, bourgeois, and proletarian aesthetics in a compelling bildungsroman about the life of Zeb Jenkins, a southern black man of the folk, who strives for bourgeois status in the North by becoming an attorney.

Although the protagonist experiences contentment in the southern folk experience, as a youth his mother's bourgeois ambitions control his life as she insists he move to the North and study law. Nevertheless, his failure to assimilate his southern folkways in the northern classroom prohibits him from advancing in law school, unlike his classmate Parker, who flourishes in the school environment despite his folk origins. Through the depiction of Parker, West presents a representative of the folk successively rising in society and obtaining bourgeois status. As in "The Envelope" and "The Typewriter," West uses a letter as the avenue to bourgeois status. When Zeb receives a letter indicating he has passed the bar exam, he feels elated. Convinced he now can practice as a lawyer, he forbids his daughter Essie from using dialect because of the family's hopes of a bourgeois status. Her mother too desires her to fulfill bourgeois expectations of a young black woman by attending college rather than becoming a dancer, which she associates with the folk and views as impractical for young black women. Zeb feels ambivalent, for while he wanted to encourage his daughter's dreams he, like Junius Murray in Jessie Fauset's *Plum Bun*, recognizes the obstacles black female artists face in a racist and sexist society. When he realizes he cannot practice law and remains part of the folk or working class, he decides his daughter must attend college and give up her dreams of being an artist. Ferguson (1987) notes that "Zeb's decision to control Essie's life evidences his willingness to repeat the same mistakes with her that his own mother made with him" (189). Although he has good intentions, Zeb seeks to destroy the artistic desire and impulse in his daughter by viewing it as an unworthy endeavor in a difficult racial climate. The title of the story belies itself, for Zeb is important in the sense that he represents countless numbers of transplanted southern blacks in search of the American Dream. Parker represents the bourgeois class through his attainment of a law degree and middle-class respectability. Zeb represents the proletarian aesthetic in his desire to put aside individual desires for the benefit of the race.

Money functions again as a central concern in "Funeral" (which appeared in the *Saturday Evening Quill* in 1930), a bildungsroman in that it charts the child's growing maturity and awareness of mortality, and a kunstlerroman in its depiction of the child using the experience as a stimulus to become a writer and transcend the pain by transforming it into artistic expression. The story recalls the impressions of Judy, the protagonist, who decides she wants to be a writer after her initiation into mortality through her uncle's death. In "Funeral," West criticizes the bourgeois aesthetic in her depiction of the preacher's sermon on Uncle Eben's death. During his sermon he posits, "Why ain't he having a big funeral in some dicty church 'stead of you asking somebody you never seen before to come round here? Cause none of you thought he was worth a high-falutin funeral" (*The Richer, the Poorer:* 68). West reveals how one man transforms a family's loss into personal gain by equating love for a deceased relative with the expense one undertakes in their funeral and the payment to the preacher. Ironically, the preacher espouses a proletarian aesthetic to fulfill his bourgeois aspirations in an attempt to glean more money from the relatives of Uncle Eben. He advocates blacks overturning society's hierarchy and structures, pointing out that "We got to organize! Us that is on top had got to help us at the bottom. But what uppity Negro will?" (*The Richer, the Poorer*: 68). Despite his plea for black unity and the toppling of rigid race and class structures, the preacher's motivation stems mostly from self interest rather than the uplift of all African Americans.

West presents the folk, bourgeois, and proletarian aesthetics by chronicling one child's initiation into death. The experience enables Judy to perceive the color, class, and community conflicts within and outside the African American community as revealed through her family. By presenting the action through the eyes of a child, West reveals the absurdity of adult greed, materialism, and self-interest in family relationships at a time of death. Like "The Typewriter," "The Five Dollar Bill," "Jack in the Pot," and "The Richer, the Poorer," "Funeral" criticizes racism and class prejudice, revealing how they divide the African American community

In "Jack in the Pot," which won the *New York Daily News* Blue Ribbon Prize in 1940, West presents a moral dilemma over whether one should spend jackpot winnings on oneself or others in need as a vehicle for meditating on class and community. The story, told from the point of view of a third-person omniscient narrator, centers on the Edmunds, a black family formerly of bourgeois status, who have become part of the folk once their stationery store goes out of business in the Great Depression. The story's premise is partly grounded in history and fact. As West points out in an interview, "Maybe forty or fifty years ago, during the Depression, if you went to the movies, you might get a chance to win something. The woman [Mrs. Edmunds] in the story, which I call my statement on poverty, won fifty dollars" (McDowell 1987: 274–75). In another interview, West notes that Mrs. Edmunds was inspired by her mother's friend, who won fifty dollars in a jackpot once (Dalsgard 1993). When one of the janitor's children (from the Edmunds's apartment complex) dies and he needs fifty dollars for the funeral, Mrs. Edmunds refuses to provide him with financial assistance.

Mrs. Edmund's guilt begins to override her self-interest, and she buys a dress for the baby to be buried in with her jackpot winnings, but it comes too late. The father has given the child's body to the medical students at a local college for experiments because he cannot afford a funeral. Ironically, the money she so jealously hoards proves of no benefit to her as her guilt-ridden conscience will not let her use it. West presents the futility of greed and materialism and the detrimental effects upon individuals in "Jack in the Pot." Mrs. Edmunds's unwillingness to share her good fortune causes her heartbreak in the end when her guilt prevents her from spending the remainder of the money. West presents a cross section of African American society and aesthetics as Mr. Johnson, a janitor in the Edmunds's apartment complex, exemplifies the folk in education, speech, and socioeconomic level. The Edmunds, on the other hand, represent a black bourgeois family fallen on hard economic times. The proletarian aesthetic manifests itself in West's moving portrayal of a family on relief and the importance of being generous in aiding and assisting others when in need.

Similarly, West meditates on class and race in "Mammy," set in New York. (It appeared in *Opportunity* in 1940.) West presents characters from a variety of backgrounds in the story (told from the point of view of a third-person omniscient narrator). The characters include a black middle-class and college-educated social worker and an affluent white family who hired a mammy, and the black southern mammy herself, a representative of the folk. West's portrayal of the mammy as a reservoir of strength and fortitude echoes Fauset's treatment of the black domestic in "Mary Elizabeth" and *Plum Bun*. The story centers on a black caseworker who must interview the former employer of a black domestic to determine whether the elderly black woman is unable to work and in need of financial aid.

West analyzes intraracial and interracial class and color conflicts in her depiction of the social worker's relationships with others. The social worker bristles at the attitude of an black elevator boy who treats her with a lack of respect when she tries to enter the elevator of the Central Park West apartment of the domestic's former employers. When the social worker meets the Colemans, the employers of the domestic, she learns that the elderly woman quit after Mrs. Coleman's daughter had a stillborn child. Although the caseworker feels the family views Mammy as a possession and not as a person, she feels obligated to situate the elderly black woman with the family because of the lack of job opportunities during the Great Depression. Mammy's folk dialect, lack of formal education, and profession distinguish her from the caseworker, who represents bourgeois middle-class black society. When Mammy claims she quit because the Colemans practiced infanticide, the caseworker attributes her statement to the displacement of the southern folk in the urban North: "Her small grievances against Mrs. Coleman had magnified themselves in her mind until she could make this illogical accusation of infanticide as compensation for her homesickness for the folkways of the South. Her move to Harlem bore this out" (*The Richer, the Poorer:* 51). However, when the caseworker spots a photo of a young woman who looks like Mrs. Coleman and discovers it is a photo of mammy's daughter, she reacts in astonishment and denial at the possibility of miscegenation in the family.

In "Mammy," West presents a story whose ending can be interpreted a number of ways. If Mammy is Mrs. Coleman's mother, then it's possible that the baby was killed for having brown skin, which would prevent them from passing as a white bourgeois family. In this sense, Mammy represents the southern folk roots of the family and its blackness. West's story serves as an indictment of colorism within the African American community and the history of miscegenation in the United States. The proletarian aesthetic manifests itself in West's criticism of racism and class consciousness in America. The story also refutes assessments of West as a writer only devoted to exploring the black bourgeoisie or Talented Tenth in her fiction. Here, in "Mammy," she draws a compelling portrait of a working-class black woman.

"The Penny" (which appeared in the *New York Daily News* in 1941) focuses on a working-class African American family struggling to make ends meet in an unidentified northern city. Appropriating the narrative strategy of the bildungsroman, West centers the story on a little boy who lies about abuse at home in order to get a penny from a class-conscious and bourgeois neighbor named Miss Halsey, who dislikes the folk. Mistaking a bruise on his face—which he acquired when he lost a penny his father gave him to buy candy—for a sign of child abuse, Miss Halsey offers to give him a penny if he will admit abuse. He lies to obtain the money. In "The Penny," West depicts class stratification within the African American community as a means of meditating on the folk and bourgeois classes. The penny represents candy, money, and the economics of exchange, for the boy feeds his penchant for candy and Miss Halsey satisfies her stereotypical notion of the poor as violent and abusive. The proletarian aesthetic is implied through the dire consequences of Miss Halsey's prejudice against the folk.

Similarly, in "The Richer, the Poorer," West deconstructs wealth and poverty. West defines the two terms in relation to spiritual and emotional rather than material goods. The title itself meditates on the folk ("the poorer") and the bourgeois ("the richer"). West presents the competing folk and bourgeois aesthetics in her depiction of two sisters—Lottie, who has material wealth, and Bess, who has lived an emotionally fulfilled life. Like Mrs. Edmunds in "Jack in the Pot," Lottie attempts to hoard her money in an effort to gain middle-class status and prosperity. As a young woman, she initially intends to use money from her cashier job for college and then decides a steady income is worth more than the gamble of succeeding or failing in college. Although her sister Bess falls in love and marries a musician, Lottie eschews marriage in favor of working because she views housekeeping as a thankless job emotionally, spiritually, and financially. Operating on a money-based aesthetic, she fails to recognize until it is too late her spiritual, emotional, and psychological bankruptcy. West presents the folk aesthetic though Bess and her husband Harry, whose connection to the folk manifests itself in his love of jazz. When Harry dies years later, he has very little in material goods to leave his wife, but she does have memories of concert trips to Europe, his horn, and good times. Harry's horn signifies his life as a jazz musician and ties to his folk roots. In West's depiction of the reunion scene between the two sisters, she reveals how a folk aesthetic often surpasses a bourgeois one. When Bess, the sister, returns to the United States to live with Lottie, she remains unimpressed with her sister's home, furniture, and lavish meal. Her stories of her life, however, reveal that rather than a life of poverty, she has lived one rich with experience. In Lottie's quest for bourgeois status, she saved and saved but never traveled or engaged in meaningful relationships with others. However, Bess, her sister, notes it is never too late to experience the joys of life. West reconfigures the rich/poor dichotomy by redefining the economics of wealth in terms of emotional well-being and interpersonal relationships. She criticizes the bourgeois aesthetic of material goods and middle-class status in favor of a folk aesthetic based on the valorization of African American art forms, life, history, and culture. The proletarian aesthetic appears in her valorization of the folk and the criticism of materialism.

In contrast, in "The Bird like No Other, " another bildungsroman that enables West to meditate on folk and bourgeois aesthetics by depicting a youth's growth and development, West focuses primarily on the bourgeois class in her depiction of a young boy's summers at a resort reminiscent of Martha's Vineyard. The story centers on Colby, his mother's friend Emily, and his visits to her cottage whenever he has squabbles with his sisters. However, one day when he is eight and comes to her home, he claims to have seen the bird of many colors his Aunt Emily tells him to watch out for whenever he comes to her cottage. Both look in astonishment at the bird before recognizing it, after the imagination's momentary transformation, as a blue jay. When Colby discovers no bird exists like the one Aunt Emily described, he realizes she told him the story to keep him quiet on summer afternoons while she busied herself in the cottage as well as a means of making him focus on nature rather disparaging his siblings. While "The Penny" depicts a boy of folk origins forced by circumstance to be disloyal to his family, "The Bird like No Other" portrays a bourgeois youth with a more positive role model who teaches him about family loyalty. The two stories can serve as companion pieces by depicting contrasting childhood experiences.

In "The Happiest Year, the Saddest Year," West returns to a loosely autobiographical account of her own childhood initiation with death as in "Funeral" through the narrative form of the bildungsroman. West appropriates the bildungsroman as a means of meditating on race, class, and gender by chronicling childhood awareness of these issues to highlight their influence on individuals. Like Judy in "Funeral," Deedee, the protagonist, comes from a middle-class African American family and must learn to reconcile initiation into death. West reveals class and color differences within African American families through her depiction of Deedee's two young cousins from Chicago, who come from a lower socioeconomic level and are distinguished by the fact that the girl is dark-skinned and the boy light-skinned. She reacts with anger, frustration, and sadness when the brown-skinned girl dies and the light-skinned child lives. Angry with God over what she perceives as color preference, she lashes out at the boy by being abusive. Unlike Judy in "Funeral," who did not have a close relationship with Uncle Eben, Deedee's love for her female cousin heightens her grief.

West depicts the family's affluence in contrast with the cousin's poverty. The family owns a summer cottage on Martha's Vineyard, which becomes the site of Deedee's and her cousin's reconciliation with the cousin's death. The two bond through their grief, becoming even closer than before the sister's passing. While the proletarian aesthetic does not play a major role in the story explicitly, the depiction of Deedee's parents and their embrace of the relatives of a lower socioeconomic level protests against class prejudice and argues for the communality of individuals.

Unlike "The Happiest Year, the Saddest Year," "The Envelope" (featuring a third-person omniscient narrator) centers on the lives of a childless adult couple, Lottie and George Henty. West uses an envelope as a means of meditating on folk and bourgeois aesthetics. The envelope's contents symbolize George's hoped-for reunion with Adrienne Hollister, a beautiful, talented, and socially mobile woman. His wife realizes the futility of his desire to relive the past. Her comment suggests that Adrienne is a member of the elite of African American society and George as her social and intellectual inferior. His wife's intuition proves correct, for the letter comes from Adrienne's daughter, who relates that Adrienne has died, and that her father, publisher Clinton Baxter, would like to receive any correspondence of hers for his records. In "The Envelope," West reveals intraracial social, intellectual, and artistic stratification in her depiction of George and Lottie, a middle-class black couple, in relation to Adrienne Baxter Hollister and her husband Clinton Baxter, who circulate in the upper echelons of society. Like Lucius Jones in "The Typewriter," Clinton's life exemplifies regret and a sense of loss at not having fulfilled his potential. West's portrayal of hierarchies and stratification within the African American community and its effect upon interpersonal relationships serves as a criticism of bourgeois pretensions and attitudes.

By meditating on folk and bourgeois aesthetics through the presentation of a troubled marriage among a black working-class couple who take in a boarder to make ends meet, West presents a thought-provoking portrait of racial and class politics in "The Roomer," which first appeared in the *New York Daily News* in 1941. Like Cleo Judson of *The Living Is Easy* and Mrs. Edmunds of "Jack in the Pot," the wife in "The Roomer" hides money from her husband, hoarding it to purchase items she believes will satisfy her desire for bourgeois status. She scorns her husband, for his income will not transform them from folk to bourgeois status. For the wife, Mike, the roomer, represents a man with bourgeois aspirations. Because the tensions between the husband's folk status and the wife's bourgeois aspirations cause friction in the home, he leaves her. West illustrates the failure of two individuals, the husband and wife, to negotiate a common aesthetic. In "The Roomer," West presents the folk aesthetic through the husband and the bourgeois aesthetic in the wife's social and economic aspirations. West subtly proposes a proletarian aesthetic suggesting the commonalty of all individuals, regardless of class.

Like "The Envelope," "Fluff and Mrs. Ripley" (also first appearing in the *New York Daily News* in 1941) centers on a middle-class couple, but the race of the characters is unmentioned, which suggests West may have wanted to focus more on class. In this story (featuring a third-person omniscient narrator), West presents a bourgeois aesthetic in a couple who try to construct their ideal of happy, middle-class home life to no avail. A store owner, Mr. Ripley desires a wife and a pet dog that reflect his view of middle-class happiness. When he buys a mastiff to fill the emptiness in his life, his wife becomes jealous of their relationship and makes him return it to the kennel, and he resentfully spends more time at work. She responds by buying a dog to keep him at home. He hates the dog, which he believes symbolizes his wife's contempt and anger at him, for Fluff does not evoke memories of Pal, his mastiff. Her devotion to Fluff, which comes to symbolize the emptiness in their marriage, disgusts him, and he leaves her.

"Odyssey of an Egg," told by a third-person omniscient narrator, focuses on the life of a lower-class man, Porky, who robs an elderly woman in an attempt to attain financial security and bourgeois status. Porky, a trade school dropout, meets an old woman who needs assistance taking her groceries home. When she dies of a heart attack after they arrive at her house, he discovers $5,000 there. He faces the dilemma of whether to call for help for the woman or pocket the money. He chooses the latter option. After he leaves her home with the money, he decides to return for more in order to obtain his dreams of bourgeois affluence. A detective mistakes him for an individual involved in a counterfeit scheme with the old woman and arrests him for fraud and murder. West reveals the futility and danger when greed, materialism, and bourgeois aspirations override one's concern for other individuals.

"About a Woman Named Nancy" (which appeared in the *Vineyard Gazette* in 1987) focuses on Nancy, a black female cook, who saves enough money to afford a cottage on Martha's Vineyard. Narrated through the point of a view of a bourgeois neighbor, the story presents the possibilities of harmony between the folk and the bourgeois through the community's acceptance of Nancy, whose affluent neighbors admire her industriousness. To the residents of the island, Nancy represents both the folk through her working-class background and the bourgeois in her acquisition of a summer cottage on the island. The narrator and Nancy's friends nurse her when she becomes ill from pneumonia. Looking after her symbolizes the narrator's and others' appreciation of folkways and the roots of the African American community. West renders a respectful portrait of a woman of folk origins whose generosity elicits understanding among the bourgeoisie, revealing the possibility of interclass harmony rather than fractionalization.

"The Maple Tree" (which appeared in the *New York Daily News* in 1957) focuses on two bourgeois couples of no specific race who live on Martha's Vineyard during the summer. In the story, told by a third-person omniscient narrator, West reveals how bourgeois aspirations and customs work to the detriment of those who favor material possessions and real estate over friendship. West portrays the maple tree that exists on the land between the two couples' homes as the symbol of tension and friction. The tree stands on a lot where a house once stood but decayed through neglect. The Comdens purchase the maple tree lot after the owner decides to sell without letting their neighbors, the Terrells, know of their intentions. When they place a fence around the tree and lot, it connotes exclusivity and separation between the Comdens and the Terrells. "The Maple Tree" illustrates how the erection of boundaries to fit one's bourgeois conception of the ideal summer home jeopardizes a friendship.

"To Market, to Market," examines bourgeois aesthetics and centers on a day in the life of a young middle-class boy sent on an errand. Instead of going directly to the store and buying the bread, the boy becomes distracted and fights for a shiny marble with neighborhood boys. By the time he retrieves the bread, he comes home late. Rather than being angry, his father shows understanding, empathizing with the child and hoping his son wins the fight he plans to engage in the next day. In "To Market, to Market" the father's understanding of the complexities of childhood enable him to forgive the boy for being late. Unlike "The Penny," the story does not focus on class or race consciousness. In its economics, the story resembles others in the collection with its concern over money, but West focuses more on childhood adventures and the child's recognition of family love.

A study of West's short fiction from *The Richer, the Poorer* reveals her preoccupation with race, class, and gender themes and the way in which the author, a closet revolutionary, explored these issues in her writing. Unlike her short stories, West's novels elicit more critical attention, yet many criticisms of West's novels overlook the proletarian aesthetic. *The Living Is Easy* (1948) appropriates the bildungsroman format or coming-of-age story in her exploration of the lives of Cleo and Bart Judson, southern black folk who migrate north in search of racial, class, and sexual equality. West presents the Judsons' experiences in the North as a microcosm of the black experience in the United States, particularly among transplanted southerners. In *The Wedding* (1995), West again appropriates the bildungsroman format in her presentation of the coming of age of Clark and Corinne Coles and their entrée into affluent Oval society in Massachusetts. West also incorporates mini biographies of key characters within the center of the text as a means of highlighting the folk roots of the black bourgeoisie, implying that elitist attitudes toward lower-class blacks signify a rejection of one's own heritage and self. In both novels, West successfully negotiates the complexity and diversity of the African American experience, effectively countering stereotypical notions of blacks as primitive, exotic, or other.

When critics note West's literary contributions and aesthetics, they often categorize her as bourgeois or genteel because of her middle-class Bostonian background. However, West's heritage and literary aesthetic transcends arbitrary labeling, for it represents a mixture of qualities. Although she attended the prestigious Boston Girl's Latin School as a teenager and later studied at Columbia University, while spending summers at her family's home in Martha's Vineyard, her family background has distinct folk roots. West's own life reveals the interweaving of the folk and bourgeois so present in her literature, as she criticizes class prejudice effectively by illustrating that middle-class blacks who look down upon the folk are rejecting an important part of their heritage. While promoting the valorization of the folk as the basis for African American culture and history, West evinces a proletarian strain that manifests itself in her life and work. Her fictionalized depictions of racial, gender, and class prejudices in *The Living Is Easy* and *The Wedding* reveal the protest or proletarian aesthetic in

Photograph of Dorothy West at booksigning for *The Living Is Easy* from the Dorothy West Collection in the Special Collections at Boston University.

her fiction. West's trip to Russia with Langston Hughes to make a film on racism in the United States in 1932 demonstrates her political activism. Her own involvement with *Challenge* (later *New Challenge*), a magazine she founded and edited from 1934 to 1937, bridged the gap between males and females as well as the lower, middle, and upper classes by providing a forum for African American artistic and literary expression (Ferguson 1987). West's adoption of a diversity of aesthetics in *The Living Is Easy* and *The Wedding* reveal her family background as well as her literary sensibilities.

The politics of literary production and reception that Fauset and Hurston faced in the 1920s and 1930s, regarding definitions of authentic African American literature as well as racism in the publishing world, also affected Dorothy West in 1948 with the publication of *The Living Is Easy*. If the novel had been serialized in *Ladies Home Journal*, it would have greatly increased West's readership and name recognition. Instead, concerns over the race of the author and the black characters featured in the text militated against its publication. West's experience calls attention to the multiplicity of ways in which black female artists and their works have been discriminated against for reasons that have no relation to artistic merit.

Previous critical assessments of *The Living Is Easy* focus primarily on her treatment of bourgeois middle-class black society. Henry Lee Moon's review for the *Crisis* (1948) notes that "Miss West has enlarged the canvas of Negro fiction and has treated a phase of Boston life which the popular novels of that city have neglected" (Ferguson 1987: 194). Recent critical assessments have also categorized the novel in relation to the bourgeois aesthetic. Alexis De Veau (1995) writes, " A compelling story of middle-class striving in a Boston black community of the early twentieth century, *The Living Is Easy* stood apart from the "'black protest literature' of its day" (73). Despite the prior critical assessments, a close reading of the text amid the social, historical, and economic aspects of the period reveals the presence of bourgeois, folk, and proletarian aesthetics.

Although "Prologue to a Life" (which originally appeared in the *Saturday Evening Quill* in 1929; it was reprinted in Knopf 1993) has received very little critical attention from West scholars, the story deserves attention for its affinities with West's 1948 novel, *The Living Is Easy*, for which it appears to be a prototype. The story centers on a married couple, Luke and Lily Kane, and their experiences as a black family in nineteenth- and early-twentieth-century America. The Boston setting, the characterization of Luke and Lilly Kane, and the theme of the American Dream connect the short story with West's novel. In the story, West meditates on the folk aspiration for a bourgeois lifestyle of material comfort, wealth, and success. The plot of the first meeting between Luke and Lilly Keane even mirrors that of Cleo and Bart Judson (the protagonists of *The Living Is Easy*), for Lily Bemis first meets Luke Kane when she accidentally falls over his bicycle. Like much of West's fiction, color/caste operates as a central theme in the text, which represents the folk and bourgeois dichotomy apparent in her fiction. Described as having golden skin and hair with a wavy texture, Lily embodies the multiethnic lines running in her background (Knopf 1993). Her speech, nonetheless, mirrors that of the black folk. She works as a domestic for a woman named Miss Trainor. In contrast, Luke, despite his delivery job, represents the emerging black bourgeoisie. His mother, Manda Cane, owns her own catering business, and he works for his mother. While he has dark skin, his heritage also reflects racial mixing in that he has blue eyes, which Lily finds an entrancing contrast to his dark skin color. He finds Lily's mildly flirtatious behavior appealing. Aware of the color/caste system , he decides that her coloring and her demeanor make her a suitable mate for him.

A romance ensues, initially beginning with meetings at the African Methodist Episcopal (A.M.E.) church, which is attended by African Americans aspiring to the black bourgeoisie of Springfield, Massachusetts. As an uneducated African American woman, Lily finds herself with few options to advance socially and economically or to express herself creatively within the public sphere. She seeks motherhood and marriage as a means of self-definition and identity. She marries Luke despite her lack of love. In this sense, Lily serves as a prototype for the coldly calculating Cleo Judson, who sees her children as symbolizing the future and the embodiment of her dreams and desires. Because Lily feels that her own prospects are limited, she hopes to bear children, specifically male sons, to fulfill the ambitions she could not achieve personally. Nearly two years after they first meet, Lily gives birth to two sons (Jamie and John).

Lily's light skin and wavy hair texture become commodities of value for her social climbing husband. Luke's mother, Manda Kane, cries at the wedding, for she realizes that her sons is attracted to Lily primarily for her physical attributes. The couple move from Springfield to Boston to begin their new lives and seek more social and economic opportunities, primarily at Lily's insistence, for she sees Boston as being a better economic opportunity and she despises the idea of living in Springfield with Luke's mother. Lily finds herself scornful of women, which foreshadows her feelings of anxiety when her third child is a female. West's language in the story mirrors Hurston's in *Their Eyes Were Watching God*, a novel in which African American characters like Mrs. Turner idolize other light-skinned blacks as godlike figures, for they worship whiteness out of internalized racism. Lily devotes much of her time and energy to the children, while Luke's lunch stand flourishes and turns into a full-fledged restaurant. As the business grows, so do the children. Her sons prove to be prodigies. John and Jamie read at the age of three, and by the time they are nine, the two boys seem like the perfect children. John's musical talent gains him acceptance at the Boston Conservatory, and Jamie becomes a mathematical genius. At the age of thirty-two, Lily's identity revolves around her role as a housewife and mother. The successful restaurant attracts the bourgeoisie in the community, primarily attorneys and medical doctors. Then, tragedy strikes when the boys are ten years old. They sink into a pond while ice skating, and not only do the boys die, but so does Lily's capacity for love and happiness. Because they represented the future for her, their death symbolizes her loss of hope. The loss of identity as a mother means her loss of self, and her relatives are desperate to help her. Her resulting depression leads to physical aliments, respiratory and heart problems. Luke tries to heal Lily through the power of God, and Lily recovers enough to function and resume sexual relations with him. As a consequence, she becomes pregnant again. Angry, she laughs bitterly when a female child is born. She views women as limited, weak, and of little value, except as potential mothers. She laughs bitterly, for she knows the irony of a female child born in a racist, sexist society, and the double jeopardy she will face as a black woman. As Lily breathes her last breath, the child cries. Luke's own ambivalent feelings about the daughter manifest themselves when he hopes, briefly, that the child, who will be motherless, has died, yet she lives and has his blue eyes. He attempts to revive Lily again using the power of God, and Lily cries and begins to sleep. West ends the story enigmatically: "Lily was dead, and Lily was not dead. A mother is the creator of life. And God cannot die" (Knopf 1993: 94). She dies in the sense that she still grieves for her dead twin sons, and she grieves for the fate that will befall her daughter as a result of her race and gender. She lives physically nevertheless. Her ability to procreate and create as a mother saves her from physical death, making her godlike and immortal, for she can be a conduit for future generations. The problematic ending of the story also mirrors to a certain extent the ending of *The Living Is Easy*, where Bart leaves Lily and she finds herself distraught. Although the couple in "Prologue to a Life" remains together, the story's ending is equally bleak and illustrates the modern temper of pessimism, fragmentation, and incompleteness.

West would flesh out the themes she explored in "Prologue to a Life" in her phenomenal novel, *The Living Is Easy*. Set in the Southern United States and Boston, *The Living Is Easy* focuses primarily on the lives of Cleo and Bart Judson, southern blacks who migrated north in search of the American dream of wealth, success, and fame. West's title is an ironic commentary on the futility of achieving personal happiness and fame through material acquisition and wealth at the cost of losing one's identity and sense of heritage. The novel depicts the movement from South to North and folk to bourgeois through the presentation of Cleo and Bart's struggle to attain wealth, social clout, and renown. West's criticism of greed and materialism, elitism, and interracial discrimination suggests that the key to African American life and culture resides in an appreciation of the folk, the proletarian sense of the communality between humans, and a necessity for the socioeconomic progress of bourgeois values but not at the expense of the community.

West presents the communal aesthetic in her depiction of Cleo and Bart's southern childhood and her migration north in search of a better life in the early twentieth century. Her depiction of Cleo and Bart's trek from the rural agrarian South to the industrialized North mirrors that of West's own parents, who left Virginia and South Carolina in quest of economic opportunity and freedom. As Frazier (1957) notes, "Although the migrants were attracted to northern cities because of opportunities of employment, the migrations were, in part, a flight from oppression to a Promised Land of freedom and equality" (24). By presenting the Great Black Migration in terms of her protagonists, Cleo and Bart Judson, West calls attention to the southern folk roots of the black bourgeois class and succeeds in criticizing prejudice, suggesting that elitism among the black bourgeoisie serves as a denial of one's heritage. West represents the folk aesthetic in her depiction of Cleo and Bart's southern childhood, their migration north, and their adjustment to urban living.

Each character reacts in a different manner to their new situation. West uses Cleo's ambivalent feelings of love and hatred toward the South and the folk as a means of meditating on color, class, and community. Like Joanna Marshall of *There Is Confusion* and Olivia Cary of *Comedy: American Style* and Mrs. Turner of *Their Eyes Were Watching God*, Cleo expresses elitist sentiments that shape her perceptions of the African American community, resulting in an estrangement from African American life and culture.[4] As Wade-Gayles (1984) asserts, "As the wife of Bart Judson, the wealthiest Black man in Boston, Cleo is cold, hostile, and manipulative" (9). In *The Living Is Easy*, West analyzes intraracial colorism. Cleo writes letters containing false information to her sisters as a means of ending their marriages with men she considers too folksy in their socioeconomic background. Because she has bourgeois aspirations, she wants her sisters to be married to middle-class black men. The plotline of writing false letters echoes Fauset's characterization of Joanna Marshall in *There Is Confusion*.[5] Cleo disapproves of her sister Lily's husband because he is a railroad porter: "She [Victoria] and Lily would be better off in Boston, where Cleo could look after them both, than in New York with one little man who spent most of his time bowing and scraping to white folks" (*The Living Is Easy*: 53). In her letter, Cleo invites her sister Lily to Boston on the pretext that she is leaving Bart and ending her marriage to him. Later, she writes a letter to Charity, her other sister, and pleads for her to move from the South to Boston to be with her and Lily. Her ambivalence about the South and her folk heritage contributes to her desire to remove her sisters from their folk environments, while simultaneously surrounding herself with family who signify the folk past for her: "All of her backward looks were toward the spellbinding South. The rich remembering threw a veil of lovely illusion over her childhood" (*The Living Is Easy*: 53). As a consequence, she attempts to reconfigure the folk and the bourgeois in her life, yet her attempts at reconciliation ultimately prove unsuccessful despite the fact that she succeeds in coaxing her sisters to come live with her.

West presents the demarcation between old and new black Boston money in her representation of the black bourgeoisie. Althea Binney's father had been a wealthy tailor, but he could not compete with department stores who could offer ready-to-wear clothing at lower prices. As a result, she teaches piano to middle-class black children to support herself. Duchess, on the other hand, represents the nouveau riche. The child of a white father and a black mother, she runs a casino that generates much money. Despite her vast financial resources, the black bourgeoisie consider her to be an outsider. Therefore, she marries Simeon Binney to achieve social status. Cleo's marriage to Bart Judson reflects her avarice and desire to obtain material possessions as she moves up the socioeconomic ladder. Similarly, Duchess desires to cement her social position by marrying a poor but respectable activist, Simeon Binney, the brother of Althea. He desperately needs her money and financial backing to make the *Clarion*, his proletarian publication, a reality. Like Philip Marshall in Jessie Fauset's *There Is Confusion*, who creates the *Spur*, and like Dorothy West herself in her establishment of *Challenge* and *New Challenge* in the 1930s, Simeon wants blacks to function as a community for the betterment of all African Americans. The purpose of his publication is to call attention to racial, class, and gender oppression.

Simeon serves as the embodiment of the proletarian aesthetic in *The Living Is Easy* through his egalitarian views. As an adult, he understands awareness of the racial, sexual, and class prejudice in the United States. When hostile whites beat him up while on a walk with his light-skinned sister, he becomes further committed to the idea that all blacks, regardless of class, face injustice. Nevertheless, he hopes the incident with the racist whites will awaken the black bourgeoisie to unite with other classes of blacks in opposition to racism. Simeon's proletarian aesthetic represents West's criticism of racial inequity in America, yet West's depiction of the unhappy marriage between Duchess and Simeon also asserts the perils of materialism as a motivation for marriage rather than love. West emphasizes the fragile nature of the black bourgeois society in her presentation of commercialization and industrialization's negative economic impact upon black businesses. Bart's fruit-importing business cannot compete with the supermarket chains, which can sell more food at cheaper prices, nor can he compete with Cleo's increasing demands for money to support their lifestyle. The black bourgeoisie, therefore, represent an elite class with a very precarious position that often cannot be sustained by individuals one or two generations removed from poverty or from sociocultural phenomena that place the black business owner at a disadvantage.

West's presentation of Bart Judson's plight represents the reality of many black businessmen of the early to mid twentieth century, including her own father, a successful entrepreneur and fruit wholesaler dubbed "the Black Banana King" of Boston. West shows the tribulation of black entrepreneurs who simply cannot maintain their businesses in the wake of urbanization, commercialization, and industrialism. The novel ends tragically, with Bart Judson as a broken-down man victimized by racism and classicism as well as his wife Cleo, whose gross materialism and lack of love for her husband create an empty marriage. He heads to New York in hopes of better economic opportunities, leaving Cleo behind in Boston. Distraught, Cleo worries about her future and bemoans her fate. West meditates on the folk and bourgeois through chronicling Cleo and Bart's rise from the folk to the bourgeois classes, yet the novel remains a proletarian statement indicting racial and class prejudice. West's *The Living Is Easy* stands as one of the most powerful commentaries on the politics of race, class, and gender in the African American literary tradition.

While nearly a half century separates *The Living Is Easy* (1948) and *The Wedding* (1995), West's last published novel before her death in 1998 represents a transition from the Harlem Renaissance to the present. The publication signifies the importance and relevance of West's insightful criticisms of race, class, and gender prejudice in African American literature today. The novel's composition and publication calls attention to the politics behind the production of African American texts. Although she began writing *The Wedding* several decades before its publication, she ceased writing the novel because of the militancy of the time: "When the black power movement of the mid 1960s erupted, West stopped working on the book [*The Wedding*], fearing its middle-class themes would be unfairly criticized" (Ferguson 1987: 195). Her trepidation over continuing the novel in the volatile Black Power climate suggests her own aware-

ness of her work as bourgeois. There was a privileging of the folk over the bourgeois aesthetic in the 1960s as black civic and political leaders tried to appeal to
the masses rather than the elite in their attempt to end racial, social, and political oppression. Nevertheless, a change in the social and political climate in the
1980s and 1990s made West believe there would be an audience for the novel,
so she resumed writing and submitted the text for publication to Doubleday
with the aid of Jackie Kennedy Onassis.

Reviews of *The Wedding* tend to address the bourgeois aspects of the novel
in its depiction of affluent black residents on the Oval, a section of a New England island. In *Ms.* De Veaux (1995) writes, "West creates an isolated world of
black and white people untouched by the civil rights movement marching toward its borders. In this world, social and economic status and light or white skin
are more valuable commodities than political consciousness and social responsibility" (73). Similarly, Rubin (1995) comments, "*The Wedding* is a finely
wrought, richly complicated novel with the suspense and focus of a short story.
It is set on Martha's Vineyard in August 1953: more specifically, in an elegant,
insular enclave of well-established professional blacks' summer residents—
known as the Oval" (11). Set in a community based upon the Oak Bluffs section of Martha's Vineyard, Massachusetts, and the rural South, *The Wedding*
spans the period from the Emancipation Proclamation to the 1950s. In *The Wedding*, West stresses the southern folk as the root of African American life and
history through the depictions of the great black migration north after slavery
as exemplified by the black progenitors of the Coles family, who signify the elite
of the Oval. The bourgeois aesthetic manifests itself in her treatment of the exclusive and affluent blacks in Martha's Vineyard who display elitism and colorism. The proletarian aesthetic manifests itself through her criticism of interracial and intraracial race, class, and gender prejudice that serve to separate rather
than unite humanity. West artfully blends the three aesthetics together as a
means of illustrating the roots of the black bourgeoisie lie in the folk experience, and the proletarian aesthetic serves as a mediator between the folk and
bourgeois. She transcends and transforms the triangular configuration of aesthetics in African American literature.

West presents the Clark Coles family as the embodiment of black bourgeois
values and sensibilities. In addition to owning the largest home on the Oval, the
Coles family represents the achievement other blacks in the community aspire
to in their quest for preeminence. College-educated and wealthy, the lives of the
Coles family reflect relative ease in comparison to even their most affluent neighbors. Clark and Corinne Coles, the parents of Shelby and Liz, portray the ideal
African American family to the outside world because they appear to be an
African American embodiment of the American dream. However, West reveals
that intraracial class and color prejudices serve to estrange the Coles family from
their community and their folk heritage. In her depiction of Ovalite society, West
connects with an important element of the black bourgeoisie—the concept of
summer homes and leisure time. West's depiction of the Oval island resort com-

munity resembles her own family history as a resident of Oak Bluffs on Martha's Vineyard in a summer home purchased by her father. The fact that West's family owned a summer home on Martha's Vineyard reveals their elite status socially and economically in comparison with most African Americans during the early twentieth century. West presents Ovalite society as an elitist settlement dominated by individuals who possess three characteristics: wealth, professional careers, and light skin. When long-time Oval resident Addie Banister rents her summer cottage to dark-skinned Lute McNeil, it signifies a defiance of Ovalite codes and standards about suitable residents. While Lute possesses the money to afford a summer cottage, his dark skin and occupation as a furniture maker reflect his working-class roots and sensibilities. Consequently, he scoffs at their ostracism of him as unfit for their society, yet at the same time he desires to be part of the elite community. Ironically, Lute reinscribes the same colorism exemplified by the Ovalites in his desire for a light-skinned black wife. West portrays his color consciousness negatively by illustrating the futility and tragedy of his obsession with Shelby Coles when he inadvertently strikes his daughter Tina with the car he is driving while attempting to take her white mother away from the island during his wife's visit to repair their broken marriage.

West both constructs and deconstructs race and class in America through her depictions of family genealogies in the Coles line through both Corinne and Clark. These narrative digressions, contained within the middle of the novel, serve as a means of linking working-class and the middle-class strains in the family history. By presenting heritage as a blend, West exposes elitism and color preferences among the Coles family as self-hatred and self-denial, the consequences of which will become spiritual emptiness. The family represents a mélange of black and white, male and female, folk and bourgeois elements. Gram (the grandmother of Corinne and the great-grandmother of Shelby and Liz), represents the bourgeois white part of the family heritage. The daughter of Colonel Lance Shelby, Gram grew up on a plantation with slaves and a mansion. Her aristocratic sensibilities temper her loyalty toward her family when the Civil War causes the family to lose its preeminence. West's presentation of Gram's life reveals the changes that come in the South after the Civil War. While Gram's family cannot readjust to life under Reconstruction, former slaves use their entrepreneurial skills for economic benefit. Like Bart Judson and his mother in *The Living Is Easy* (modeled after West's own father who ran a successful restaurant in Richmond, Virginia) and like Joel Marshall and his mother in Fauset's *There Is Confusion* , the black slave Melisse becomes a successful caterer and earns enough money to send her son Hannibal north for an education. As the blacks' standard of living increases, Gram's family's meager savings dwindle, resulting in her daughter Josephine's decision to marry Hannibal although he is black. Josephine and Hannibal's union represents a marriage of the folk and the bourgeois class, as he provides her with economic security. In turn, she provides him with a sense of social cachet, prominence, and an aristocratic past.

West illustrates the absurdity of such a position when the upper echelons were often only a generation or two removed from poverty.

When Hannibal receives his doctorate from a northern university and a position as professor at a Washington, D.C., college, he relocates his family to the area. His family embodies the racial and class stratification there. West's depiction of the city has an authenticity. As Frazier (1957) notes, "Because of its relatively large professional class, including teachers in the segregated public school system, doctors, dentists, and lawyers, and large numbers of Negroes employed in the federal government, Negroes in the nation's capital had incomes far above those in other parts of the country" (164). West connects to the preeminence of Washington, D.C., as a cultural center for blacks aspiring to bourgeois status. Members of the elite Washington, D.C., society depicted in the novel pay close attention to money and skin color, a factor that militates against the darker-skinned individuals and in favor of the lighter-skinned ones.

To the "blue-vein" society depicted in *The Wedding*, skin gradation signifies a marker of gentility and aristocratic background.[6] Like Olivia Cary in Fauset's *Comedy: American Style* and Mrs. Turner in Hurston's *Their Eyes Were Watching God*, the blue-vein society practices a rigid color prejudice that tempers their treatment of other blacks. Hannibal's skin color signifies the absence of white blood, a marker of racial miscegenation. Given his educational background, the blue-vein society deems him worthy of a professorship and later a presidency of a college in Washington, D.C., yet it marginalizes him as a dark-skinned black man. The blue-vein society's origins stem from the class of free mulattos of the pre–Civil War era who attempted to maintain their status after the war ended. In an attempt to distance themselves from the darker-skinned and/or the folk, many formed exclusive organizations or separate communities as Russell, Wilson, and Hall (1992) have noted: "The elite group of those who had been free before the war, in many cases for generations, called themselves the 'bona fide' free and reacted to the upheaval by forming exclusive social clubs based on color and class, which provided an effective way to maintain the old hierarchy" (25). *The Wedding* reveals the prevalence of these attitudes as expressed through Hannibal's marriage to a white woman (believed to be a light-skinned black woman), which exemplifies the fulfillment of his entry into the black bourgeois class of Washington, D.C., and the blue-vein society. By the early 1950s (the time of the novel), color and class consciousness are still important.

West meditates on race and class in American society. When dark-skinned Liz decides to marry a dark-skinned black doctor, her family disapproves because of his low origins. Her fiancé's name of Linc proves symbolic, for he links the low and high history of the Coles family. Liz and her fiancé elope due to Corinne's prejudice against Linc's parents. Corinne considers his parents to be inferior because Linc's parents are working class. Liz has dark skin but does not internalize the prejudices of Corinne: "Her mother blew the trumpet of praise for marriage to her own kind, if not color, the right color being preferable but not as mandatory as the right class. That class and the posture it demanded had given her the self assurance to feel that no barrier was insurmountable, and to say with ease that she looked white but wasn't" *(The Wedding:* 90). Class overrides color distinctions in Ovalite society. Linc's professional accomplishments will not win him the pseudo-aristocratic ties.

The marriage of Clark and Corinne in *The Wedding* serves to propagate the idea of a refined, genteel, and light-skinned class of blacks. As a young doctor, Clark attends a medical workshop at the Washington, D.C., college of which Hannibal serves as president. Clark moves in the upper echelons because of his profession and family background, as a consequence becoming an "acceptable" suitor for Corinne: "As the youngest of three brothers, all successful general practitioners who lived prosperously on Striver's Row in Harlem (a street so called because of the prominence and pretensions of this envied and imitated group of professional men and their pretty wives), he was determined to excel in any area that offered a challenge" *(The Wedding:* 104). Despite his attraction to Sabina, a dark-skinned student at the school, the rigid color and class code prevents the development of a relationship with her because the young woman is excluded from social functions. Finding in Corinne a socially acceptable mate, he proposes and further reinforces a hierarchy of class and power among the middle-class black bourgeois society. Although Clark views himself as cultured and a member of the bourgeoisie, his family heritage lies in the southern folk. His grandfather, Preacher Coles, was a self-educated field hand who rose to prominence through the gift of oratory and his acumen in building homes, selling produce, and acquiring livestock, after marrying a mulatto washwoman.

Despite their folk origins, both parents possess the determination and will to rise socially and economically, and their son Isaac, Clark's father, becomes the embodiment of their dreams. Recognizing that financial stability can be passed on from generation to generation, Preacher saves his money to ensure his progeny's place in the black bourgeois world. In *The Wedding,* West depicts the Great Migration north as embodied by Isaac Coles's journey with Amy Norton, a white spinster who insists that he leave the South to fulfill his destiny. Like Cleo and Bart Judson of *The Living Is Easy,* he leaves in search of economic opportunity and freedom. When Isaac boards the train with Amy Norton, his journey reflects that of many blacks at the turn of the century, questing after the American dream: "All over the South such sacrificial scenes were taking place, the giving of gifted colored children to the North when their mettle could be tested, their potential realized. Most of them would always be exiles. No free man returns to the yoke, but the South that was in them was in them to stay. What lingered was not the harshness of its whites, or the hovels of its blacks, but the beauty of its land, the abundance of its beauty" *(The Wedding:* 139).

West illustrates that the folk and southern heritage remain in an individual as expressed through an appreciation for the rural and agrarian history of the

South despite the racial, sexual, and class discriminations. The South remains embedded within the individual wherever he or she travels in life. Presenting a folk aesthetic in *The Wedding* through a valorization of the South, West illustrates the importance of the South and folkways as the basis of African American life.

West details the rise from the folk to the bourgeois in the Coles family through Isaac's exposure to the world of Martha's Vineyard (where Amy's family owns a summer home). The exposure as a youth has a profound effect upon the shaping of his consciousness and his attitudes toward race, class, and gender. His ascent from the folk to the bourgeoisie parallels the rise of the black bourgeois society in America at the turn of the century. When Isaac earns a scholarship to Harvard University to study medicine, he reflects his father's ambitions that the son advance to Striver's Row in Harlem. Marriage to a schoolteacher provides Isaac with respectability and stability in the eye of his patients: "There were too many advantages: marriage gave a busy doctor a home where he could get a meal without waiting for a table and a wife to mend his shirts, keep his social life in order, and give him sons to carry on his name" (*The Wedding:* 153). The marriage also provides social and economic stability to his wife, who views the union as the ultimate for an African American woman of her time. Viewing money and social prominence as barometers of success, his wife becomes a real-estate owner, as money and property serve to provide her with the fulfillment that she lacks in a loveless marriage.

West reveals how the Great Black Migration north coincides with the bourgeois community as his wife collects capital from her apartments. Ironically, she recreates the very conditions from which they fled in the South, substandard housing for others. The money and the prominence that her role bestows upon her initially quell any guilt she feels about their plight. Isaac and his wife play a major role in the lives of the southern folk in Harlem. While he ministers to their physical aliments, she benefits from the money they pour into her dilapidated apartments, further cementing the couple's entrance into the bourgeois class. While her motives result from a desire for material gain, his emerge from the need to see himself as the savior of the race, attempting to help promote the existence of one who would become a great race leader.

West presents the Coles as the arbiters of taste and affluence in black bourgeois society, yet she clearly indicates the cost to their spiritual and emotional well-being as greed and avarice overcome concern for the welfare of others and the community. Buoyed by her financial success, Isaac's wife appears altruistic in her charity balls to aid the underprivileged. Their mimicking of bourgeois white society further reinscribes racial, class, and gender hierarchies within the African American community. Greed, materialism, and the desire for social preeminence characterize the "charity" balls rather than concern for the plight of their fellow African Americans. Issac's wife's estrangement from the folk represents her distance from her African American heritage and identity: "She did not for a moment identify with the people of the ghetto, any more than she identified with their common ancestors in Africa" (*The Wedding*: 163). West depicts the schoolteacher's spiritual vacuum as a result of her estrangement from her folk origins. When Isaac's wife finally immerses herself in the folk as part of a project to gain entrance into a white women's social welfare organization by observing and recording experiences of tenement dwelling, she recovers her sense of self, heritage, family, and identity as a black woman. Initially, the differences in clothing, speech, housing, and behavior unsettle her. Isaac's wife feels as if she is communicating with individuals from a foreign country, but as she spends more time with them the chasm grows smaller. Her interaction with the southern folk forces her to reassess her life, ambitions, and goals and come to terms with her heritage as an African American. Her desire to aid the standard of living of the folk and desire for a settlement house reveals the proletarian aesthetic in *The Wedding*. The folk recover her spiritual self as she gains a connection with God and a charitable desire to benefit the community by donating to the church. Hence, she seeks to negotiate the triangularity of her world.

West's interweaving of past and present in *The Wedding* reveals the power of coming to understand the triangularity. Clark's union with Corinne represents the marriage of two socially prominent individuals, who on the surface seem to be the ideal African American family, but the foundation upon which the marriage rests reflects more on superficial connections than passion or love. Because Clark never married Sabina, the woman he most loved in college because of her dark skin color and low social class, his daughter Shelby's wedding stirs ambivalent feelings in him. His long-term affair with the dark-skinned Rachel (who reminds him of Sabina) reflects his regret over allowing his bourgeois aspirations to dominate his existence. When Clark decides to exchange a bourgeois wife with the proper social cachet for a true love in Rachel (a nurse who works for him), he had already waited too late. Although Rachel once had bourgeois hopes of eventually marrying Clark, she opts for a city employee who will meet her needs. Although materially rich, Clark is spiritually poor. While he has money, wealth, and social preeminence, his life reflects an emptiness. He has broken with his heritage. Although a self-made man, Isaac valorized hard work over leisure. Although he desires social and economic achievement, he still retains many of the values of the working-class poor. But it is clear that Clark's inability to negotiate the triangularity is what prompts his tragic downfall. His rise to power brought many accompanying consequences. West suggests that the black bourgeois class must behave responsibly in the acquisition of power by not reinscribing the dangerous hierarchies of race, class, and gender. For Clark, Shelby's wedding for love rather than social or material gain represents the possibilities of freeing the family from the trappings of completely bourgeois motives in their relationships.

The community remains stunned at Shelby's choice in a mate when she could have become engaged to any of the eligible light-skinned black men in the Oval community. Because of their estrangement from their folk roots, the black Ovalites have little appreciation for jazz as an art form despite its African American origins. They valorize professions such as doctor, lawyer, and architect over that of jazz musician. Corinne finds the prospect of her daughter's marrying Meade, a white jazz musician, particularly horrifying because the eldest, Liz, also marries someone she considers beneath her daughter. Liz marries a dark-skinned black man from a working-class background despite her mother's reservations. Even though he is a doctor, Corinne still looks down upon him because of his dark skin and low socioeconomic origins. Liz and Shelby defy the family history of marrying light-skinned blacks to continue the blue-vein society of the Oval. West accurately portrays and deftly criticizes color and class consciousness through the two women's decisions to defy social customs that define color, class, and community. For Shelby, Lute represents the allure of a black man who represents the folk and the possibilities of connecting to that aspect of her heritage through him. Conversely, Shelby represents the attainment of Lute's bourgeois aspirations. Although his current wife, Della, comes from an affluent white family in Boston, Lute views light-skinned Shelby as a means of gaining access to the black bourgeoisie world he so desires to enter. When his overweening ambition to obtain Shelby ends in his beating up Della, who has come to visit him on the island, and drive her away from the Oval so he can continue to pursue Shelby, he inadvertently hits his daughter, Tina, with the car and kills her. The accident has an impact upon the Oval community, emphasizing the futility and destructiveness of color and class prejudices. West presents the effects of the tragedy among the members of the community, for it forces them to reassess their views on color, class, and community. The tragic accident reaffirms Shelby's decision to place love above color and class distinctions (unlike Lute) and marry Meade. For Gram, the accident has significance also, for it makes her recognize that the race and class distinctions she so heartily clings to represent malignant and destructive forces. When she grasps Liz's dark-skinned child, it signifies an acceptance of the roots of the Coles family and her attempt to negotiate the challenge of African American history.

Although published in 1995, Dorothy West's *The Wedding* depicts the futility and tragedy of elitism, which characterizes her earlier work *The Living Is Easy*. As in *The Living Is Easy*, the southern past represents the foundations of African American culture and community. Individuals who elevate bourgeois values over their folk heritage suffer. Both *The Living Is Easy* and *The Wedding* signify West's crowning achievement in negotiating the wealth, triangularity of heritage, and power of the African American experience. Similarly, West's understudied autobiographical essays and short stories from *The Richer, the Poorer* illustrate how her family's collective history shaped her predilection toward exploring the politics of race, class, and gender in her writings. Far from being a member of the black bourgeoisie far removed from the folk, West's life and artistic creations represent a proletarian outcry against injustice, proving the presence of a revolutionary mind.

## NOTES

1. Jessie Fauset had difficulty getting the Frederick A. Stokes Company to accept her 1931 novel *The Chinaberry Tree* for publication because they believed her presentation of black middle-class life was unrealistic. As a consequence, she contacted Zona Gale, a respected white female novelist known for her realistic literary works, to write an introduction verifying its authenticity.

2. Difficulties with Fauset's publisher, Frederick A. Stokes, in having her manuscript for *The Chinaberry Tree* accepted, and the control which Charlotte Osgood Mason held over the production, distribution, and reception of Hurston's work in the late 1920s and early 1930s reveals the constraints and restraints under which the two women sought to create literary works. West's interpretation of the decision by the editors of *Ladies Home Journal* not to serialize *The Living Is Easy* reflects the complicated politics of literary reception and publication in African American literature.

3. All stories and essays by West cited herein, with the exception of "Prologue to a Life," are from *The Richer, the Poorer.* New York: Doubleday, 1995.

4. In Jessie Fauset's *There Is Confusion* (1924) and *Comedy: American Style* (1933), characters such as Joanna Marshall and Olivia Cary destroy the lives of family members with their elitism. In Zora Neale Hurston's *Their Eyes Were Watching God* (1937), Mrs. Turner's racial self-hatred causes her to dislike dark-skinned blacks like Tea Cake and favor light-skinned blacks like Janie as she wishes that mixed-race blacks could mix with whites or form their own class.

5. In *There Is Confusion* (1924), Joanna Marshall sends a letter to Maggie Ellersley, who comes from a lower socioeconomic background, informing the young woman that she should not pursue a relationship with Philip Marshall, her brother.

6. The term *blue vein* describes blacks of mixed-race ancestry who established organizations and institutions in which membership was based upon one's socioeconomic class and skin color. Russell, Wilson, and Hall (1992) note that "Membership was considered an honor, and the 'blue veiners' and 'bon tonners' were thought to have the finest of bloodlines. In practice, however, admission to a blue vein society depended not on family background but on skin color. An applicant had to be fair enough for the spidery network of purplish veins at the wrist to be visible to a panel of expert judges" (25).

## REFERENCES

Adams, Katherine H. 2001. *A Group of Their Own: College Writing Courses and American Women Writers, 1880–1940.* Albany: State University of New York Press.

Dalsgard, Katrine. 1993. "Alive and Well and Living on the Island of Martha's Vineyard: An Interview with Dorothy West." *Langston Hughes Review* 12, no. 2: 28–44.

De Veaux, Alexis. 1995. "Bold Type: Renaissance Woman." *Ms.* Magazine, May/June, 73.

Ferguson, Sally Ann. 1987. "West, Dorothy." *Dictionary of Literary Biography: Afro-American Writers from the Harlem Renaissance to 1940*, eds. Trudier Harris and Thadious Davis. Detroit: Gale.

Frazier, E. Franklin. 1957. *Black Bourgeoisie: The Rise of a New Middle Class in the United States.* New York: Macmillan.

Knopf, Marcy, ed. 1993. *The Sleeper Wakes: Harlem Renaissance Stories by Women.* New Brunswick, N.J.: Rutgers University Press.

Miller, R. Baxter. 2000. "Café de la Paix: Mapping the Harlem Renaissance." *South Atlantic Review* 65, no. 2: 73–94.

Moon, Henry Lee. 1948. "Review of Dorothy West's *The Living Is Easy.*" *Crisis* 55, no. 10: 308.

Rubin, Merle. 1995. "Racial Pride and Prejudice Drive a Family-Centered Novel." *Christian Science Monitor*, 2 February, 11.

Russell, Kathy, Midge Wilson, and Ronald Hall. 1992. *The Color Complex: The Politics of Skin Color Among African Americans.* New York: Harcourt Brace Jovanovich.

Wade-Gayles, Gloria. 1984. "The Truths of Our Mothers' Lives: Mother-Daughter Relationships in Black Women's Fiction." *SAGE: A Scholarly Journal on Black Women* 1, no. 2: 8–12.

Willis, Susan. 1987. *Specifying: Black Women Writing the American Experience.* Madison: University of Wisconsin Press.

# Conclusion

Examining Jessie Fauset, Zora Neale Hurston, and Dorothy West in relation to the triangle of aesthetics constituting African American literature—the folk, the bourgeois, and the proletarian—sheds new light on their works and opens the door for future scholarship on these three writers. From her position as a literary editor for the *Crisis*, membership in the NAACP, and experience as a schoolteacher, Jessie Fauset is often characterized as a writer of the bourgeois tradition. In contrast, Zora Neale Hurston, who represented herself as a product of all-black Eatonville, Florida, and collected folklore is often presented as the embodiment of literature reflecting the folk aesthetic. Dorothy West, the daughter of a wealthy Boston fruit importer, is often neglected in studies of the Harlem Renaissance because her first novel did not appear until after the literary period ended, though she published a number of short stories during the 1920s and 1930s. When she is discussed as a Harlem Renaissance writer, she is often considered a writer of the bourgeois aesthetic because of her middle-class background. Work by all three writers contains elements of the three aesthetics. While this study ostensibly focuses on their novels, when necessary their short fiction, articles, and autobiographical essays have been analyzed as well.

This study adopts a variety of critical approaches, including historical and feminist in an effort to better understand the relationship between narrative technique and formal elements in the construction of aesthetics. Admittedly, each critical school has its strengths and weaknesses. Historical approaches provide a sense of the social, economic, and political forces that produce a work but sometimes obscure more formal (theme, plot, character, symbols) elements. Feminist approaches examine the roles of women in a text, while sometimes not thoroughly examining history, class, or formal aspects. With all this in mind, a combination of historical, and feminist approaches offers the best available approach for analyzing the connection between narrative technique and aesthetics in the fiction of Fauset, West, and Hurston. Rereading their works illustrates how they transcend and defy the labels that have been bestowed upon them in terms of aesthetics by chroniclers of literary history. All three writers present a fusion of folk, bourgeois, and proletarian aesthetics in their works. The complex nature of their literary legacy manifests itself in their appropriation of narrative strategies in relation to formal elements of character, plot, theme, and symbolism. The bildungsroman signifies the protagonist's coming of age, while the kunstlerroman represents a special type of bildungsroman, which focuses on the artist's development. First person and third person omniscient narration provide the means of exploring an individual or several individuals' growth.

The folk aesthetic encompasses literature that celebrates the commonplace and the ordinary. Folk literature presents characters of lower socioeconomic levels who frequently speak in dialect or nonstandard English. Characters may live in the rural South or industrial North. Writers of the folk aesthetic often focus on the rich cultural tradition of African American society. The bourgeois aesthetic, in contrast, reflects the middle-class culture. Characters tend to be highly educated with professional jobs. Gentility, refinement, and highbrow culture are central qualities of the bourgeois tradition. Literature of the bourgeois aesthetic has a variety of settings ranging from small communities to big cities. Of the three aesthetics, the proletarian aesthetic functions as the most overtly political. Also known as protest fiction, it challenges racism, class prejudice, and sexism. Literature of the proletarian aesthetic tends to be didactic in the call for racial, sexual, and class unity. Writers of the proletarian aesthetic blend art and politics in their exploration of the social, political, and economic conditions in the United States. Works may be naturalistic or realistic in tone, as they display the protagonist's attempt to negotiate external or internal factors that impede development in American life.

Fauset's novels—*There Is Confusion, Plum Bun, The Chinaberry Tree, Comedy: American Style*—and her short stories (such as "The Sleeper Wakes," "Double Trouble," and "Mary Elizabeth") appropriate the bildungsroman and the kunstlerroman in their treatment of the African American female artist's struggle to succeed. While elements of the folk and the proletarian aesthetic appear in her novels, the bourgeois aesthetic predominates in Fauset's valorization of refinement, gentility, and culture. Hurston's *Jonah's Gourd Vine, Their Eyes Were Watching God, Moses, Man of the Mountain, Seraph on the Suwanee,* "Spunk," Sweat," "The Gilded Six Bits," and "The Bone of Contention" feature the bildungsroman and the kunstlerroman in their portrayal of the individual's struggle for voice and identity in an often racist, sexist, and elitist world. Although Hurston displays the bourgeois and proletarian aesthetics, the folk aesthetic prevails in her presentation of the oral storytelling tradition. Of the three, Dorothy West was the longest-living writer. West's novels *The Living Is Easy* and *The Wedding* and the essays and short stories from *The Richer, the Poorer* feature the folk and bourgeois aesthetics, respectively, in her depiction of both the working and middle classes in the South and in the North. Nevertheless, her works are often more didactic than those of her two contemporaries. Her role as founder and editor of *Challenge* and *New Challenge* as well as her trip to Russia to make a film on race relations in the United States attests to her activism. As her work is presently being reissued, scholars and critics are recognizing the confluence of art and politics in her work.

This study strives to provide a fuller and better-developed understanding of works by Jessie Fauset, Zora Neale Hurston, and Dorothy West. There are many directions in which future scholarship might lead. Some may consist of other critical approaches, including deconstruction, psychoanalytic, or New Historical readings, among others. Reader response may also prove valuable in interpreting the fiction of Fauset, Hurston, and West. Other scholars may discover narrative techniques embedded within the works of the three writers that have not been addressed in this examination or explore the formal elements from other critical approaches. Continual examination and inquiry into the literary legacy of Fauset, Hurston, and West will only enrich our understanding of African American aesthetics and, hence, the wonderful diversity of American literature.

This study of Fauset, Hurston, and West has a variety of motivations. First, although an increasing number of works on the Harlem Renaissance, and in particular women writers, is being published, much of the available scholarship (with the exception of that on Hurston) consists of biographical treatments and anthologies. Historically, Hurston, Fauset, and West have been positioned in opposition to one another as representatives of different values, aesthetics, and backgrounds. West, in particular, has been underread, undervalued, and often overlooked or jettisoned from studies of the Harlem Renaissance because her novel *The Living Is Easy* was not published until 1948 and *The Wedding* not until 1995. The anthology *The Richer, the Poorer* was first published in 1995. The labeling of West as an example of the black bourgeoisie, in an environment that tends to emphasize the folk as the epitome of "authentic" African American literature militates against West, who is often cast as apolitical and out of touch with the masses despite the fact that her work values the folk and carries a strong protest voice. Fauset, too, (despite her role as editor and mentor) is often overlooked or undervalued for her role in the Harlem Renaissance. Because she experimented with the novel of manners and her texts often focus on marriage, she sometimes is read as reactionary or conservative, yet her subversive rendering of race, class, and gender illustrates the power of her texts. Without Fauset, fewer voices might have been heard during the Harlem Renaissance. While Hurston finally achieved, after her death, critical acclaim and a role in the American literary canon, most of the criticism focuses on *Their Eyes Were Watching God* (1937), while not addressing her other novels or her numerous short stories. Also, the focus on the folk over the proletarian and bourgeois renders an incomplete picture of Hurston as a literary stylist and artist. This rereading seeks to examine these authors' major and minor works, presenting the texts in relation to one another as a means of reflecting on the politics of race and gender embedded within these texts. Hopefully, this study will help continue the path of criticism on this triumvirate of writers who contributed so much yet received such little acclaim throughout much of their lives.

Opportunities for women writers, particularly African American women writers, have increased since the period of the Harlem Renaissance, particularly dating back to the period of time in which Hurston, Fauset, and West first appeared on the Harlem scene. The Civil Rights Movement of the 1960s and the Women's Rights Movement of the 1970s created a climate in which the academy, publishing houses, journals, magazines, and newspapers became more receptive to their works. As a consequence, writers such as Toni Morrison, Alice Walker, and Gloria Naylor share a critical and commercial success that Fauset, Hurston, and West never experienced during their lifetimes. Toni Morrison's Nobel Prize for Literature in 1993, Walker's Pulitzer Prize for *The Color Purple* (1992), and Gloria Naylor's American Book Award–winning first novel *The Women of Brewster Place* (1982) testify to the honors bestowed upon the current generation of African American women writers. Not only have Morrison, Walker, and Naylor won major awards, but their works reach a general reading audience and even intersect with popular culture, as both Walker's *The Color Purple* and Morrison's *Beloved* were adapted to the screen for major motion pictures, and *The Women of Brewster Place* was broadcast as a television movie. Nevertheless, the politics of race, class, and gender still reverberate throughout the texts of these three contemporary writers, just as in those of their predecessors. Not surprisingly, contemporary African American writers use history to explore the collective consciousness of African Americans and the nation. Themes such as slavery, women's and men's roles, the struggle of the female artist, family, motherhood, race relations, and class prejudice reverberate in texts of Harlem Renaissance writers, and contemporary African American writers continue to explore these themes, either consciously or unconsciously. Alice Walker views Hurston as a type of literary foremother, of whom she writes evocatively in her collection *In Search of Our Mothers' Gardens*. However, it can be argued that Fauset, West, and Hurston serve as types of literary foremothers for all contemporary African American female writers who also explore the folk, bourgeois, and proletarian aesthetics in their works, illustrating the interconnectedness of these strains in an articulation of life and experience. Jessie Fauset, Zora Neale Hurston, and Dorothy West wove together the strands of African American history to create a lasting legacy. Their work stands as a testimony to the excellence of their literary craft and spirit as they articulated the power of the New Negro Movement from the perspective of African American women.

# Selected Bibliography

## SUBJECT WORKS

Fauset, Jessie. *The Chinaberry Tree and Selected Writings*. Boston: Northeastern University Press, 1995. (Originally published in 1931.)

———. *Comedy: American Style*. New York: G. K. Hall, 1995. (Originally published in 1933.)

———. *Plum Bun: A Novel Without a Moral*. Boston: Beacon Press, 1990. (Originally published in 1929.)

———. *There Is Confusion*. Boston: Northeastern University Press, 1989. (Originally published in 1924.)

Hurston, Zora Neale. *Folklore, Memoirs, and Other Writings*, ed. Cheryl Wall. New York: Library of America, 1995.

———. *Novels and Stories.*, ed. Cheryl Wall. New York: Library of America, 1995.

West, Dorothy. *The Living Is Easy*. New York: Feminist Press, 1982.

———. *The Richer, the Poorer*. New York: Doubleday, 1995.

———. *The Wedding*. New York: Doubleday, 1995.

## SECONDARY WORKS

Abrams, M. H. *A Glossary of Literary Terms*. Fort Worth, Tex.: Harcourt Brace, 1993.

Adams, Katherine H. *A Group of Their Own: College Writing Courses and American Women Writers, 1880–1940*. Albany: State University of New York Press, 2001.

Allen, Carol. *Black Women Intellectuals: Strategies of Nation, Family, and Neighborhoods in the Works of Pauline Hopkins, Jessie Fauset, and Marita Bonner*. New York: Garland, 1998.

Bell, Bernard. *The Afro-American Novel and Its Tradition*. Amherst: University of Massachusetts Press, 1987.

Bone, Robert. *The Negro Novel in America.* New Haven, Conn.: Yale University Press, 1958.

Bontemps, Arna, ed. *The Harlem Renaissance Remembered.* New York: Dodd, Mead, 1972.

Brawley, Benjamin. "The Negro in American Fiction." Pp. 959–65 in *The Prentice Hall Anthology of African American Literature,* eds. Rochelle Smith and Sharon L. Jones. Upper Saddle River, N.J.: Prentice Hall, 2000.

Brigham, Cathy. "The Talking Frame of Zora Neale Hurston's Talking." *College Language Association* 37, no. 4 (1994): 402–19.

Carby, Hazel. *Reconstructing Womanhood: The Emergence of the Afro-American Woman Novelist.* New York: Oxford University Press, 1987.

Dalsgard, Katrine. "Alive and Well and Living on the Island of Martha's Vineyard: An Interview with Dorothy West." *Langston Hughes Review* 12, no. 2 (1993): 28–44.

Davis, Angela Y. *Women, Race and Class.* New York: Random House, 1981.

De Veaux, Alexis. "Bold Type: Renaissance Woman." *Ms. Magazine,* May/June 1995, 73.

Du Bois, W. E. B. *The Souls of Black Folk.* New York: Penguin, 1989.

DuPlessis, Rachel Blau. *Writing Beyond the Ending: Narrative Strategies of Twentieth-Century Women Writers.* Bloomington: Indiana University Press, 1985.

Fauset, Arthur Huff. "American Negro Folk Literature." Pp. 238–44 in *The New Negro: Voices of the Harlem Renaissance,* ed. Alain Locke. New York: Simon and Schuster, 1997.

Felton, Estelle. "Review of *Jonah's Gourd Vine,* by Zora Neale Hurston." Pp. 4–5 in *Zora Neale Hurston: Critical Perspectives Past and Present,* ed. Henry Louis Gates. New York: Amistad, 1993.

Ferguson, Sally Ann. "West, Dorothy." *Dictionary of Literary Biography: Afro-American Writers from the Harlem Renaissance to 1940,* eds. Trudier Harris and Thadious Davis. Detroit: Gale, 1987.

Frazier, E. Franklin. *Black Bourgeoisie: The Rise of a New Middle Class in the United States.* New York: Macmillan, 1957.

Graham, Lawrence Otis. *Our Kind of People: Inside America's Black Upper Class.* New York: Harper Collins, 1999.

"Harlem Renaissance." *Vanity Fair,* September 2001, 192–93.

Hedden, Worth Tuttle. "Review of *Seraph on the Suwanee,* by Zora Neale Hurston." Pp. 35–36 in *Zora Neale Hurston: Critical Perspectives Past and Present,* ed. Henry Louis Gates. New York: Amistad, 1993. Originally published in 1948.

Hemenway, Robert. *Zora Neale Hurston: A Literary Biography.* Urbana: University of Illinois Press, 1977.

Holloway, Karla F. C. *The Character of the Word: The Texts of Zora Neale Hurston.* New York: Greenwood Press, 1987.

Holman, C. Hugh, and William Harmon. *A Handbook to Literature.* New York: Macmillan, 1992.

Honey, Maureen, ed. *Shadowed Dreams: Women's Poetry of the Harlem Renaissance.* New Brunswick, N.J.: Rutgers University Press, 1989.

Howard, Lillie P. "Seraph on the Suwanee." Pp. 267–79 in *Zora Neale Hurston: Critical Perspectives Past and Present,* ed. Henry Louis Gates. New York: Amistad, 1993.

Huggins, Nathan. *Harlem Renaissance.* New York: Oxford University Press, 1971.

Hull, Gloria. *Color, Sex, and Poetry: Three Women Writers of the Harlem Renaissance.* Bloomington: Indiana University Press, 1987.

Hutchinson, George. *The Harlem Renaissance in Black and White.* Cambridge, Mass.: Harvard University Press, 1995.

Hutchinson, Percy. "Review of Moses, Man of the Mountain, by Zora Neale Hurston." Pp. 27–28 in *Zora Neale Hurston: Critical Perspectives Past and Present,* ed. Henry Louis Gates. New York: Amistad, 1993. Originally published in 1939.

Jenkins, Wilbert. "Jessie Fauset: A Modern Apostle of Black Racial Pride." *Zora Neale Hurston Forum* 1, no. 1 (1986): 14–24.

Johnson-Feelings, Dianne, ed. *The Best of the Brownies Book.* New York: Oxford University Press, 1996.

Knopf, Marcy, ed. *The Sleeper Wakes: Harlem Renaissance Stories by Women.* New Brunswick, N.J.: Rutgers University Press, 1993.

Lewis, David Levering. *When Harlem Was in Vogue.* New York: Oxford University Press, 1989.

Lewis, Vashti Crutcher. "Mulatto Hegemony in the Novels of Jessie Redmon Fauset." *College Language Association* 35, no. 4 (1992): 375–86.

Locke, Alain. "Review of *Their Eyes Were Watching God,* by Zora Neale Hurston." P. 18 in *Zora Neale Hurston: Critical Perspectives Past and Present,* ed. Henry Louis Gates. New York: Amistad, 1993. Originally published in 1938.

Locke, Alain, ed. *The New Negro: Voices of the Harlem Renaissance.* New York: Simon and Schuster, 1997.

Lowe, John. *Jump at the Sun: Zora Neale Hurston's Cosmic Comedy.* Urbana: University of Illinois Press, 1994.

Lupton, Mary Jane. "Bad Blood in Jersey: Jessie Fauset's *The Chinaberry Tree.*" *College Language Association* 27, no. 4 (1984): 383–92.

Marsh-Lockett, Carol P. "Whatever Happened to Jochebed? Motherhood As Marginality in Zora Neale Hurston's *Seraph on the Suwanee.*" Pp. 100–110 in *Southern Mothers: Fact and Fictions in Southern Women's Writing,* eds. Warren Nagueyalti and Sally Wolff. Baton Rouge: Louisiana State University Press, 1999.

McDowell, Deborah E. "Conversations with Dorothy West." Pp. 265–82 in *The Harlem Renaissance Re-examined,* ed. Victor A. Kramer. New York: AMS, 1987.

———. Introduction to *Plum Bun* by Jessie Fauset. Boston: Beacon Press, 1990.

———. "Lines of Descent/Dissenting Lines." Pp. 230–40 in *Zora Neale Hurston: Critical Perspectives Past and Present,* ed. Henry Louis Gates. New York: Amistad, 1993.

McLendon, Jacquelyn Y. *The Politics of Color in the Fiction of Jessie Fauset and Nella Larsen.* Charlottesville: University Press of Virginia, 1995.

Miller, Nina A. "Femininity, Publicity, and the Class Division of Cultural Labor: Jessie Redmon Fauset's *There Is Confusion.*" *African American Review* 30, no. 2 (1996): 205–20.

Miller, R. Baxter. "Café de la Paix: Mapping the Harlem Renaissance." *South Atlantic Review* 65, no. 2 (2000): 73–94.

Rubin, Merle. "Racial Pride and Prejudice Drive a Family-Centered Novel." *Christian Science Monitor,* 2 February 1995, 11.

Russell, Kathy, Midge Wilson, and Ronald Hall. *The Color Complex: The Politics of Skin Color Among African Americans.* New York: Harcourt Brace Jovanovich, 1992.

Shockley, Ann Allen. *Afro-American Women Writers 1746–1933: An Anthology and Critical Guide.* Boston: G. K. Hall, 1988.

Slaughter, Frank G. "Review of *Seraph on the Suwanee.*" Pp. 34–35 in *Zora Neale Hurston: Critical Perspectives Past and Present,* ed. Henry Louis Gates. New York: Amistad, 1993. Originally published in 1948.

Speisman, Barbara. "Voodoo As Symbol in Jonah's Gourd Vine." Pp. 86–93 in *Zora in Florida,* eds. Steve Glassman and Kathryn Lee Seidel. Orlando: University of Central Florida Press, 1991.

Sundquist, Eric J. "'The Drum with the Man's Skin': *Jonah's Gourd Vine.*" Pp. 39–75 in *Zora Neale Hurston: Critical Perspectives Past and Present,* ed. Henry Louis Gates. New York: Amistad, 1993.

Sylvander, Carolyn Wedin. "Jessie Fauset." *Dictionary of Literary Biography: Afro-American Women Writers from the Harlem Renaissance to the Present,* ed. Trudier Harris and Thadious Davis. Detroit: Gale, 1987.

———. *Jessie Redmon Fauset, Black American Writer.* Troy, N.Y.: Whitston, 1981.

Untermeyer, Louis. "Review of *Moses, Man of the Mountain,* by Zora Neale Hurston." Pp. 26–27 in *Zora Neale Hurston: Critical Perspectives Past and Present,* ed. Henry Louis Gates. New York: Amistad, 1993. Originally published in 1939.

Wade-Gayles, Gloria. "The Truths of Our Mothers' Lives: Mother–Daughter Relationships in Black Women's Fiction." *SAGE: A Scholarly Journal on Black Women* 1, no. 2 (1984): 8–12.

Wall, Cheryl, ed. "Zora Neale Hurston: Changing Her Own Words." Pp. 76–97 in *Zora Neale Hurston: Critical Perspectives Past and Present,* ed. Henry Louis Gates. New York: Amistad, 1993.

———. *Women of the Harlem Renaissance.* Bloomington: Indiana University Press, 1995.

Wallace, Margaret. "Review of *Jonah's Gourd Vine,* by Zora Neale Hurston." Pp. 8–9 in *Zora Neale Hurston: Critical Perspectives Past and Present,* ed. Henry Louis Gates. New York: Amistad, 1993. Originally published in 1934.

Washington, Mary Helen. "'I Love the Way Janie Crawford Left Her Husbands': Emergent Female Hero." Pp. 98–109 in *Zora Neale Hurston: Critical Perspectives Past and Present,* ed. Henry Louis Gates. New York: Amistad, 1993.

Willis, Susan. *Specifying: Black Women Writing the American Experience.* Madison: University of Wisconsin Press, 1987.

———. "Wandering: Hurston's Search for Self and Method." Pp. 110–29 in *Zora Neale Hurston: Critical Perspectives Past and Present,* ed. Henry Louis Gates. New York: Amistad, 1993.

Wintz, Cary D. *Black Culture and the Harlem Renaissance.* Houston: Rice University Press, 1988.

Wright, Richard. "Blueprint for Negro Writing." Pp. 965–73 in *The Prentice Hall Anthology of African American Literature,* eds. Rochelle Smith and Sharon L. Jones. Upper Saddle River, N.J.: Prentice Hall, 2000.

———. "Review of *Their Eyes Were Watching God,* by Zora Neale Hurston." Pp. 16–17 in *Zora Neale Hurston: Critical Perspectives Past and Present,* ed. Henry Louis Gates. New York: Amistad, 1993. Originally published in 1937.

# Index

## About the Author

SHARON L. JONES is Assistant Professor of English at Earlham College, where she teaches African American literature, humanities, modern literature, 19th-century literature, and contemporary literature. She is coeditor of *The Prentice Hall Anthology of African American Literature* (2000).